REDEMPTION SONG

First published in 2008 by
Liberties Press
Guinness Enterprise Centre | Taylor's Lane | Dublin 8 | Ireland
LibertiesPress.com | info@libertiespress.com
Editorial: +353 (1) 415 1287 | sean@libertiespress.com
Sales and marketing: +353 (1) 415 1224 | peter@libertiespress.com

Trade enquiries to CMD Distribution
55A Spruce Avenue | Stillorgan Industrial Park | Blackrock | County Dublin
Tel: +353 (1) 294 2560
Fax: +353 (1) 294 2564

Distributed in the United States by
Dufour Editions | PO Box 7 | Chester Springs | Pennsylvania 19425

and in Australia by
InBooks | 3 Narabang Way | Belrose NSW 2085

Copyright © Niall Stanage, 2008

ISBN: 978–1–905483–57–0

2 4 6 8 10 9 7 5 3 1

The author has asserted his moral rights.
A CIP record for this title is available from the British Library.

Cover design by Sin É Design
Internal design by Liberties Press
Set in Garamond

Printed in Ireland by Colour Books | Baldoyle | Dublin 13

REDEMPTION SONG

AN IRISH REPORTER INSIDE THE OBAMA CAMPAIGN

NIALL STANAGE

LIB
ERT
IES

To my mother,
For her sense of gentleness;
And my father,
For his sense of justice.

CONTENTS

PREFACE

He had something special. I can remember the instant when I knew it for sure.

On 11 February 2008, I went to see Barack Obama speak in Baltimore. There was nothing outwardly momentous about the occasion. Baltimore is the biggest city in the state of Maryland, which was due to hold its Democratic Party primary the next day. The newspaper columnists and TV pundits were not overly excited about the contest. Obama was expected to beat Hillary Clinton comfortably, which he did.

I had already watched the young Illinois senator experience disorientating lurches between success and failure. The previous month, I had been at his election night party when he nudged American politics towards a new era by winning the Iowa caucuses, the first battle in the primary process. Five days later, I saw him go down to defeat against Clinton in New Hampshire. He had seemed so certain to win that at least three British newspapers, tempted into impetuosity by deadline pressures and the transatlantic time difference, ran front-page stories that assumed his victory.

It was clear that something extraordinary was flaring around Obama. My doubts centred on its depth and durability. I found my answers in Baltimore.

I walked through the streets of the port city in search of the 1st Mariner Arena. It was a Monday afternoon – not exactly prime time for a large-scale political rally – and the air was frigid. When I finally got to the venue, I stood slack-jawed. About 45 minutes before the doors were due to open, the line to see Obama stretched almost the full distance around the cavernous hall. It was a quarter of a mile long at the very least, and five or six people broad. The crowd, perhaps two-thirds of whom were African-American, were bundled up against the weather. They stamped their feet, thrust their hands into their armpits and muttered about why the organisers would not let them in early. But nobody was giving up and going home.

They duly filled the 13,000-seat arena to capacity. There was a sharpness to their support for the candidate that I had not seen before, even in Iowa or New Hampshire. Obama seemed aware of it too.

His speeches in those early days regularly included a line about how everyone who turned up to vote in the presidential election, which was then almost nine months away, could take heart from one thing: 'The name "George W. Bush" will not be on the ballot.' The remark always went down well. In Baltimore, the reaction was thunderous. Obama held his microphone out towards the crowd like the singer of a rock band – albeit a diffident, besuited one – the better to pick it up.

The moment that hit me with such force came soon afterwards. Obama was talking about the ethos that he believed had come to characterise the Bush White House. This, again, was a fixture of his speeches at the time. He would accuse the administration of cynicism, inequity and incompetence – and he would usually be met with a nodding of heads and the occasional whoop of approval, rather than an ovation. There were no big applause lines in that particular passage.

I was standing in the media enclosure on the floor of the arena as the attack on Bush concluded. A small group somewhere in the seats over my right shoulder began to chant. 'It's your time!' they shouted. It was spontaneous, not like the slogans of 'Yes, we can' and 'O-ba-ma' that had become part of the aural furniture of the candidate's gatherings. The voices were ardent, and the words were instantly picked up around the auditorium. I gazed up into the stands. It looked like a cross between a religious revival and a cup final. There were white and Hispanic and black faces, and they all seemed transported. Thousands of arms and outstretched index fingers were moving in unison, pointing at Obama.

'It's your time!' the voices rang out, louder and more insistently. 'It's your time!'

Even Obama seemed taken aback. He hesitated, and smiled a bit uncertainly. Then he recovered. 'It's *your* time,' he told the crowd, stressing the middle word like a teacher delivering a gentle correction.

In fact, both the politician and his public were right. The fates had aligned, matching an abundantly gifted candidate with a nation in dire need of uplift. When Obama had launched his presidential bid a year before, he had introduced a spark of enthusiasm into a political culture that had seemed grim and desiccated. The spark had caught. It had ignited the kind of passionate mass movement that blazes into life no more than once in a generation. Now his supporters were as desperate as Obama – maybe more so – for it to succeed.

It was their time.

*

Obama's opponents would often complain that the media were essentially in his pocket. Chris Matthews, the host of a political talk show, famously declared after one Obama speech: 'I felt this thrill going up my leg.' Lee Cowan, a political reporter for NBC News, talked about the 'energy' that attended Obama's events and added: 'It's almost hard to remain objective, because it's infectious.' The remarks were made early in the Democratic primary process, and they infuriated Clinton supporters. Later, after Obama had clinched his party's nomination for the presidency, they would pop up in a campaign video released by John McCain.

The criticism sounded plausible. But the reality was more complicated. News reporters, rightly conscious of the need to appear objective, tend to shy away from talking about things that cannot be easily measured, like emotional intensity. But their preferred template of ostentatious 'fairness' – 'candidate X said this and candidate Y said that' – can obscure as much as it reveals.

During most of the Democratic primaries, the enthusiasm of the crowds that came to see Obama ran at a higher pitch than it did among those who turned out for Clinton. Everyone who was present knew it.

When people like Cowan sought to communicate this reality, they were accused of fawning. But to avoid talking about such tricky subjects was to ignore the heart of the Obama story. He had touched something in the national mood. You could hear it in the cheers from the stands, and could see it afterwards, in the tears that stained many cheeks.

Stacie Laverne brought her five-year-old son to see Obama at the Baltimore rally. She wanted him to be able to say that he had seen the man who – maybe – would be the first black president. 'This is all about emotion,' she told me. Lamar Shields was also in attendance that day. 'People want someone who feels connected to them – that feels their hunger, feels their pain,' he said. 'And I think people can relate to hope. It's the only thing that brings people together.'

The upfront emotionalism of the Obama campaign led to accusations that it was insubstantial. In fact, Obama had policy prescriptions for every major issue facing America. He could explain them with fluency and in detail, and they were laid out on his website for anyone who wanted to read them. But it was not his position papers that marked him out. He could inspire people, and he had arrived centre-stage at a time when they badly needed inspiration.

*

Goodwill alone would never have carried him to the White House. Plenty of Democratic candidates in the past had been embraced by the party's most fervent supporters, only to fall far short of electoral glory. If Obama was to avoid that fate, his candidacy would need steadiness and steel. The team of advisors who surrounded him provided both. I spoke with them throughout their quest, and soon realised that the 'No Drama Obama' label that had attached itself to the campaign told only half the story.

The top triumvirate of aides – David Axelrod, Obama's chief strategist; David Plouffe, his campaign manager; and Robert Gibbs, his communications director and senior advisor – had the kind of personal bond with the candidate that was rare in the mercenary world of political consulting. Axelrod's association with Obama went back the furthest. Despite his languorous demeanour, you soon learnt to read the signs that betrayed the emotions which swept through him on both the good nights and the bad ones. In Texas, on the evening when Obama lost the Democratic primary in that state, he seemed disconsolate. By the time I boarded the Obama campaign jet less than three weeks before the election, things were going right, and the unusual lightness of Axelrod's mood suggested he knew it.

If the 'no drama' motto did not tell the whole truth, it at least illuminated an important part of it. Firstly, the people at the top of Obama's campaign liked each other, which was unusual in high-level politics. As a consequence, they never whispered criticisms of each other into the ears of the press – a practice that was commonplace among Clinton and McCain aides. Secondly, their visceral belief in Obama never clouded their vision. Presidential campaigns often get buffeted by the winds of the latest controversy. The Obama team's eyes remained locked on their objective: acquiring the 270 electoral votes required to win the White House.

They diligently built an infrastructure capable of harnessing – and maximising – the popular support that swelled behind Obama. The organisation grew into something gigantic, eventually boasting more than 3 million fundraisers and 1.5 million active volunteers. I listened to Plouffe talk in October 2008 about how the grassroots movement amounted to a huge storm that was going to crash down and overwhelm the Republicans. He did not say it in the vainglorious manner common to other people in his profession. He mentioned it quietly but firmly, as if he were stating a fact. Time proved him right.

*

Obama himself often perplexed those of us in the media. We kept searching for some sense of what he was like 'behind the mask' – until a lot of us concluded that, really, there was no mask.

This was not to suggest that Obama was a saint. His self-confidence could soar to hubristic heights at times and he could be prickly, especially when he was tired. But the incidents reporters cited as evidence of these traits were hardly indicative of deep-seated psychological turmoil. The most famous example of his grouchiness came during a particularly miserable period of the primaries. Obama was never at his cheeriest in the early morning, and he grew irritated when a reporter shouted a question about the Middle East at him as he ate breakfast. 'Why can't I just eat my waffle?' he responded wearily.

Most of the time, he remained imperturbable, sometimes eerily so. On the plane, as the days ticked down to the presidential election, I watched him clown around with Axelrod and, at a stop near Disney World, tease the photographers by asking how much they would pay him to put on a Mickey Mouse hat he had found.

Even on the night of his ultimate victory, he seemed almost preternaturally composed. Photos taken behind the scenes as the results came in showed him sitting calmly on a couch with his mother-in-law. He delivered his speech a short time later without a stumble or a hesitation. The moment was heavy with the weight of history – and Obama seemed to bear it with ease.

His private thoughts when he contemplated the road he had travelled remained unknown to everyone but his wife, Michelle. Still, to watch his progress from close quarters was a journalist's dream. Reporters always want to find themselves working on a good story. The Obama candidacy was the most amazing one anyone covering it had ever witnessed.

On the night he won the presidency, I spotted a photographer in the press tent whom I had befriended during the campaign. She was young and smart, and not given to extravagant displays of emotion. I walked over to the desk and looked over her shoulder at her laptop screen. She was flicking through pictures she had taken of America's next First Family less than an hour before.

I put my hand on her back and, when she turned around, I saw that she was crying. She got up, hugged me and said: 'Do you know how lucky we are to have seen this?'

Even as I write those words, less than a week later, they sound corny. But, standing in that tent in Grant Park on 4 November 2008, I knew exactly what she meant. I said so, and hugged her back.

Like my photographer friend, I had the privilege of a ringside view of history. As I watched Obama claim the presidency, I thought of all the times I had seen him in draughty school halls and theatres, all the miles clocked up on the campaign trail, all the days when an ending like this had seemed more like a fragile, flickering hope than a serious possibility.

I knew just how many things needed to come together for Barack Obama to be elected to his nation's highest office. I knew how improbable his journey had been. And, deep down, I knew something else.

I would never see anything quite like it again.

NIALL STANAGE
HARLEM, NEW YORK
10 NOVEMBER 2008

1

THE SPEECH

Barack Obama wanted an omelette.

It was a Tuesday in the midsummer of 2004, and dawn was edging over the east coast of the United States. Obama, a state level legislator who would turn 43 eight days later, was still unknown to most Americans. Waking in his room at the Hilton Back Bay Hotel in Boston, he knew he was beginning the most vital 24 hours of his political career. He needed food.

It was only 6 AM. The hotel restaurant would not open for another half an hour. Aides found an all-night diner nearby. They brought back the boss's order: a green-pepper omelette made with egg whites.

Obama had plenty to ponder over breakfast.

The Democratic Party's quadrennial national convention was in full swing. Four thousand three hundred party activists had descended on the biggest city in Massachusetts. The media heavily outnumbered them: there were 15,000 journalists in town.

In two days' time, the Democrats would officially – and flamboyantly – nominate Senator John Kerry, a lantern-jawed Vietnam war veteran and a Boston resident, as their presidential candidate. A month later, down the coast in New York, Republicans were due to take part in their own festival of extravagance to endorse President George W. Bush's re-election bid. They would do so in the famous Madison Square Garden arena, barely three miles from where Ground Zero still gaped. The election, everyone agreed, would be close.

Obama was billed as the convention's keynote speaker. The title sounded more impressive than it really was.

Four years before, the Democrats had convened in Los Angeles and nominated Vice President Al Gore to face Bush, then the governor of Texas. Gore – who, his party hoped, would extend the ethos of President Bill Clinton's administration without the libidinous sideshows – had chosen Congressman Harold Ford Jr to deliver the keynote address.

Ford was a young African-American, and a political moderate. He was spoken of inside the party as a rising star. The similarities between him then and Obama now were striking. Ford's 2000 speech had not done him any harm. It had not done him a great deal of good either. Smooth, airy and inoffensive, it had been well received on the night and almost instantly forgotten.

That was the fate that befell most keynote speakers. They tended to hew close to the hackneyed template of American political rhetoric: a safety-first approach that the top brass in both parties, ever-anxious to quench any spark of unpredictability, were happy to encourage. You had to go back two decades to find a keynote address that anyone really remembered. Mario Cuomo, then the governor of the state of New York, had thrilled the hearts of the Democratic Party faithful in 1984 with a fiery oration in San Francisco.

Obama's performance was expected more closely to resemble Ford's than Cuomo's. If he had read a *New York Times* preview of the convention earlier in the month, he would surely have noticed the reporter's prediction that the young senator 'may be overshadowed on Tuesday night by Mr Kerry's wife, Teresa Heinz Kerry'.

Heinz Kerry would not be his only competition. Senator Edward Kennedy – jowly and grey now, but still a totemic figure for many Democrats – would speak too. Kennedy could be sure of a rapturous reception. Boston was his home town.

Howard Dean, the former governor of Vermont, would also go to the podium that night. Dean had flared briefly in the presidential primary as an insurgent candidate running against those, like John Kerry, who were entrenched in the party establishment. His campaign had come to nothing, but he remained beloved among the Democratic grassroots.

Fortunately, Obama did not lack confidence – even if he had become expert at giving the appearance of modesty. He still began his speeches with a reference to the many ways he had heard his surname mangled, most memorably as 'Alabama' or 'Yo Mama'. He had given a short interview the previous day to *USA Today*, the biggest-selling newspaper in the country, and had been sure to set the bar of expectations low. 'I think making sure I don't drone on is important,' he said.

This self-deprecation underlined Obama's awareness that he was not yet a national figure. But he also knew that he could be on the cusp of becoming one. Among the political cognoscenti, word was spreading. His bid for a place in the 100-member US Senate, representing Illinois, had seemed like a long shot when he first announced it in January 2003. It didn't look that way any longer.

The national Democratic leadership believed that Obama's candidacy represented one of the party's best chances to gain a Senate seat in a challenging year. It was that cold political calculation, as much as an appreciation of the rising star's undoubted oratorical gifts, that had resulted in Obama being asked to give the keynote speech.

A handful of journalists had also begun suggesting that there was something unusual about the tall man with the big smile and the sticky-out ears – something different, maybe even something unique.

Magazines like the *New Yorker* and the *New Republic* had run sympathetic profiles. The most perspicacious observations of all had come from a *New York Times* columnist, Bob Herbert.

'Remember the name Barack Obama,' Herbert had counselled his readers in an article that ran on 4 June. 'You'll be hearing it a lot as this election season unfolds.

'His partisans describe Mr Obama as a dream candidate, the point man for a new kind of politics designed to piece together a coalition reminiscent of the one blasted apart by the bullet that killed Robert Kennedy in 1968,' Herbert wrote.

'In a political era saturated with cynicism and deceit, Mr Obama is asking voters to believe him when he talks about the values and

verities that so many politicians have lied about for so long. He's asking, in effect, for a political leap of faith.'

Herbert was the first media commentator to identify the core of
Obama's appeal – an appeal that would propel him through Boston
and into the Senate, and would eventually sustain his run for the White
House. For now, though, everything rested on the speech. Obama had
begun drafting it back in Springfield, the Illinois state capital. Terry
Link, a fellow state legislator who would become one of his closest
friends, told me: 'He basically wrote it in one night, sitting in his hotel.
It was his speech, and it showed to the world who he was.'

Obama jotted down his lines longhand on a yellow legal pad, keeping half an eye on the basketball game on TV. Later, he would joke that
he was glad he had composed the address before he had dwelt on the
significance of the occasion, and nervousness and writer's block had
been given a chance to kick in.

He had honed the words with the people he most trusted. Prime
among these – with the exception of his wife, Michelle, a razor-sharp
Princeton- and Harvard-educated lawyer who had been raised in modest circumstances on Chicago's South Side – was David Axelrod.

Axelrod, six years Obama's senior, had been something of a boy
wonder in the journalistic world. In the mid-1980s, not yet 30, he had
given up a prime position with his adopted home town's main newspaper, the *Chicago Tribune*, to plunge into the even murkier realm of political strategising.

No one doubted Axelrod's capacity for ruthlessness when circumstances demanded it. He had once run a negative ad against a client's
rival in which TV clips of the opponent were slowed down and translated into black and white, producing an effect that seemed to resemble old newsreel footage of Adolf Hitler.

Despite that – and despite the belligerent-sounding nickname
('Axe') that had attached itself to him – Axelrod was something of an
oddity. He was a quietly spoken, drily humorous figure in a milieu
awash with bombastic self-promoters. His dominant features were a
droopy moustache, a comb-over and dark eyes – a combination that
had led one writer to compare him to 'an exotic rodent'. He looked

melancholy in all but his most ecstatic moments.

Axelrod also seemed ill at ease with the cynicism that his Washington-based counterparts wore like a badge of honour. He knew that sometimes you had to play rough to win. Yet when he expressed regret about that fact, somehow his words rang less hollow than you expected.

'I believe there is nobility in politics. I believe there is great good that can be done,' he would tell the *Washington Post* more than two years after the Boston convention. 'I know my business, and the technology of polling groups and focus groups – all of what we do – in some way contributes to an atmosphere of cynicism. I try to fight that. I can't say I'm totally blameless. I think everyone in this business has a hand on that bloody dagger.'

Every time I spoke to Axelrod, I found myself thinking of Toby Ziegler from the TV series *The West Wing*. Like the fictional White House communications director, idealism and a mournful acceptance of the ways of the world seemed to co-exist within him.

Axelrod and Obama had met in the hurly-burly of Chicago's political circles and had become friends. When the consultant had signed on for Obama's Senate run, his credibility pulled other pros into the young candidate's orbit. By the time of the convention, Robert Gibbs was serving as Obama's chief media aide. An affable but tough southerner, hefty and bespectacled, Gibbs had left Kerry's presidential campaign only months before, in protest at the firing of a colleague.

Obama and his advisors thought the speech had something going for it. They just weren't sure exactly what it was. Obama had to send the text for clearance to the Kerry campaign in advance. To his relief, it came back with few changes. At one point, in the days leading up to the speech, Michelle Obama was brought in to watch her husband practise his delivery. 'Her assessment was that I wasn't going to embarrass the Obama family,' Barack said.

After breakfast, Obama was whisked through a series of TV interviews. The questions were mostly polite and light. So were the answers. 'I like to tell people that, although I'm skinny, I'm tougher than I look,' he quipped on NBC's *Today*.

That afternoon, Obama sought refuge with his family and advisors. As the hour of the speech drew near, there was a lengthy debate over which tie he should wear. 'We finally settled on the tie that Robert Gibbs was wearing,' Obama would later write. Then there was a visit to Teresa Heinz Kerry and, finally, there was just Obama and Michelle, sitting backstage. He stepped into the spotlight as a band played the old, civil rights-tinged Impressions hit, 'Keep On Pushing'.

Obama betrayed some signs of nervousness as the speech began, though few people were familiar enough with his speaking style to know it. He stumbled over a couple of words. His body language, normally so natural, seemed a touch forced. He looked like a man reminding himself to look animated.

Early in the address, he gave a posthumous nod to his parents. He said that, despite disparate backgrounds, they 'shared an abiding faith in the possibilities of this nation. They would give me an African name, "Barack", or "blessed", believing that in a tolerant America, your name is no barrier to success.' He got his first burst of real applause for that line, and it seemed to put him at ease.

Then the speech took an interesting turn. Most politicians who mount the podium at conventions take the easiest route to winning applause. Often, they just run down a list of party shibboleths and depart. Obama assumed that the audience was capable of grasping a more thoughtful argument. He understood those on the Left who wanted the government to help the marginalised, of course; but he also sympathised with those who argued that too heavy an emphasis on government intervention corroded personal responsibility. The bulk of the American people, he insisted, had no wish to confine themselves to ideological pigeonholes.

'The people I meet in small towns and big cities and diners and office parks – they don't expect government to solve all of their problems. They know they have to work hard to get ahead, and they want to,' he said. 'Go into any inner-city neighbourhood, and folks will tell you that government alone can't teach our kids to learn. They know that parents have to teach, that children can't achieve unless we raise their expectations and turn off the television sets and eradicate the slander that says a black youth with a book is acting white.'

The applause erupted. The acclaim sounded different from the perfunctory response to a politician hitting a well-honed line. African-American delegates were among those cheering loudest of all.

Obama continued through a standard, though effective, statement of the benefits Kerry would bring to the country. Then came the couple of minutes of rhetoric that would change the trajectory of his life.

'Alongside our famous individualism, there's another ingredient in the American saga: a belief that we are all connected as one people,' he began quietly. 'If there's a child on the South Side of Chicago who can't read, that matters to me – even if it's not my child.'

The volume of his delivery began to build. 'If there's a senior citizen somewhere who can't pay for their prescription drugs, and [is] having to choose between medicine and the rent, that makes my life poorer – even if it's not my grandparent. If there's an Arab-American family being rounded up without benefit of an attorney or due process, that threatens my civil liberties.'

The crowd were on their feet now. Obama let the applause start to subside before plunging on. 'Even as we speak, there are those who are preparing to divide us: the spin-masters, the negative-ad peddlers who embrace the politics of "anything goes".

'Well, I say to them tonight, there is not a liberal America and a conservative America; there is the United States of America. There's not a black America and a white America, a Latino America, an Asian America; there's the United States of America.'

Down on the convention floor, there was bedlam. People were roaring their approval. Some were weeping. Robert Gibbs and David Axelrod were down there too. Gibbs leaned into Axelrod. 'Are you seeing what I'm seeing?' he asked.

'The pundits!' Obama went on. 'The pundits like to slice and dice our country into red states and blue states: red states for Republicans, blue states for Democrats. But I've got news for them, too. We worship an awesome God in the blue states, and we don't like federal agents poking around in our libraries in the red states. We coach Little

League in the blue states and, yes, we've got some gay friends in the red states.

'There are patriots who opposed the war in Iraq, and there are patriots who supported the war in Iraq. We are one people, all of us pledging allegiance to the Stars and Stripes, all of us defending the United States of America.'

He could have stopped there and been fêted as the star of the night. He didn't, wrapping up instead with a tribute to America itself and to things more personal: John Kerry's war service, and vice-presidential nominee John Edwards' working-class roots, and his own complicated history. At the centre of it all lay a word he would use a lot more in the years to come: hope.

'I'm not talking about blind optimism here . . . I'm talking about something more substantial. It's the hope of slaves sitting around a fire singing freedom songs; the hope of immigrants setting out for distant shores; the hope of a young naval lieutenant bravely patrolling the Mekong Delta; the hope of a millworker's son who dares to defy the odds; the hope of a skinny kid with a funny name who believes that America has a place for him too. Hope in the face of difficulty! Hope in the face of uncertainty! The audacity of hope!'

The speech has passed into legend now. There are other American orations that are more famous, more important or simply better. But none has so instantly transformed a relative unknown into a political supernova.

Terry Link had been watching his friend from one of the skyboxes high in the arena. 'I was very nervous about it because, you know, you want someone you like to hit a home run,' he told me. 'So, all through the speech, I'm watching him and I'm watching how the crowd is reacting at the same time. By the time he finished that speech, tears were coming out of my eyes. He hadn't just hit a home run, he'd hit a grand slam.

'But I was embarrassed too; I was sort of dabbing at the side of my eyes with my jacket because I didn't want the other people to see how emotional it had made me feel. So eventually I look around – and everyone else has tears in their eyes as well.'

Obama's address had an almost cinematic sweep. Its political genius lay in the many different, sometimes clashing, things it praised: the greatness of America and the efforts of those who strained against its injustices; the national credo of rugged individualism and the craving of its people for a connection to something greater than themselves; the possibility of honourable disagreement and the deeper loyalties that united all of its citizens. Perhaps, at one level, Obama tapped into something as grandiose as a desire for national healing and as basic as an appetite for civility.

He certainly tapped into something. The reaction of the media was as instantaneous, and as feverishly positive, as that of the audience. Jeff Greenfield, a CNN analyst, proclaimed it 'one of the really great keynote speeches of the last quarter-century'. On MSNBC, Howard Fineman of *Newsweek* lauded Obama as 'the best argument for the American dream that's around in politics'.

It was left to Chris Matthews, an Irish-American who had served as a speechwriter to President Jimmy Carter before turning to a career in broadcasting, to trump them all. 'That is an amazing moment in history right there. It is really an amazing moment. A keynoter like I've never heard,' the excitable Matthews announced. Then he came straight out and said what others had already begun to murmur: 'I've just seen the first black president there.'

The newspapers that followed the next morning were no less adulatory. Kennedy, Dean and Teresa Heinz Kerry were mentioned only as afterthoughts to the new wunderkind. And although the main focus soon shifted to John Kerry and his looming battle with Bush, the hosannas for Obama were heard for the rest of the week.

'A superstar is born,' wrote *Chicago Tribune* columnist Clarence Page exultantly. 'America fell in love with Barack Obama,' William Raspberry chimed in on the editorial page of the *Washington Post*. And when it came to the reception accorded to the state senator for the rest of his time in Boston, the *New York Times* put it most pithily: 'The next day, Barack Obama owned the town.'

Obama made the most of the publicity. He raised $70,000 for his Senate bid during his time in Boston. When he left, he embarked on a five-day tour of Illinois. The crowds that showed up were beyond even his campaign's expectations. The enterprise, the Chicago-based journalist and author David Mendell wrote, resembled 'a 1,600-mile victory lap'.

As for Obama, he made sure to keep up the appearance of humbleness. 'Apparently the speech turned out OK Tuesday,' he told one group of voters in Kewanee, a small city 150 miles west of Chicago. He said it with a smile.

*

Obama showed his best side in Boston. His triumph at the convention led many to conclude that he was a political natural whose gifts had been fully formed for years but had gone undiscovered beyond the state of Illinois. If the reporters and profile-writers had delved into his earliest days in electoral politics, a rather different picture would have emerged, however – one that would have unsettled some of the candidate's new-found fans.

A love of politics did not seem to course through Obama's veins in the way it did for, say, Bill Clinton. Back in Arkansas in the late 1970s, Clinton had become the youngest governor in the nation, aged 32. When Obama was the same age, in 1993, he was still splitting his time between various community organising activities and legal work.

When he finally decided, in 1995, to seek the modest office of state senator, he did so with a peculiar blend of ambivalence and ruthlessness. His opportunity arose when a congressman in Chicago, Mel Reynolds, was ensnared in a sex scandal and resigned. An existing state senator, Alice Palmer, decided that she would give up her safe berth representing the 13th District and run for the House of Representatives seat vacated by Reynolds.

Palmer and Obama had long admired each other. Obama sought and received a guarantee from Palmer that, should she lose her race in the special congressional election, she would not then double-back and try to keep her state Senate seat.

One of the most revealing glimpses of the young contender came in a December 1995 interview with the *Chicago Reader*, an alternative weekly newspaper. Whereas the Obama of presidential politics would be subtle, deft and focused on transcending ideological and racial differences, back then he sounded callow and often teetered on the brink of sanctimony.

Having solicited money from rich donors, he expressed disquiet about having done so, promising that 'once I'm known, I won't need that kind of money'. He complained about the reluctance of other Chicago politicians to back him, and suggested that the problem was their moral cowardice. They 'warn me I might be too independent,' he said.

Most startling of all was Obama's complex view of the racial divisions in American society. Though he noted that African-Americans who 'are only talking about racism as a barrier to our success are seriously misled', this was only a preface to a larger point. 'This doesn't suggest . . . that these African-American tribal affinities aren't legitimate,' he said. 'Historically, African-Americans have turned inward and toward black nationalism whenever they have a sense, as we do now, that the mainstream has rebuffed us, and that white Americans couldn't care less about the profound problems African-Americans are facing. But cursing out white folks is not going to get the job done.'

Obama may well have been factually accurate in that analysis. But it would be hard to imagine presidential candidate Obama placing such emphasis on the idea that whites did not care about blacks, or suggesting that 'cursing out white folks' was an understandable, if inadequate, response. In any case, concerns about whether Obama was quite as noble as he claimed were soon swirling around.

Alice Palmer's bid for Congress fizzled out. She ran third in a Democratic primary won by Jesse Jackson Jr, the son of the well-known civil rights leader. (Jackson would go on to win the general election and take his place in Congress, where he still serves.) She then reneged on her promise to Obama and sought to retain her state Senate seat after all.

Obama had other ideas. All candidates were required to present a petition of support from over 700 of the district's voters in order to get on the ballot. Obama put a legal team to work challenging the validity of the signatures Palmer had presented. He did the same thing with other candidates who posed little threat. It worked. His challenges were upheld, clearing the field of all his competitors.

According to the letter of the law, Obama's people had done nothing wrong. And when asked about the episode 12 years later, Obama made the argument that 'If you couldn't run a successful petition drive, then that raised questions in terms of how effective a representative you were going to be.'

It was still an odd course to adopt for a man who, just four years previously, had headed a voter registration project. Those who worked with him at the time remember a candidate who was not quite as free of internal conflict about his actions as he would later claim to have been.

'He wondered if we should knock everybody off the ballot. How would that look?' one of his campaign consultants, Ronald Davis, recalled in an interview with the *Chicago Tribune*.

'I don't think he thought it was, you know, sporting,' a volunteer, Will Burns, added. 'He wasn't very proud of it.'

He did it nonetheless. And, come January 1997, he was on his way to Springfield as a state senator.

*

Many of Obama's new colleagues treated him with scepticism, in part because of his trumpeted commitment to ethics reform, and in part because they found him haughty.

Rich Miller, a journalist who ran a newsletter devoted to politics in the Illinois capital, told the *Chicago Reader* in 2000: 'Barack is a very intelligent man. He hasn't had a lot of success here, and it could be because he places himself above everybody. He likes people to know he went to Harvard.'

Obama's ascetic image among his fellow lawmakers was leavened a bit by his participation in the poker school that met every Wednesday night at Terry Link's Springfield home. The card night had begun, Link told me, because he and Obama barely drank, and they wanted something else to do with their free time other than hanging out, joy-lessly and soberly, in bars.

Link recalled his friend's cautious poker style with a laugh. 'He was not what you could call a riverboat gambler,' he said. 'He was the kind of guy who would figure out the odds and calculate his chances of winning before he did anything.'

Larry Walsh, another state senator, was also a regular member of the card school. When I spoke to him in late 2008, he remembered, with obvious fondness, that there seemed to be only one person who could break Obama's concentration on the game.

'We used to tease him because he'd get a phone call from Michelle, and he'd be gone for 20 or 30 minutes,' Walsh said. 'He was a newly-wed and we had all been married quite a while. So we'd tease him about talking all lovey-dovey over the phone. But they definitely were in love – and it still shows to this day.'

Walsh told me that, when he first met Obama, it had taken the young legislator's 'big toothy smile' to win him over. Walsh, a farmer (and built like one), had previously noticed only that Obama was 'lanky, with kind of a weak handshake'. But the grin 'created the feel-ing that this guy really liked you,' he said. (He also added approvingly that 'Michelle has put some weight on him' since then.)

Both Walsh and Link said that it had taken time before the wari-ness with which Obama was regarded by some peers began to melt. Other African-American politicians from Chicago were among the ici-est of all towards the new arrival. Obama's Harvard background made it seem that he was 'not really a neighbourhood kind of guy', as Link put it delicately.

Rickey 'Hollywood' Hendon, a flamboyant man whose nickname was a reference to his connections in the entertainment industry, often clashed with the future presidential contender, according to colleagues in the legislature.

By the time I spoke to him in 2008, however, he was keen to down-play the extent of the tensions that had existed. (He had even taken to wearing an Obama cap to prove his loyalty.) He claimed that he had merely been fond of Alice Palmer and had lacked any kind of comparable personal history with Obama.

'We knew what Alice Palmer stood for, and there were questions as to what Barack stood for,' Hendon told me. 'People knew we could depend on Alice Palmer on the issues. I loved her, and if I told you I loved Barack, that would be a lie. I just didn't know him.'

Kimberly Lightford, another African-American state senator from Chicago, who was elected after Obama and clearly looked up to him, laughed when I paraphrased Hendon's remarks for her. She said that the hostility was much more severe than Hendon was suggesting.

'I was the chair of the Senate black caucus and that stuff interfered with my meetings,' she recalled. 'Rickey would say to me: "He's arrogant." And I would say: "No, he's confident." I used to tell Rickey he was just jealous. And I do think there was a "big brother-little brother" thing going on. Rickey wondered who this guy was, to come in and start stealing the attention.'

In any case, Obama soon became impatient with his position in Springfield. He decided to contest an election for a seat on Capitol Hill. With the benefit of hindsight, this would be seen as a pivot upon which his career turned. It would not end in glorious victory but in a huge defeat – 'a spanking', as he would later put it himself.

One of the archetypes of local, urban politics in America is the erstwhile black radical turned mainstream politician. Bobby Rush was just such a man. A co-founder of the Illinois Black Panther Party, Rush had once posed with a pistol and encouraged African-Americans to take up arms in self-defence. He had gradually moved away from militancy as he climbed the ladder of elected office. First, he became a member of Chicago City Council. Then he won election to Congress in 1992.

In 1999, Rush made an ill-advised decision. He decided to challenge the sitting mayor of Chicago, Richard M. Daley. Rush received only 28 percent of the votes cast and, to widespread surprise, barely won a majority of the African-American vote.

His poor performance led potential rivals to think that, come the next congressional election, he could be beaten. Among those who held that view was Barack Obama. His friends were almost unanimous in telling him that he was wrong. 'I thought he would lose,' one African-American backer in Chicago told me, thinking back to those days. 'I thought he would not make a dent into Bobby Rush, and I told him so.' Obama wouldn't listen to them. He should have done.

Rush had been politically active within his community for the best part of 30 years. Though some griped that the former Panther was less attentive to his constituents' concerns than he had once been, he had not committed any egregious misdeeds. And Obama's efforts to explain why Rush should be ejected from office were fuzzy at best. 'Congressman Rush exemplifies a politics that is reactive, that waits for crises to happen, then holds a press conference, and [he] hasn't been particularly effective at building broad-based coalitions,' Obama told the *Chicago Reader*.

Obama was presenting himself as a political reformer. But the cause of reform can seem like an abstraction to voters who are struggling with the basic necessities of life, a category into which many people on the South Side of Chicago had the misfortune to fall.

Rush pulled no punches in using Obama's background against him. 'He went to Harvard and became an educated fool. We're not impressed with these folks with these eastern elite degrees,' he said.

There was often a note of hurt in the older man's words, too. 'I felt as though I had been betrayed,' he would recall several years later. 'I had befriended Barack many years ago, and I thought that he was someone who I could count on.'

Rush trounced Obama by a margin of two to one. The man who emerged from that defeat seemed different to his friends and his colleagues in Springfield. He was chastened, and less inclined to clamber up onto the moral high ground.

'He was very disappointed when he didn't win,' Larry Walsh recalled. 'His mood was very down. I can remember one night, we were playing [cards] and everybody was sort of hesitant to bring it up: "Why did the wheels fall off?"'

At a subsequent game, months afterwards, something changed. Obama abruptly stopped the general chit-chat, according to Walsh, and announced with a smile: 'OK everybody, say "I told you so."' A frank discussion of everything that had gone wrong in the congressional race followed. 'I think by that time he was accepting what had happened,' Walsh said. 'He was getting ready to move past it.'

*

In time, Obama set his sights on the US Senate. It looked like an absurdly impetuous move, given his unremarkable track record. Another loss would effectively end his political career. He had promised Michelle that if he did not win this time, he would find something more worthwhile – and family-friendly – to do. The race was seen, she said, as 'a last hurrah' for him.

The shape of the campaign was uncertain. It was assumed that the incumbent senator, the Republican Peter Fitzgerald, would run for re-election, even though he was not particularly popular within his party. There was no telling who might emerge to challenge Obama for the Democratic nomination.

Obama officially entered the field on 21 January 2003. 'LEGISLATOR IN RACE TO UNSEAT FITZGERALD', ran the headline on the nine-paragraph *Chicago Tribune* story the next day. His most serious Democratic opposition would emerge later, in the shape of financier Blair Hull.

The contest would ultimately take a bizarre course – something which would prove both a blessing and a curse for Obama. He would indeed make it to the Senate. But key opponents, both Democratic and Republican, would immolate themselves in such spectacular fashion that critics would always be able to make light of his achievement. 'My victory proved nothing,' he would later lament.

Fitzgerald announced in April 2003 that he would retire, throwing the Republican contest wide open. Among the Democrats, Obama usually ran third or fourth in polls of the seven-member field for the rest of the year.

The Democratic primary was set for 16 March 2004. Late in 2003, Hull, who had initially been polling behind Obama, surged to the front of the pack.

The reason was simple: money. Hull had made his fortune when a stock-trading firm he controlled was sold for $531 million. He was willing to spend up to $40 million to win the seat, he said.

Things began to look grim for Obama as February rolled on and Hull maintained his lead. Obama would later reminisce about calling supporters to tell them not to panic. 'I would hang up the phone . . . and I would wonder to myself if perhaps it was time to panic after all,' he acknowledged.

Then the rich man's campaign fell apart. Under pressure from the media, he released divorce records regarding a woman to whom he had twice been married, Brenda Sexton. Among the paperwork was an order of protection Sexton had taken out against him. Hull, Sexton claimed, had threatened her life, had hit her on the shins and was 'a violent man with an ungovernable temper'.

Hull's poll ratings dropped like a stone. He inflicted further damage on himself by taking out a full-page ad in the *Chicago Tribune* in which he proffered an explanation that was, at best, inept: 'Here are the facts: she kicked me three times, I asked her to stop before finally hitting her leg, and I used some bad language. That is the sum total of what happened.' Claiming a right to self-defence might have been justifiable from a legal standpoint but it was never going to be politically effective.

Some political insiders claimed to see the hand of David Axelrod in the disclosure of marital strife. Before plumping for Obama, Axelrod had discussed working for Hull and had learnt some of the details of his personal life. Axelrod has always adamantly denied having any part in pushing the embarrassing information into the public domain. A reporter for the *Chicago Tribune* did claim, however, that the Obama campaign team had done its level best to keep the story running once it appeared.

Hull's support collapsed. Obama won the primary in a canter, securing 53 percent of the vote. Dan Hynes, a well-established Chicago politician, got 24 percent, Hull only 11 percent. 'It was huge for him,' Larry Walsh said.

The victor's speech to supporters at a rally that night peaked in a refrain that would be heard across America a few years hence. Obama said that, at the start of the race, 'the conventional wisdom was that we could not win. We didn't have enough money. We didn't have enough organisation. There was no way that a skinny guy from the South Side with a funny name like Barack Obama could ever win a statewide race.

'Sixteen months later, we are here. And Democrats from all across Illinois – suburbs, city, downstate, upstate, black, white, Hispanic, Asian – have declared: "Yes we can! Yes we can! Yes we can!"'

*

With the Democratic nomination secured, the real battle loomed against the standard-bearer of the Republican Party. Jack Ryan, a social conservative who bore more than a passing physical resemblance to John Kennedy Jr, JFK's son, had emerged as the Grand Old Party's candidate. Ryan was another multimillionaire. His fortune had been made when Goldman Sachs, in which he was a partner, went public.

By May, things were looking good for Obama. One opinion poll showed him up by 16 points. The next month, things looked even better. A scandal similar to the one that had finished off Blair Hull sank Ryan.

The *Chicago Tribune* and a television station in the city sued for the right to see Ryan's sealed divorce papers. Adding some Hollywood glamour to the story, Ryan's ex-wife was an attractive and well-known actress, Jeri Ryan. To the horror of the Ryan campaign, a judge in Los Angeles found in the media's favour. The candidate had previously assured the Illinois Republican Party that, even if the records did become public, there was nothing in them that would cause him serious embarrassment. That would have been fine – had the assertion not been a whopping lie.

In fact, Jeri Ryan had testified that her then-husband had taken her to sex clubs in New York and Paris against her wishes. In a declaration of 9 June 2000, she recalled the New York trip, during which, she said, the future senatorial candidate had brought her to 'a bizarre club with cages, whips and other apparatus hanging from the ceiling. Respondent [Jack Ryan] wanted me to have sex with him there, with another couple watching. I refused.'

Of the club in Paris, her statement read in part: 'I told him I thought it was out of his system. I told him he had promised me we would never go. People were having sex everywhere.'

Ryan tried to tough it out for a while, but his efforts – including a reference to the Paris venue as 'an avant-garde nightclub' – were as ineffective as Blair Hull's had been. He exited the race before the month was out.

Illinois Republicans were left with a headache of monumental proportions. Obama had the battlefield to himself. The more he came to be seen as a white-hot favourite, the more difficult it was to attract any credible Republican into the race. At one stage, rumours swirled that the party might recruit Mike Ditka, the extrovert former head coach of the Chicago Bears football team. But by mid-July Ditka had ruled himself out.

Then came Obama's triumph at the Boston convention. The Republicans were now in a state of desperation. Just how grim their predicament had become was revealed when they finally unveiled their candidate: Alan Keyes.

Keyes was not even a resident of Illinois. His home was in Montgomery County, Maryland, almost 700 miles from Chicago. Keyes was a perennial candidate, and a perennial loser. His dismal electoral record was a consequence of both his ultra-right religious views and his propensity for peculiar personal behaviour.

As a candidate in a 1992 Senate race in Maryland, he had decided to pay himself a handsome salary out of campaign funds. Four years later, while running for president, he had been detained by police after trying to gatecrash a debate from which he had been excluded.

In the three months between Keyes' announcement and the election, he lived up – or rather down – to every expectation. Launching his candidacy, he predicted not just that he would win but that 'the victory [will be] for God'. Later, he drew comparisons between himself and Abraham Lincoln, and said that Jesus would not vote for Obama because of his pro-choice position on abortion.

Another lively moment came when, on a radio show, Keyes described homosexuality as 'selfish hedonism'. The host asked if this meant that Mary Cheney, the lesbian daughter of Keyes' party col-league, Vice President Dick Cheney, was a selfish hedonist. 'Of course she is,' came the reply. 'That goes by definition.'

As Election Day approached, virtually everyone accepted that Obama was in an impregnable position. In the end, only the margin of victory was a surprise: Obama received 3,597,456 votes to Keyes' 1,390,690. That translated as a 70 percent to 27 percent win. It was the biggest margin of victory in a US Senate race in Illinois history.

The Obama campaign splashed out $100,000 on a victory party that night in the Hyatt Regency Hotel in Chicago. There were ice sculptures bearing the slogan 'Obama: Only One America'. The room was crammed with 2,000 supporters. The man who was assured of becoming only the fifth black senator in American history hit the stage shortly after 9 PM, and the cries of 'Yes we can!' rang out again.

Obama's victory was the single bright flare in a dark night for the Democrats. It was obvious to all but the most desperate diehards that John Kerry had lost the presidential election to George W. Bush. The result was made official the next day.

Democrats had woken up on Election Day believing that Kerry could win. Now, bleary-eyed on the morning after, they were trying to dilute their disappointment by casting around for a new hero. Could the senator-elect from Illinois be their man?

'I am not running for president. I am not running for president in four years. I am not running for president in 2008,' a bemused Obama told reporters in his campaign office.

As the questions persisted, he almost began to plead. 'Come on, guys,' he protested. 'It's a silly question. Guys, I am a state senator. I was elected yesterday. I have never set foot in the US Senate. I have never worked in Washington. And the notion that I am somehow going to start running for higher office, it just doesn't make sense.'

Times change.

2

LEAP OF FAITH

Hermene Hartman opened the package that had arrived at her office and found yet another book from a first-time author. There was a letter with it too. The message was not from a publicity agent but from the writer himself. In it, he explained who he was and asked whether she would consider reviewing his memoir. Hartman, a well-known figure within the more affluent sections of Chicago's black community, was unfamiliar with him. His name was unusual: Barack Obama.

Hartman was the publisher of *N'Digo*, a Chicago magazine catering to an African-American readership. The book was *Dreams From My Father*, Obama's tale of growing up as a biracial American. His efforts to promote the book in that summer of 1995 may have been intended to advance whatever literary ambitions he held. They also had a secondary purpose. Obama was inching towards entering the state Senate race at the time. A boost in his profile in the locality – even the relatively modest one that might be delivered by a book review in *N'Digo* – would be more than welcome.

Hartman agreed to meet Obama in person. She was immediately 'quite impressed with him', she told me. 'Since that day, I have always been very impressed with his listening ability, which is so unusual. When he asks questions, he really listens to the answers.'

Obama pressed her for a review. 'He was very dedicated and very determined,' Hartman recalled. She eventually declined, despite his persistence. 'I thought the book was a little exotic for the audience,' the publisher said. 'I didn't think it fitted with our core readers.'

Still, Obama's approach to Hartman had not been entirely in vain. 'I told him I thought he was someone to watch, and we became friends,' she said. Hartman would soon become a central player in a group of influential Chicagoans who would back Obama's earliest political campaigns. Revealingly, she emphasised that the members of this group mostly came from the African-American business community. Churches had traditionally been the conduit from which aspiring black politicians had emerged; Obama, not for the first or last time, would take a different route.

'We said to him, "Please do not go to the ministers,"' Hartman noted. '"We need a different model."'

*

The first edition of *Dreams From My Father* had a respectable print run of 20,000 copies, garnered some positive reviews and was even published in Japan. But Obama himself described its sales as 'underwhelming'. Anyone who bought a copy signed by the young author, and held on to it, made a wise choice: today, their purchase could be worth up to $5,000.

When his memoir was re-released in 2004, Obama did not need to write any beseeching letters to would-be reviewers. The new edition hit the shelves in August, just after his speech at the Democratic National Convention. By Christmas, with his Senate victory in the bag, it had spent 14 weeks on the *New York Times* best-seller list. By the summer of 2008, Obama was the Democratic nominee for president and *Dreams From My Father* had racked up over a hundred weeks as a best-seller. Total sales had surpassed 900,000 copies.

Obama's new-found political celebrity was, of course, the root of the success of the 2004 edition. It was also helped on its way by the strikingly atypical story he had to tell.

Obama had been born in Hawaii on 4 August 1961 to Ann Dunham, a white native of Kansas, and Barack Obama Sr, a black Kenyan. His parents had met at the University of Hawaii. Obama wrote in his memoir that his parents had married the year before his birth, although he acknowledged that virtually everything around the ceremony seemed 'a bit murky'. *Time* magazine noted in an April 2008 story that, contrary to Obama's belief, court records gave the marriage date as 2 February 1961 – by which time the 18-year-old Kansan would have been three months pregnant with her son. Neither friends nor family were invited to the wedding, and Obama told *Time*: 'I never probed my mother about the details. Did they decide to get married because she was already pregnant? Or did he propose to her in the tra-ditional, formal way? I suppose, had she not passed away, I would have asked more.' (Obama's mother was diagnosed with cancer and died in 1995, aged 52.)

Whether Dunham and Obama married in 1960 or 1961 would have made no difference to one major issue. As Obama noted in *Dreams From My Father*, many Americans would have thought of a stark, cold term to describe such a union: 'miscegenation'. 'The word is hump-backed, ugly, portending a monstrous outcome: like "antebellum" or "octoroon", it evokes images of another era, a distant world of horse-whips and flames.'

('Antebellum', a Latinate term that literally means 'before war', was typically used in reference to the pre-Civil War American South, while 'octoroon' was a degrading label from the same epoch for a person who could be discriminated against because one of his or her great-grandparents was African-American. The latter term may have fallen out of use by the time Obama's parents met, but the racist attitudes it had underpinned were anything but ancient history.)

Black-white marriage was still illegal in more than half of the 50 US states in 1960. It was only in 1967 that the Supreme Court finally dealt the death blow to these injustices by declaring the state of Virginia's ban on interracial marriages unconstitutional. The plain-tiffs in the Supreme Court case were a woman of African-American and Native American heritage and her white husband, whose names – Mildred and Richard Loving – meant, in a happy quirk of history, that the case's standard appellation would forever be *Loving* v. *Virginia*.

The Obamas' marriage, however, was not to be some Hollywood-style parable about the power of love to overcome all obstacles. It was much messier than that.

Barack Obama Sr left the family when his son was just two. Initially, he went to Harvard University alone, on a scholarship. His wife would tell her son years later, in a rare show of enmity towards Barack Sr, that her husband had been offered a more generous scholarship at another university, the New School in New York City, the terms of which would have been sufficient to support all three of them. 'But Barack was such a stubborn bastard, he had to go to Harvard,' she added.

Dunham would divorce Obama Sr shortly afterwards, and he would return to Kenya. Barack Obama would see his father only once more, at the age of 10, when the older man would come back to Hawaii to visit his son, his former wife and his former in-laws. The experience seems to have been excruciatingly awkward for all concerned.

For a while after returning to his newly independent homeland, Obama Sr was on the rise, working as an economist for the Kenyan government. But tribalism – in addition to run-ins with other officials and, eventually, with President Jomo Kenyatta – put paid to his chances of further advancement. In later years, he would fall into bitterness and excessive drinking.

By 1982, Barack Obama – then known as 'Barry' – was a student at New York's Columbia University. He was making breakfast one morning when he received a phone call in his dingy apartment. The line was so bad that he had to ask the caller, who was in Nairobi, to repeat who she was.

'Aunt Jane,' the voice came back across the ocean. 'Listen, Barry, your father is dead. He is killed in a car accident. Hello? Can you hear me? I say, your father is dead. Barry, please call your uncle in Boston and tell him. I can't talk now, OK, Barry. I will try to call you again.'

The call was cut off, Obama remembered, 'and I sat down on the couch, smelling eggs burn in the kitchen, staring at cracks in the plaster, trying to measure my loss.'

*

Despite such turbulent beginnings, *Dreams From My Father* is far from being an unrelenting lament. Obama noted that he had no recollection of his father prior to the latter's departure from the family home. 'At the point where my own memories began,' he wrote, 'my mother had already begun a courtship with the man who would become her second husband.'

That man was Lolo Soetoro, an Indonesian. Obama writes about him with fondness for the most part, and his descriptions of Indonesia, where the family moved when he was six, are vivid and joyful. He lived there for four years. A half-sister, Maya Soetoro, was born in 1970; she and Obama remain close to this day. The tensions that were, in time, to pull apart his mother's second marriage gradually became apparent, however. Barack was sent back to Hawaii to live with his maternal grandparents, his mother promising that Maya and she would join him within a year.

Stanley and Madelyn Dunham were an intriguing couple. 'Gramps' and 'Toot', the young Obama called them – Toot from 'tutu', the Hawaiian word for 'grandparent'. The couple had moved several times from their native Kansas, driven in part by Stanley's restlessness and by his belief that a big opportunity was always around the next corner. Stanley had been lured to Hawaii by the promise of the money to be made in the wake of the former territory's admission as a full US state in 1959 and, more specifically, by the offer of running a furniture shop.

The Dunhams were not overtly political and would certainly not have seen themselves as liberals per se. Yet they possessed a basic decency that inoculated them against the more common bigotries of their time.

When Ann was still a child, they had lived in Texas for a while. Toot worked at a local bank. A mannerly woman, she would share the time of day with her colleagues, including an African-American caretaker she would later remember only as 'Mr Reed'.

As Barack Obama told it: 'While the two of them chatted in the hallway one day, a secretary in the office stormed up and hissed that Toot should never, ever, "call no nigger 'Mister'".'

During the same period, Toot came home from work one day to

find her daughter being taunted by other children because she was reading books in the garden with another girl, who was black. 'Nigger lover,' the bullies shouted, dispersing when Toot appeared. When Stanley called some of the other children's parents to complain, he was met with a near-universal response: 'You best talk to your daughter, Mr Dunham. White girls don't play with coloureds in this town.'

At least Hawaii was a little more relaxed about ethnicity. Obama at first excelled academically, gaining entrance on a scholarship to Honolulu's most elite school, Punahou Academy. His mother and Maya did indeed arrive back from Indonesia, and for three years the trio lived together in an apartment only a short distance from the school. It was a time of relative harmony and stability for the family, but Ann, who was now studying for a master's degree in anthropology, eventually decided to go back to Indonesia to do fieldwork. Maya was to go with her, and Barack was asked whether he wanted to join them. He declined. 'I doubted what Indonesia now had to offer and wearied of being new all over again,' he recalled.

Obama was also becoming caught up in the typical tumults of adolescence. In his case, the confusion was exacerbated by questions about his racial identity. 'I was trying to raise myself to be a black man in America, and beyond the given of my appearance, no one around me seemed to know exactly what that meant.'

Obama's disorientation deepened, and it bred the classic teenage blend of resentment and apathy. His academic performance tapered off, though the extent of his rebellion does not seem to have been especially dramatic: he won a place at a respected Los Angeles university, Occidental College, without much apparent effort. He had chosen Occidental casually – the deciding factor was that he had met a girl from close to Los Angeles while she was in holiday in Hawaii.

It was not until Obama transferred to New York after two years on the west coast that he began to find his path once more. He arrived in the city in August 1981 in inauspicious circumstances – as he relates it, he spent his first night sleeping in an alley after no one answered the door at the apartment he had been told he could live in. Things improved over the next two years: he ran every day, fasted on Sundays and otherwise devoted himself to his studies. He graduated from Columbia in 1983 with a degree in political science.

Obama's new seriousness of purpose was not immediately hitched to a specific goal. In time, he decided that he would become a community organiser. In his memoir, he would mock himself for a deficiency that his opponents would years later accuse him of: vagueness.

'There wasn't much detail to the idea,' he recalled. 'I didn't know anyone making a living that way. When classmates in college asked me just what it was that a community organiser did, I couldn't answer them directly.'

There was another flaw in Obama's vaguely conceived master plan. As graduation approached, he had written to every organisation and progressive-minded official he could think of. No one wrote back.

He reconciled himself to a year of 'more conventional work' and joined a business research company. From there, he went on to a dissatisfying job with a government reform group and, later, to a casual post passing out flyers on behalf of an aspiring local politician. 'The candidate lost and I never did get paid,' Obama observed tartly.

Then, just when he had 'all but given up on organising', his luck changed. A call from an activist in Chicago came through. The man, who was white – Obama gave him the alias 'Marty Kaufman' in the book, though in reality he was Gerald Kellman – was candid about what he needed: someone smart and black. His idea was to bring together working-class people of all races to help save or replace manufacturing jobs, which the city was losing at a rapid rate. He offered Obama $10,000 a year to join him. Obama went for it.

*

For the next three years, community organising would be Obama's life. It was an uphill battle, trying to engage people in places like Altgeld Gardens, a struggling public housing estate – or, as Obama would bluntly put it, 'a place to house poor blacks'. The Gardens, he wrote, 'seemed in a perpetual state of disrepair. Ceilings crumbled. Pipes burst. Toilets backed up.'

Still, he enjoyed modest successes during his first stint in Chicago.

He helped bring a job centre to the area. And a group of citizens whom he had helped organise pressured the city's housing authority, which had been blithely indifferent to their concerns, into examining their homes for asbestos.

The asbestos victory came after the residents and Obama had made a bus trip to the authority's offices to confront officials directly. Their achievement made no national headlines; it created no stir beyond the housing projects of the South Side. Yet it seemed to prove some grand ideas: that government could be held accountable to the people and that, if citizens banded together, they could force through real changes. On the journey back home, the residents were thrilled. As for their organiser: 'I changed as a result of that bus trip, in a fundamental way. It was the sort of change that's important not because it alters your concrete circumstances in some way (wealth, security, fame) but because it hints at what might be possible and therefore spurs you on, beyond the immediate exhilaration, beyond any subsequent disappointments, to retrieve that thing that you once, ever so briefly, held in your hand. That bus ride kept me going, I think. Maybe it still does.'

Breakthroughs like the asbestos issue were special in part because they were so rare. Most of the time, community organising was a grind and change came in tiny increments – if at all. After three years, Obama applied to Harvard Law School. He was accepted, and left Chicago.

His time at Harvard and beyond is dealt with only as an addendum in *Dreams From My Father*, which instead reaches its emotional climax with a visit to Kenya to visit the grave of his father.

It was at Harvard rather than in the more hard-scrabble climes of Chicago that Obama came to public attention. In February 1990, he became the first African-American president of the *Harvard Law Review*. The position was such a golden ticket to the highest echelons of the legal world that it was fought for tooth and nail. (Perhaps the closest, if inexact, parallel to the role in Irish or British universities is the presidency of the Oxford Union debating society.)

The achievement was significant enough to draw the attention of the national media. 'FIRST BLACK PRESIDENT OF HARVARD LAW REVIEW

ELECTED', the Associated Press trumpeted on 5 February. Obama told the news agency that his election should not be seen as 'a symbol that there aren't problems out there with the situation of African-Americans in society.' He did allow, though, that it 'sends a signal out that blacks can excel in competitive situations like scholarship. It's also a sign of progress.'

Leaving Harvard, Obama abjured the big law firms in New York and Washington, instead returning to Chicago. In 1992, he threw himself into a voter registration drive – the one that supporters of Alice Palmer would recall bitterly when Obama conspired to keep her off the ballot in the state Senate race four years later. It was called Project Vote and its slogan was 'It's A Power Thing'. Obama invoked Malcolm X in a bid to grab the attention of young African-Americans who were far removed from the traditional political system.

'Today, we see hundreds of young blacks talking "black power" and wearing Malcolm X T-shirts,' he told the *Chicago Sun-Times* in August 1992, 'but they don't bother to register and vote. We remind them that Malcolm once made a speech titled "The Ballot or The Bullet" and that today we've got enough bullets in the streets but not enough ballots.'

Project Vote registered over 100,000 new voters in the city. For Obama, the drive's success was another feather in his cap. So too was his decision, made shortly afterwards, to join one of Chicago's best-known civil rights law firms. Obama alludes to his legal work at the very end of *Dreams From My Father*. As his memoir finishes, the real story of his rise to power was just beginning.

The book itself became a key factor in Obama's ascent after its reissue in 2004. It solidified the sense that he was a politician apart. That idea had his biracial identity at its core, but it also encompassed other, less solemn, issues. For a start, he could write. The book is notable for the grace of its prose and its author's sense of how to tell a story. Joe Klein, an author and a political columnist for *Time*, described it as 'maybe the best-written memoir ever produced by an American politician'.

Obama's literary skill seemed to go hand in hand with candour and sensitivity – two qualities not much associated with politicians in America or anywhere else. As the book's success grew and Obama's political star rose ever higher, great attention was paid to his admission of teenage drug use, which had included dabbling with cocaine. His depiction of universal emotions – regret, confusion and loneliness among them – was perhaps more significant, at least in helping him develop the passionate following that would sustain his run for the presidency.

During his days as an organiser, for example, one of his father's other children, Auma, came to visit him in Chicago. Having doubts about her boyfriend and about her own capacity for intimacy, she asked Obama whether he had any similar tensions in his personal life.

'Well . . . there was a woman in New York that I loved,' he answered. 'She was white. She had dark hair, and specks of green in her eyes. Her voice sounded like a wind chime. We saw each other for almost a year. On the weekends, mostly. Sometimes in her apartment, sometimes in mine. You know how you can fall into your own private world? Just two people, hidden and warm. Your own language. Your own customs. That's how it was.'

Obama went on to tell Auma how uncomfortable he had felt when a visit to a country house owned by his lover's family revealed the enormous gulf in their backgrounds. He pushed the woman away, he said, partly out of fear that he would eventually be sucked into her world. When Auma asked him if he ever heard from her, he told her that he had got a postcard at Christmas, that she had met someone else, and that, in any case, he had his work to focus on.

'Is that enough?' Auma asked.

'Sometimes,' Obama replied.

There is nothing life-changing about the episode, and the mystery woman is never mentioned again. Yet try imagining a similar vignette springing from the pen of, say, Hillary Clinton or John Kerry, never mind George W. Bush. For them to reveal such real, messy humanity – and to express it with such tenderness – seems almost unthinkable.

Dreams From My Father was important not just for its acuity and its skill. It also solidified one of Obama's most precious assets: people liked him.

*

For all of Obama's ambition, his insistence at the start of his Senate career that he had no plans to run for the Oval Office in 2008 seems to have been genuine. 'The intention never was to do it,' Terry Link told me. 'We talked about the speculation. He would call me from various places as he was travelling around and I know for sure he had no intention of doing it.'

Further evidence lies in a series of meetings that were held early in 2005. The glow from the convention speech still clung to Obama. *Dreams From My Father* was selling and selling. The biggest fear he and his advisors had was that expectations would build to such a height that he could not possibly meet them.

They came up with a strategy that paid little heed to what would happen in 2008. It became known as the 2010–2012–2016 plan.

Obama's six-year Senate term would run out in 2010. As that year loomed, he would have to decide whether to run for re-election or have a tilt at becoming governor of Illinois, a position that would be up for election at the same time. A victory in either of those races would leave the coast clear to think about a White House run in 2012. If, in the meantime, a Democrat (most likely Hillary Clinton) had won the presidency in 2008, that person would surely seek re-election in 2012. This, in turn, would mean that Obama would not get his chance until 2016.

The first phase of the strategy crafted by the Obama team called for him to knuckle down in the Senate. He was so coated in stardust at the time that he needed to prove that he was not going to lose touch with the needs of the people who had elected him. With that in mind, Obama spurned the requests of TV producers who wanted him as a guest on the big national talk shows for most of that year. He generally avoided nationally orientated speaking engagements as well, although he made an exception for the NAACP, one of America's oldest civil rights organisations.

He would also use his talent for self-deprecation to ease his way into his colleagues' good graces. As late as March 2006, he would make light of his public image. 'I've been very blessed,' he told the crowd at the Gridiron Dinner, a jovial if sometimes cringe-making Washington occasion at which journalists and politicians poke fun at each other. 'Keynote speaker at the Democratic convention. The cover of *Newsweek*. My book made the best-seller list. I just won a Grammy for reading it on tape. Really, what else is there to do?' He paused and smiled: 'Well, I guess I could pass a law or something.' Less than a year later, he would announce his candidacy for the presidency of the United States.

Obama's ability to construct a path to the door of the White House was testament to his prodigious talents and to the sense of freshness associated with him. Even so, those things on their own, in a different time, would not have been enough to sustain a relative novice in a serious bid for the highest office in the land.

In order to back Obama for president in 2008, the American people would have to be prepared to take on some degree of risk. As Bill Clinton would grumpily put it months later, even selecting Obama as the Democratic Party's candidate would require a willingness 'to roll the dice'.

There was one 'perfect storm' scenario that not even Obama had thought much about as he embarked on his Senate career. Americans' anxiety about the direction in which their nation was heading could grow deeper and broader; their disgust with the culture of Washington could grow stronger; and their hunger for a new direction could grow ravenous. If all of that happened, quickly enough and with enough intensity, then they might decide to give the dice a roll in 2008.

This meant that there was one person who was capable of creating the conditions in which the new senator could become a bona fide presidential contender. It was the man whose second term at 1600 Pennsylvania Avenue was just beginning.

*

The American electorate gave George W. Bush the benefit of the doubt in the 2004 presidential election. Many of them would come to regret it.

Bush won re-election in the face of a war that was already beginning to go awry and an indifferent economy. His victory could be partly ascribed to his campaign's depiction of John Kerry as prone to expediency and waffling, yet that was not the whole story.

In November 2004, many of his compatriots were willing, rightly or wrongly, to give Bush credit for having kept the US homeland safe from terrorist attacks in the three years since the horrors of 9/11. Like any Republican candidate, he could also rely on support from the large slice of the electorate that consistently agrees with the party's core tenets of low taxation, military strength and conservative moral values.

If Bush's first administration had been controversial, his second was a fiasco. The most obvious and most serious example was Iraq. The benighted country had held its first democratic general election ten days after Bush had been sworn in again, but that did nothing to arrest its trajectory towards chaos. Violence spiralled for much of the next two years. By the summer of 2006, the *Iraq Coalition Casualty Count* website was recording bloodshed at a level that was almost apocalyptic: 1,063 Iraqi civilian deaths in July, 2,733 in August, 3,389 in September.

A tragedy at home blasted a hole in Bush's domestic credibility. In the last week of August 2005, Hurricane Katrina formed in the Gulf of Mexico. When the storm crashed into Louisiana and Mississippi, catastrophe ensued. The levees protecting New Orleans, which lay below sea level, broke. In that city alone, more than 700 people died. The total death toll was over 1,800.

The grim statistics were only part of the reason why Bush was so damaged by Katrina. The sheer inadequacy of the government's response to the hurricane was astonishing. Many of the deaths occurred after the storm had passed; people perished from dehydration; bodies lay in the street for days. The president's approval ratings, which had been anaemic before the tragedy, turned sharply downwards afterwards. They never recovered.

There were other failures too. The first big domestic initiative of Bush's second term – reform of the social security system – ran aground. When a vacancy came up on the Supreme Court bench, he nominated Harriet Miers, who had been his personal lawyer before becoming White House counsel. The choice horrified even many Republicans, who saw it as blatant cronyism. Pressure was eventually exerted on Miers to withdraw her name from consideration.

Fiscal conservatives grew increasingly appalled by the nation's spiralling budget deficit. At the same time, Bush's seemingly incongruous support for liberalisation of the immigration system offended the most nationalistic segments of his base.

The wider world offered no succour. By mid-2006, Iran's nuclear programme was continuing to gather pace. On 5 July, North Korea tested seven long-range missiles, including two that were thought to have sufficient range to reach Alaska. Israel, with US backing, fought a bloody and pointless battle with Lebanon's Hezbollah guerrillas through July and August. All in all, it felt to many Americans as though the wheels were coming off.

As 2006 wore on, Obama edged back into the limelight. The Democrats hoped to make gains in the midterm elections in November. Obama had begun to rival Bill and Hillary Clinton as the hottest possible guest for party fundraising events. He toured the country, boosting the coffers of colleagues seeking office – and, in the process, building up a sizeable reservoir of goodwill.

Obama still did not appear to be giving any serious thought to leaping into the 2008 presidential race. Besides, he had a new book lined up for release in the autumn. Not even Obama at his most cocky could have envisaged the kind of reception that book would receive, or where it would lead.

*

As a piece of writing, *The Audacity of Hope* paled by comparison to *Dreams From My Father*. Obama's relative anonymity when he wrote his first book in the mid-1990s had given him the liberty to be self-revelatory and raw. Now, his fame, and the likelihood that he would seek higher office at some point, conspired to produce a more cautious, formulaic work. Axelrod and more junior members of his staff had scrutinised the drafts as Obama had written them, combing them for formulations or admissions that might cause him trouble down the line.

Audacity's literary quality came to matter little. The book set off the first real outbreak of Obama-mania. The media fed part of it. There was an appearance on *Oprah*, a photo shoot for *Men's Vogue* and magazine covers galore – including one from *Time* headlined 'WHY BARACK OBAMA COULD BE THE NEXT PRESIDENT'. But there was something else going on, something which it was well beyond the power of the press to confect.

When Obama scheduled a book signing in Chicago, the queue to see him began forming just after 4 AM. A 1,450-seat hall in Tempe, Arizona, sold out almost immediately. The same thing happened in Seattle, at a concert hall with a capacity of 2,500.

In the first three weeks after going on sale in mid-October, *The Audacity of Hope* sold an extraordinary 182,000 copies. One astonished independent bookshop owner told the *New York Times*: 'Obama is out of the ballpark completely.'

The book does have some charms, especially in its more personal moments. Obama recalled how he had kissed Michelle for the first time after buying her ice cream ('It tasted of chocolate,' he revealed), and how, more than a decade into their married life together, he would be mocked by their elder daughter Malia, then eight, for being so uncool as to try to shake hands with her friends. (The couple had one other child, Sasha, who was almost three years Malia's junior.)

The broader purpose of *The Audacity of Hope* was to make the argument that partisanship had infected and corroded America's public life. Obama wrote about 'the gap between the magnitude of our challenges and the smallness of our politics'. He lamented a political culture that had become debased to the point where it had come to resemble the empty tribalism of a sports match.

His road map to get out of the cul-de-sac could, at times, be distinctly lacking in detail. Yet the lack of specifics did nothing to dim the enthusiasm so many Americans felt for Obama. In fact, it may have added to it, since it allowed people to project whatever they desired onto him. Either way, the hysteria fuelled even more speculation about the senator's ambitions.

The official position remained that he was not running for president. According to David Axelrod's account, the candidate and his aides agreed that serious discussion of his plans for 2008 would have to wait until after the midterm elections.

Obama had already begun thinking about the idea with a new earnestness and urgency. When I spoke to Terry Link, he recalled a rally for another Illinois Democrat that both he and Obama had attended in the lead-up to Election Day: 'He and I were just walking together, away from the crowd, and we were talking. That was the first time I had ever said to him: "I think you're ready to do it." By that stage, he was contemplating it seriously.'

During a 22 October appearance on *Meet the Press*, the most widely watched of all the national political talk shows, Obama let it be known for the first time that his stance had shifted. 'Given the response I've been getting the last several months, I have thought about the possibility,' he told host Tim Russert.

The elections went well for the Democrats. The party regained control of both the Senate and the House of Representatives, and leading figures in the Republican Party, including Senator George Allen of Virginia and Senator Rick Santorum of Pennsylvania, lost their seats.

The next day, the Obama team met over pizza. The discussion stretched over four hours. There were few flights of fancy. The talk focused on practical matters: how much money Obama would need to raise, what the logistical challenges were, and, of course, whether he could win.

'Anyone who tells you that he is 100 percent certain that Senator Obama's running doesn't know him,' Axelrod told *Salon*. 'He's still working it through.'

There was another reason for Obama's reticence. Michelle was significantly more sceptical about a run for the presidency than anyone else in his inner circle. She had a plethora of worries. How would the media attention affect Malia and Sasha? Could Barack win without compromising himself and thus becoming just another politician? Was there a realistic plan to win the nomination and the presidency or was this just some dangerous brew of book-inspired euphoria and wishful thinking?

'Even when we had that discussion [at the rally], I remember him saying, "This is going to have to be a family decision",' Terry Link said. 'It was going to be their decision, not his. He knew the magnitude of this. He knew what they would have to go through, so he sat down and contemplated it with her.'

The Obama family headed for Hawaii over Christmas. There, Michelle and Barack would have a chance to talk over the pros and cons a final time. Aides scrambled to put the infrastructure for a bid in place. If Obama decided not to run, it would be easy enough to dismantle whatever had been prepared; if he decided he was in, and his operation wasn't up to scratch, the whiff of amateurishness could wreck his chances before he had a chance to get out of the starting blocks.

The new year dawned. Whether in genuine uncertainty or in an attempt to erect a smokescreen, Obama's advisors let it be known that the senator was unlikely to announce anything before President Bush's annual State of the Union address on 23 January.

Then, suddenly, he was in. On 10.06 AM on 16 January 2008, Obama filed papers to form a presidential exploratory committee. He released a video on his website to explain the decision to supporters. Dressed in an open-necked shirt, Obama asserted that he knew 'how hungry we all are for a different kind of politics'.

He and Hillary Clinton stood only a couple of yards apart later that day on the floor of the Senate. Each studiously ignored the other. Four days later, Clinton announced that she was entering the race. 'I'm in, and I'm in to win,' she said. Her advisors insisted that she had always intended to declare her candidacy that day, though media speculation that she had moved the date forward due to concern about Obama's challenge continued regardless.

There was little real combat between the camps in the next couple of weeks. On 10 February, a sunny but bitterly cold day, Obama officially launched his campaign in front of 15,000 people in Springfield, Illinois. It was the same place where Abraham Lincoln, the president who had ended slavery, had risen to prominence. The crowd was keen to get an eye-witness view of modern history being made.

Obama took to the stage with his wife and daughters in tow. Michelle, Malia and Sasha were wrapped up against the elements: the temperature was minus 14 degrees centigrade. Obama, bareheaded and without gloves, would later admit that a heater had been secreted at the base of the podium at which he stood.

His breath curled in the air as he expounded once again on the need for a new kind of politics. In one of the most widely replayed lines from his address, he insisted: 'I know I haven't spent a lot of time learning the ways of Washington. But I've been there long enough to know that the ways of Washington must change.'

There was another passage from the speech that was more important than most people realised at the time. 'This campaign can't only be about me,' he told the crowd. 'It must be about *us* – it must be about what we can do together. This campaign must be the occasion, the vehicle, of your hopes and your dreams. It will take your time, your energy and your advice – to push us forward when we're doing right, and to let us know when we're not. This campaign has to be about reclaiming the meaning of citizenship, restoring our sense of common purpose, and realising that few obstacles can withstand the power of millions of voices calling for change.'

If Obama were to win, he would have to prove those words true. If the battle for the Democratic nomination became an exercise in conventional political warfare, Hillary Clinton had the weaponry to outgun him.

Obama's chances depended on hundreds of thousands of people answering his call and offering not just their money and their votes but passionate engagement with his cause. If the former community organiser could breathe life into a true national movement, he was in with a shot. It was a big 'if'.

3

GIRDING FOR BATTLE

It was a Saturday night in a hotel in New Hampshire and, to the amazement of just about everyone, Hillary Clinton seemed on the verge of breaking into 'The Locomotion'.

The evening had gone well. Clinton had drawn a bigger audience than anyone could remember to an annual fundraiser for the local Democratic Party. The speech she delivered had held the crowd rapt. When it was over, 'You Ain't Seen Nothing Yet' blared from the speakers and well-wishers crammed the podium. They jockeyed to get close to the woman who, at that moment, seemed highly likely to become the first female presidential nominee of a major party.

Clinton, a wide smile on her face, mock-strutted from one side of the stage to the other, her arms rolling in imitation of the pistons of a train just as the old sixties dance move demanded.

It was a rare moment of levity from a woman who usually clasped her earnestness like a shield. That weekend in March 2007, ten months before New Hampshire would become the crucial second state to vote in the contest to select the Democratic candidate, Clinton seemed more at ease in her own skin than usual.

Perhaps it was the introduction that had done it. Kathy Sullivan, an old Clinton ally, was retiring after eight years as chairperson of the state party. As she handed over the microphone, she asked the audience to welcome 'the great, wonderful, fabulous, divinely attractive and brilliant senator from the state of New York, Hillary Rodham Clinton'.

'I hope the press is listening to "divinely attractive",' Clinton began, a gentle jab at those of us peering at her over our laptops from the back of the room. 'Next time somebody says, you know, "I'm not crazy about her hair" or "What on earth did she think when she put that outfit on?", I'm going to say . . . ' She paused, as if to draw the audience closer in, then threw her head back theatrically. 'Well, all I know is that in New Hampshire, they think I'm divinely attractive.' The crowd roared, startled by her uncharacteristic flamboyance.

The evening may not have been an official Clinton campaign event, but it felt like one. Hillary badges and stickers seemed to adorn the clothes of every other person strolling through the foyer of the Nashua Sheraton Hotel. 'For one thing, she's a woman – that's a big thing,' Susan Caldwell of Raymond, New Hampshire told me when I asked why she was already a firm supporter of the former First Lady. 'She's committed to the same things I am committed to: she's for women and families and children and health care, and those are all important to me. I met her a few weeks ago; she came across very warm, very connected.'

Clinton herself swiftly turned from her humorous opening to more serious matters. Much of the American public had become 'invisible' to George W. Bush and his allies, she argued. 'If you are a hard-working single parent who can't afford health insurance, or a small-business owner who worries about energy costs, or a student who can't afford to continue college, you are invisible to this administration,' she said. 'For six long years, President Bush and the Washington Republicans have looked right through you.'

Clinton offered up a few more American archetypes, then added: 'They're not invisible to us. They're certainly not invisible to me. And when we retake the White House, they will no longer be invisible to the president of the United States.'

There was one person who was apparently invisible to Clinton, though. She made no reference to Barack Obama during her 25-minute speech. The omission was hardly accidental. Clinton had decided, in conjunction with her senior advisors, that she should present herself as the inevitable victor in the Democratic contest. Attacking or otherwise acknowledging her rivals would only boost their stature, so the thinking went.

There were plenty of reasons to believe the strategy might work. Clinton had been arguably the dominant personality in the party since Al Gore had lost the presidency to Bush in 2000. On that Election Day, as her husband prepared to leave office, Clinton had won election to the Senate, the only First Lady ever to do so. She had coasted to a 12-point victory in New York over a little-known Republican, Rick Lazio.

(Clinton was elected to the Senate on the same day as three other women. Between then and the end of 2008, a further six female senators would be elected, bringing the total number of women to have served in the body over its 219-year history to 37.)

On Capitol Hill, Clinton earned plaudits for her unexpected willingness to find common ground with Republicans and for her prodigious workrate. When she ran for re-election in 2006, she crushed her opponent, John Spencer, by 67 percent to 31 percent.

By then, no one seriously doubted that Clinton would seek the presidency in 2008. During her first run for the Senate, she had tried to defang allegations that she was a carpetbagger by promising to serve out her full term if elected. She had conspicuously declined to repeat that pledge in 2006.

The notion of Clinton's strength as a candidate was inseparable from her husband's exalted reputation in the party. Bill Clinton had been the first Democrat since Franklin Delano Roosevelt to serve two full terms as president; indeed, he was only the second Democrat to have won a presidential election since 1964. He was the most formidable fundraiser in the party's history and had a lifetime of favours he could call in from local Democratic office-holders and activists. All in all, the conventional wisdom was that Hillary Clinton held too many organisational assets to be beaten. But it wasn't quite as simple as that.

One of Clinton's biggest problems was straightforward: considered in isolation from her fame and her last name, her political skills could look distinctly modest. She had proven a drag on Bill Clinton's first run for the presidency, causing uproar with comments that appeared to denigrate traditionalist women. In particular, one snippy remark in response to questions about aspects of her legal career – 'I suppose I could have stayed home and baked cookies and had teas' – took years for her to live down.

Things did not improve when the Clintons made it to the White House. Hillary took on an enormous responsibility – reform of the US health care system – and her stewardship proved disastrous. The task force she chaired met in secret, at her insistence. The proposal it produced was over 1,000 pages long and was impossible to explain with any lucidity. She refused to compromise on the bill – something she would later admit was a serious error – and it died before even coming to a vote in the Senate.

Clinton had another weakness that was often overlooked because it did not fit into the overall narrative that surrounded her. The implicit message of much of the press coverage she received was that she was diligent and disciplined, which she was. But as a consequence, it was assumed that she was the epitome of consistency on the campaign trail, which she was not.

A few days before her impressive appearance at the New Hampshire fundraiser, I had seen Clinton address an audience in Washington that, on paper, looked tailor-made for her. Emily's List is an organisation that helps Democratic women who support abortion rights get elected across the US. Clinton, speaking at the group's annual luncheon, should have been the heroine of the hour. Once the applause that greeted her initial appearance had died down, she droned through a flat oration weighted down with clichés. The life drained from the room.

A week later, Judith Warner referred to the event in the *New York Times*. 'Hillary's a real tear-stopper,' she wrote. 'She has a voice that is metallic and somewhat atonal. She has the sentence structure and cadences of a political science professor.'

Clinton's weaknesses were not limited to matters of style and temperament. One issue loomed above all else in those early months on the trail: Iraq. Back in October 2002, the Senate had debated whether or not to give Bush the authority to use force in Iraq. Clinton's contribution had been a rather tortuous speech that paid lip service to both sides of the argument. She had voted to give the president what he wanted. She was one of 29 Democrats to do so; 21 had voted against.

Grassroots Democrats, however – the people who would now form the bulk of the electorate in the state-by-state primaries – had always been much more dubious about the war than the party leadership in Washington. They liked the fact that Obama, then a state senator, had come out unequivocally against the conflict before it had begun. Clinton's vote raised doubts that had dogged her for a long time. What did she really believe? Was she prepared to stand on principle even when it was not expedient to do so?

Clinton complicated matters further by adopting a curious stance when she was criticised for the Iraq vote. She would not apologise outright for it but neither, for obvious reasons, was it feasible for her to argue that she had been right. Instead, she settled on an answer that she repeated at almost every campaign stop: had she known then what she knew now, she would not have voted to authorise the use of force.

The formulation had been arrived at out of fear that if she apologised for the vote, Republicans would accuse her of being a flip-flopper. Yet Clinton's explanation left many Democratic audiences dissatisfied. If she was implicitly acknowledging that she had been wrong, they wondered, why not make a clean breast of things and say so?

During a town hall meeting in the small city of Dubuque, on one of her first trips to Iowa, I watched the crowd shift uneasily as a man told her that her position seemed like 'a way of saying: "I'm not responsible for my vote."' 'I have said many times that I take responsibility for my vote,' Clinton responded icily. She then changed the subject, criticising Bush's conduct of the war. Among the crowd that night was Tracy Nowack, a recent arrival in Iowa from neighbouring Illinois. Clinton, she told me, was 'very much what I expected'. She did not say it with enthusiasm.

As the race kicked off in earnest, two factors were pulling Clinton in opposite directions: she had enormous advantages but, respected rather than loved, she was far from being the perfect candidate. The question for Obama was whether he could come across as credible enough to stand a chance of derailing her.

(John Edwards was the only other member of the eight-person Democratic field who could pose a realistic challenge to Clinton, and even his chances of overall victory were regarded as slim. The other candidates were New Mexico governor Bill Richardson, Senator Joe Biden, Senator Chris Dodd, Congressman Dennis Kucinich and former senator Mike Gravel.)

*

Obama passed one of the first tests more emphatically than anyone had expected. Money was always going to be an issue for any candidate going up against the Clinton machine. In late 2006, with Obama's entry into the race far from certain, two of his key advisors, Steve Hildebrand, a veteran Democratic operative, and Pete Rouse, the publicity-shy head of his Senate office, had got in touch with Julianna Smoot.

Smoot was a hyper-competitive North Carolinian who had become a major player on the financial side of Democratic politics despite her relative youth. (She had just turned 40 when she was approached about Obama.) Obama's aides wanted Smoot to pitch to become his fundraising director, but they also wanted a realistic assessment of how much the senator could raise if he got into the contest. They already had a figure in their heads: $12 million by the time the first quarter ended on 31 March 2007. A 'take' on that scale would at least ensure they would not be blown out of the water by Clinton, they believed.

Smoot drew up a plan and encouraged Hildebrand and Rouse to set a more modest goal: $9 million. Obama would need to set aside ten hours each week to make fundraising calls, she cautioned – an enormous investment of time, given the gruelling schedule that faces any serious candidate. Though Smoot's findings made Obama's aides realise the scale of the challenge they faced, her level of preparedness impressed them. She was hired.

The estimates that Smoot, Hildebrand and Rouse had arrived at would, as it turned out, not have been enough to avert disaster. On

1 April, the Clinton campaign announced that it had raised $26 million for the quarter. No one else had come close to such a sum at a comparable stage of the electoral cycle.

The Clintonites' celebratory feelings soon turned to a sense of foreboding. The Obama camp did not immediately release its figures. In politics, such studied hesitancy does not bespeak embarrassment; it usually means that a campaign is keeping back good news in order to create the biggest possible bang. So it proved. Obama had raised almost $25 million. It was an astonishing figure for a candidate who had begun the race without any established national network.

The deeper you drilled down into the figures, the better they looked for Obama. More than 100,000 people had contributed to his campaign, twice as many as had given to Clinton's. Also, under the technicalities of US election law, donations to candidates were capped at $2,300 for the primary. Individuals could give an additional $2,300, but only with the proviso that the second tranche of money could not be used until the recipient became the party's official candidate and started the general election campaign. Almost all the money Obama had raised – $24.8 million – could be used in the primary. For Clinton, that figure was only $19.1 million.

The fundraising surge continued throughout the spring and into early summer. During the second quarter, Obama raised $32.5 million to Clinton's $27 million.

Obama's fundraising performance fed a message that his campaign aides loved to propagate: that Clinton was the establishment candidate, favoured by party insiders and a wealthy elite, while Obama was the fresh-faced insurgent propelled by popular support.

That notion was already trickling into popular culture in intriguing and sometimes bizarre ways. Homemade videos related to the campaign began appearing on sites like YouTube. Two of the most popular were a version of Apple's famous '1984' ad which had been manipulated to place Hillary Clinton in the role of Big Brother (or Sister), and a music video from 'Obama Girl'.

Even professional admen expressed admiration for the 1984 clip. It potently framed the idea of Clinton as a presumptuous, controlling figure who might – just might – be overthrown by the renegade Obama. The knowing video for Obama Girl's song, 'I Got a Crush . . . on Obama' played off R'n'B and hip-hop stereotypes to amusing effect. Its direct political consequences were unknowable: even the actress who played Obama Girl, Amber Lee Ettinger, would later admit that she failed to vote in the primary in her home state of New Jersey. But the video would go on to be seen more than 10 million times by October 2008, advancing the idea of Obama as the preferred candidate of younger voters.

Obama struggled to find his footing when it came to other aspects of the race. He got off to a bad start when, the day after launching his candidacy, he referred to American lives lost in Iraq as having been 'wasted'. It was a silly mistake, and Obama knew it. 'I was actually upset with myself when I said that, because I never use that term,' he immediately told the biggest newspaper in Iowa, the *Des Moines Register*.

There were other errors, too. At the first televised debate, held in late April, Obama was asked what he would do in response to another terrorist attack on the United States. His answer concentrated on relief efforts and the importance of good intelligence. Much to the delight of the Clinton team, it omitted any mention of retaliation.

June brought the worst foul-up of all – and one that infuriated the usually placid Obama. His staff sent out a memo to reporters suggesting that Hillary and Bill Clinton had overly close ties to India and that they were linked to companies that were outsourcing American jobs. There were two further twists: first, the memo had been sent out with the instruction that its contents should not be attributed to the Obama campaign; second, its headline referred to 'Hillary Clinton (D-Punjab)' – at best a poor joke, at worst an unsupportable suggestion that she was more interested in the welfare of Punjabis than Americans. The memo's tone and the sneaky way in which it sought to propagate damaging material about an opponent seemed to make a mockery of Obama's pledge to practice a new kind of politics.

Obama complained that the memo had been sent without his knowledge. It was, he said, 'stupid and caustic'. Behind the scenes, he would later recall to Richard Wolffe of *Newsweek*, he was 'the most angry I've been in this campaign'. He told his staff that, in future, if they were 'even going close to the line', they needed to ask for his clearance.

As the long summer wore on, some of the excitement that Obama's candidacy had initially generated wore off. The candidate was criticised for not taking the fight to Clinton more directly in the debates. His demeanour, some supporters believed, was too mild and professorial.

Even the pace of fundraising seemed to be falling away. Obama's total third-quarter take of $20 million was weak. Clinton beat him in that period, announcing a total of $22 million. Her campaign released the news on the day Obama was due to give a big speech on Iraq, starving him of media oxygen and adding to his team's frustration. The very next day brought a new nationwide poll. It gave Clinton an apparently impregnable 33 percent lead over Obama.

Obama's key lieutenants, including David Axelrod and Robert Gibbs, were reduced to trying to staunch panic. They argued forcibly – and with some justification – that national polls did not matter. The name of the game, they insisted, was to win in Iowa, the first state to vote – a result that would so shake up the race that the polls would change instantly.

In truth, the picture was so mixed that it was almost impossible to get a clear read. So long as you looked at the situation from the angle recommended by the likes of Axelrod and Gibbs, there was indeed some cause for confidence. In Iowa, Obama's poll numbers had begun to move up again. More to the point, the Obama team was devoting inordinate attention to nurturing its local-level organisation.

Tom Harrington's experiences were typical. Harrington was a 56-year-old university professor who lived and worked in the small city of Ames. A member of the Iowa Democratic Party's State Central Committee, he had first been drawn to Obama when he saw him speak in Ames the day after announcing his candidacy.

Two things about the young senator had been magnetic even then, Harrington told me. The first was that Obama seemed 'more idealis-tic' than other major figures in the party. The second was his capacity to inspire. Harrington knew that the organisers of that first rally thought beforehand that they would be doing well to draw 2,000 people. Seven thousand showed up.

Harrington's three teenage children, normally oblivious to politics, had been insistent about coming along. 'That guy has to be our president,' one of his sons told him afterwards. Harrington shook Obama's hand after his speech finished, informed him of his position in the state party, and pledged that he would do anything he could to help him win the caucuses. Obama told the professor to make sure that he gave campaign workers his contact details before he left. 'We'll be getting in touch,' the candidate added.

Harrington subsequently became a local organiser for Obama. Much to his delight, he found that the central campaign was happy to devolve enormous decision-making power to volunteers like him. 'We did pretty much whatever we wanted, and they facilitated us in that,' the professor said. 'Their slogan was "Respect, Include, Empower", and they really lived up to it.' This attitude was close to revolutionary in national American politics, where campaigns are often controlled from a distant headquarters with a rigid hand.

Harrington and his fellow volunteers made the most of their independence. They held house parties, inviting acquaintances who were still undecided and hoping that their own enthusiasm would win these people over. Female supporters each chipped in $5 to buy an ad in a local newspaper. The ad listed all of their names and declared their allegiance to Obama, the intent being to convince other Democratic women that it was acceptable to support someone besides the former First Lady.

News of these kinds of activities filtered back up the campaign chain – strengthening Axelrod and the others in their belief that support for Obama was building. Yet they still needed a moment that would serve to crystallise their case, confirming the doubts they believed many Democrats harboured about Clinton. At the end of October, it came.

The occasion was yet another televised debate, this one from Philadelphia's Drexel University. Clinton had a couple of uncomfortable moments early on but, as the debate began winding down, she seemed to have escaped serious damage. Then she tripped.

The issue was whether or not illegal immigrants should be eligible for driving licences. Though immigration in general was a hot topic, the question was peripheral to the main debate. It seemed that Clinton was asked about it only because the governor of New York state, Eliot Spitzer (who would later resign after his patronage of prostitutes was uncovered), had advocated a policy under which licences would be issued.

Clinton's initial answer praised Spitzer for trying 'to fill the vacuum left by the failure of this administration to bring about comprehensive immigration reform'. She added that there were 'several million' illegal immigrants in the state of New York and that 'they are driving on our roads. The possibility of them having an accident that harms themselves or others is just a matter of the odds.'

Clinton expressed no reservations about the plan. Yet when one of the long-shot candidates, Senator Chris Dodd, stated that he did not support the granting of licences, Clinton broke back in. 'I just want to add, I did not say that it should be done,' she said, 'but I certainly recognise why Governor Spitzer is trying to do it.'

The interjection provoked audible dismay from the crowd. In cross-talk between her and Dodd, Clinton denied having said that the proposal 'made sense', which in fact she had said in the past and went on to say again sixty seconds later.

One of the debate's two moderators, Tim Russert, claiming he wanted to make sure of what he had just heard, asked Clinton specifically if she supported Spitzer's plan. The best Clinton could offer in response was an accusation: 'This is where everybody plays "gotcha".'

If there was an instant that shifted the tide against Clinton in the run-in to the primaries, this was it. The central point, as Obama and Edwards realised, was not whether or not Clinton backed licences for illegal immigrants. It was that her contorted answer seemed like prima facie evidence of a trait her critics had long ascribed to her: a tendency to speak out of both sides of her mouth. Like her husband, who infamously testified that whether he had told the truth in a particular instance depended upon 'what the meaning of the word "is" is', Clinton was exhibiting an unappealing slipperiness.

Edwards was the first to pounce. 'Unless I missed something, Senator Clinton said two different things in the course of about two minutes,' he said. Obama chimed in immediately afterwards. 'I was confused on Senator Clinton's answer,' he said. 'I can't tell whether she was for it or against it, and I do think that is important.'

Clinton's messy performance got enormous coverage – and it had an effect. The last major Iowa poll taken before the debate had given the New York senator a 10-point lead over Obama. In the first one taken afterwards, she was only three points ahead. The furore came at a perfect time for Obama. A huge event in Iowa was looming.

The Jefferson-Jackson dinner in Des Moines would attract around 9,000 of the Democratic Party faithful. That night, Obama took to the stage immediately after Clinton. The format played to his strengths: while Clinton still had the edge on him in debates, he was by far the more rousing podium speaker.

Beginning by setting out the myriad failures of the Bush administration – including 'a war that should have never been authorised and should have never been waged' – Obama implicitly but unmistakably linked Clinton to a kind of standard political campaigning which, he asserted, was not up to the challenges of the day. 'The same old Washington textbook campaigns just won't do in this election. . . . Not answering questions 'cos we are afraid our answers won't be popular just won't do.' The speech ended with a promise to 'keep the American dream alive for those who still hunger for opportunity, who still thirst for equality' – and with a massive ovation.

'Should he win the Iowa caucuses,' David Yepsen, Iowa's most respected political journalist, wrote the next day, 'Saturday's dinner will be remembered as one of the turning points of his campaign, a point where he laid down the marker and began closing on Clinton.'

The view looked the same from where Tom Harrington was sitting. 'That evening went really well,' he remembered. After the speech, Harrington had turned to other Obama supporters who were there with him. 'This is it!' he said.

*

By the end of November, the sense that the ground was shifting was palpable. On 29 November, I went to see Obama speak at the famous Apollo Theater in Harlem. The New York neighbourhood savours its reputation as the capital of black America, but the crowd that night was racially diverse. It was huge, too, wending its way around more than a city block in the bitter cold.

Inside, Chris Rock introduced Obama. The comic praised the audience for being 'on the right side of history' and also added that they would be 'real embarrassed' if Obama won without their support. They would, he suggested to laughter, say to themselves: 'I had that white lady. What was I thinking? *What* was I thinking?'

The sense of Obama as both an African-American trailblazer and a healer of racial enmity gained ground that night. A passage towards the conclusion of his speech served simultaneously as a tribute to the black civil rights movement and, more generally, to the power of collective action.

'I will never forget that the only reason I am standing here today is because somebody, somewhere, stood up for me,' he began. 'And because that somebody stood up for me, somebody else stood up, even when it was hard, even when it was risky, even when it wasn't popular.

'And because a few people stood up, a thousand more stood up. And then a million more stood up. And standing up with courage and conviction, somehow they were able to bring about a transformation of this nation.'

Seated close to me in the balcony was George Patton Jr, a 76-year-old African-American. He had risen unsteadily to his feet at several of the more impassioned moments of Obama's speech. After Obama left the stage and people began filing out, I asked him what he thought of the event.

He waved his ticket stub aloft. 'I am going to have this framed for my granddaughter, for my great-granddaughter,' he said. 'This is a historic event.'

But was he confident Obama would prevail over Clinton? 'He has the courage and the vision and the decency to speak the truth,' he said.

A husk of emotion caught in his throat. 'The truth will always prevail in the end.'

*

With just over a month left before voting would begin, campaigning accelerated to a breakneck pace. Clinton, trying to stem the Obama surge, ended up playing into his hands. Three days after Obama's Harlem event, a new poll put him three points clear in Iowa. The former First Lady, campaigning in the state, was asked whether Obama had a character problem. 'It's beginning to look a lot like that,' she replied.

When Clinton had come under pressure from her opponents in debates, she had insisted that Democrats should keep their fire trained on Republicans and desist from attacking each other. Now that principle was beginning to look rather flexible. In a soundbite that was to become emblematic of her approach, at least in the minds of her critics, Clinton welcomed the onset of negative campaigning. 'Now the fun part starts,' she said.

That night, I saw Obama speak at a fundraiser in Boston. More than 2,000 people showed up. 'I just got back from Iowa, where it appears we're doing pretty good,' he said, to cheers. 'It's amazing how you go from being DOA [dead on arrival] to being a genius in about three weeks.'

His supporters' enthusiasm reached fever pitch when he drew an unlikely trump card in the shape of a woman whom all of America could identify from her first name: Oprah.

The chat show host Oprah Winfrey had announced her support for Obama in May and had hosted a fundraiser for him at her California home in September. Her decision to appear on the stump for him was of a different order of magnitude.

Winfrey's star power, and the level of trust she had built up with her audience, was immense. She had never before campaigned for a politician. The expectations that surrounded her first appearance, in Des Moines, Iowa on 8 December, were enormous. The day itself brought appalling weather – driving snow, ice and temperatures that did not get above minus 10 degrees centigrade. I watched the crowds stream through the doors of the city's Hy-Vee Hall, the hundreds becoming thousands. In the end, around 18,000 people came out that Saturday.

Winfrey's arrival on stage was greeted with an ear-splitting roar. Two things stood out about her speech, aside from the wall-to-wall media coverage it generated. One was the degree to which she had evidently bought into the burgeoning Obama-mania; the other, the forcefulness with which she stuck the boot into Hillary Clinton.

Her references to Obama were almost ecstatic. 'A politician who has an ear for eloquence and a tongue for the unvarnished truth,' she called him. Her speech concluded with the breathy insistence that 'I am here to tell you, Iowa, he is The One.'

Though she did not mention the former First Lady by name, much of her speech seemed to be aimed at rebutting attack lines the Clintons had used against Obama. The crux of the Clinton argument was that Obama was insufficiently experienced, whereas Hillary's years in Washington meant that she was better equipped to achieve real change. Winfrey did not have much time for that.

'We can recognise that the amount of time you've spent in Washington means nothing unless you're accountable for the judgements you made,' she said.

Obama's remarks were received at least as well as Winfrey's, but it was her emergence – and the footage of the two of them embracing – that was the real story of the day.

David Axelrod understood as much. I found him loping around the media benches towards the rear of the hall. His usual mournful expression had been replaced by a distinct cheeriness. He praised Winfrey's 'genius'. The value of her speech, he told me, was in attracting such a massive crowd, to whom 'Senator Obama gets the chance to make his pitch'.

Axelrod was not going to lose his moorings, however. I asked him about the increasingly harsh tone of the Clinton team's attacks upon his candidate. He exhaled slowly. 'Yeah,' he said sardonically. 'She loved us when we were 30 points behind.'

I had spoken to several audience members on their way out of the Winfrey event, and most had offered positive but unremarkable sentiments. After almost everyone else had left to navigate the treacherous roads outside, I found two sisters, Kenosha and Celina Carr, sitting side by side on a bench in the foyer.

They were young – Kenosha was seventeen ('But I'll be eighteen before election day,' she told me), and Celina just fourteen – and they were waiting for an older family member to pick them up and take them home.

Despite their youth, they knew every twist and turn of the campaign. Excitement about Obama's candidacy bubbled up constantly. There was something more substantial than mere exuberance in their words, too: something idealistic but not naive. They could not fully explain what was special about Obama, but they could feel it in their gut.

'He sees the reality of things. He *gets* the issues,' Celina told me.

'I wish people would know what is going on in the world,' Kenosha added. 'He represents the kind of politics we have been trying to get people like our parents to vote for for so long.'

And Hillary? 'She just seems like the candidate who wants to destroy everything,' Kenosha said. 'At the moment, all I'm hearing are mean things and dirty things from her.'

Clinton's supporters would have argued vigorously against that idea. Yet polling suggested that Kenosha's viewpoint was one that a large number of Democrats shared. Earlier that summer, when a Clinton victory had seemed almost inevitable, a CNN poll in New Hampshire had asked Democrats which of the candidates they considered most likeable. Obama topped the poll with 40 percent. John Edwards claimed 20 percent. Clinton registered a dismal 14 percent. A similar poll by the same organisation, conducted two weeks before the Oprah event, had asked Democrats whom they rated as most honest and trustworthy. Clinton came fourth.

*

The Clinton camp was rattled now, its anxiety manifesting itself in the use of ever more aggressive tactics. A Clinton campaign co-chair in New Hampshire, Bill Shaheen, gave an interview to the *Washington Post* in which he raised the issue of Obama's teenage drug use and went on, without evidence, to float the idea that Obama may have been a drug dealer.

Shaheen resigned. As the row continued, Clinton's chief strategist, Mark Penn – a man who would become more and more controversial as the campaign wore on – appeared on *Hardball*, the influential political talk show hosted by Chris Matthews. Clinton's guru was standing beside Joe Trippi, a top aide for John Edwards; David Axelrod was on a satellite link. When Axelrod raised the question of whether dodgy tactics were covertly encouraged by the higher ranks of the Clinton campaign, Penn seemed to prove his point. Never the most effective TV performer, he said with an unmistakeable smirk that 'The issue related to cocaine use is not something that the campaign was in any way raising.'

Trippi was so stunned by the crudeness of the manoeuvre that he sprang to defend Obama before Axelrod could get a word in: 'I think [Penn] just did it again,' Trippi spat. 'He just did it again. Unbelievable. He just said "cocaine" again.' The debate over drug use, he added, was 'garbage, and it needs to stop'.

No sooner had that row faded than Bill Clinton came to the fore. The former president sat down with Charlie Rose, a well-respected journalist who hosts an eponymous long-form interview show on public television. The interview was largely concerned with Clinton's new book, *Giving*. When Rose turned his attention to the presidential race, Clinton got increasingly worked up.

His irritability seemed to have its foundations in a sense of pique. Obama and his supporters had begun defining the bitter partisanship that attended Clinton's time in the White House as part of a broader malaise in American civic life. 'If you listen to the people who are most strongly for [Obama], they say basically we have to throw away all these experienced people because they have been through the wars of the nineties,' Clinton complained. 'And what we want is somebody who started running for president a year after he became a senator because he's fresh, he's new, he's never made a mistake and he has massive political skills. And we're willing to risk it.'

As Clinton went on – and on – an element of condescension seemed to creep into his remarks. He said that he got 'tickled' watching Obama and added that, if experience didn't matter, 'in theory, we could find someone who is a gifted television commentator' to run for president.

Rose mentioned on-camera that the former president's aides were trying to end the interview. His handlers had presumably realised that, whether his points were valid or not, they would create the kind of distraction that his wife could do without. It was only the first of many odd interventions Bill Clinton would make.

By now, every new poll caused a tremor. In Iowa, one survey had Clinton up by four points. Another said that Obama was ahead by three. In New Hampshire, Clinton's once-mighty lead had almost evaporated.

For Obama, the questions seemed starker as the final sprint loomed. A defeat in Iowa would finish him, confirming the apparent ineluctability of Clinton's progress. His young volunteers felt that things were shifting his way, but their older comrades remembered all those idealistic Democrats who, over the years, had gone down to defeat at the hands of the establishment.

Obama had the magic. You could feel it at his rallies. You could hear it in the catch in George Patton's voice in Harlem, in the zest of the Carr sisters in Des Moines. How much power and propulsion could that magic provide? Clinton and Obama had been campaigning all year. By Christmas Day, as they took a 24-hour respite with their families, the first votes were just nine days away. It was crunch time.

4

YES WE CAN!

The small commuter jet drifted low, headed for Des Moines Airport. It was New Year's Day, and there was less than 60 hours left before the Iowa caucuses would begin. Looking out of the window, I was reminded that the process by which the most powerful nation on earth elects its leader is mesmerisingly eccentric.

Beneath the plane was a vast, snowy expanse, pockmarked by only a handful of tiny villages and some isolated farmhouses. Iowa is twice the size of the Republic of Ireland, but Ireland is three times as densely populated. Des Moines, Iowa's biggest city, is home to just 200,000 people.

If you were putting together an election calendar from scratch, you would presumably want the vital first state to be in some way representative of the nation as a whole. Iowa is not even close. Its population is disproportionately old, rural-dwelling and, above all, white. Two and a half percent of Iowa's inhabitants are black. (African-Americans make up 12.8 percent of the US population; they account for 37 percent of the total in the 'blackest' state in the union, Mississippi.) African-American presidential aspirants who had preceded Obama – by far the most credible of whom was Jesse Jackson – had never bothered to compete seriously in Iowa, preferring to conserve their energies for more hospitable states.

At the turn of the year, when campaigning and caucusing take place, the so-called Hawkeye State is also skin-strippingly cold.

Temperatures of minus 20 degrees centigrade are common. The harsher the weather gets, the more likely it becomes that the caucuses will be dominated by hardcore supporters. The less committed simply stay at home.

In the caucuses – the word comes from a Native American term meaning 'a gathering of the tribal chiefs' – the idea of a secret ballot is discarded. Iowa Democrats show their support for one candidate or the other by standing together in one area of a meeting room. On 3 January, Obama supporters would stand in one spot, Clinton supporters in another, Edwards supporters in another, and so on. The most marginal candidates would then be eliminated, after which their supporters would be cajoled by representatives of each of the frontrunners to join their group. These idiosyncrasies had their charm – if you did not think too hard about how the leadership of the free world could be at stake.

In six of the previous eight presidential campaigns, the Democrat who had received the most support in Iowa had gone on to become the party's nominee. The 2008 election calendar was unusually compact, and winning Iowa was therefore seen as more important than ever. It was assumed that the shot of momentum a triumph delivered would carry the winner to victory in New Hampshire as well. The Iowa caucuses were to be held on a Thursday night; the New Hampshire primary was set for the following Tuesday.

All of this explained why Obama and Clinton had each spent around $20 million in the state. Obama's national campaign manager, David Plouffe, had moved to Iowa to spearhead his effort. The intense, boyish Plouffe was David Axelrod's business partner and his equal within the campaign. In theory, Axelrod looked after the candidate's message and political strategy, while Plouffe plotted the logistical course to the nomination. In practice, the distinction was often meaningless.

The campaign manager's surname, pronounced as if it rhymes with 'fluff', earned him the soubriquet 'Plouffe Daddy' from Obama's younger backers. He was genuinely liked by those who laboured alongside him, despite a reputation for parsimony that became a standing joke. He would insist on campaign workers from Chicago driving the 330 miles from their headquarters to Des Moines, rather than have the campaign pay the modest air fare. Axelrod would say with a smirk that anyone who tried to get more than one hand towel from the dispenser in the toilets at HQ would cause a sign reading 'See Plouffe' to pop up.

Plouffe's public profile, especially early in the campaign, was much lower than Axelrod's. That was no accident, and caused him no unease. He had an almost congenital dislike of the spotlight. He could sometimes spare a few words for reporters on a specific topic but he almost never granted full-length interviews. The *New Republic* magazine once reported that when Plouffe found out that he was to be included in another national publication's list of the 50 most influential people under the age of 45 – the kind of exposure other political strategists would kill for – he got himself removed from it.

Plouffe had one especially crucial asset in the campaign's early days: he had an intricate knowledge of Iowa's political landscape. He had worked for Iowa senator Tom Harkin over several years in the early 1990s and had later been employed by Congressman Richard Gephardt, whose constituency lay in the neighbouring state of Missouri and who had won the Iowa caucuses during his first presidential bid, back in 1988.

The Obama campaign had got a big boost on New Year's Eve. The final poll from the *Des Moines Register* gave the Illinoisan a seven-point lead over Clinton. The other campaigns complained that the poll was based on overly optimistic projections about how many people would turn out. Plouffe seemed to half-agree. If the projections held up, 'we're headed for a good night', he told the *Washington Post*. But, he added circumspectly, 'a poll is not going to caucus. Therein lies the challenge.'

The national movement Obama had envisioned way back at his Springfield announcement speech was beginning to take root and grow. In Iowa and New Hampshire, it was at its strongest. Plouffe's volunteers knocked on 50,000 doors across Iowa on the last Saturday before the caucuses. In the last three days, they made 150,000 phone calls.

On New Year's night, I drove west. Obama was to speak in Council Bluffs, a city of about 60,000 people. It nestled in the midst of hostile territory for the presidential hopeful. Western Iowa is significantly more conservative than the state's eastern reaches, and the local congressman, Republican Steve King, had made his name as a vociferous opponent of illegal immigration. (In March 2008, King would further distinguish himself by claiming that an Obama victory in the presidential election would provoke 'dancing in the streets' from al-Qaeda and other radical Islamic groups.)

The turnout was strong. About 1,000 people braved the cold and showed up in a hall at Iowa's School for the Deaf. The candidate's speech was similar to the one I had heard late the previous year in Harlem, Boston and elsewhere. But, with everything now on the line, Obama's attacks on his opponents were sharper, his attempts to rebut any doubts about him more vigorous.

He pushed back hard against the theory – advanced relentlessly by the Clinton campaign – that he would be a weaker candidate to face the Republicans than the former First Lady. 'I beat every single Republican. I beat 'em all,' he said, referring to the most recent opinion polls.

Obama had a vice-like grip on the mantle of change. It was the one big theme on which Clinton, with her family baggage and her years in Washington, could not compete with him. He maximised this asset at every opportunity. His campaign events in those final days in Iowa were entitled the 'Stand for Change' tour. In Council Bluffs, he got some of his biggest applause for asserting that 'Washington is in its last throes' – a remark that, at least by implication, painted the Clintons and the Bushes as different sides of the same tarnished coin. Without naming Hillary Clinton, he also castigated those who claimed to be able to chart 'a bold new course' in foreign policy while being 'steeped in conventional thinking'. Longtime observers of Obama's career had always argued that he had more iron in his soul than his sunny image would suggest. Now he was proving it.

There was excitement in the hall that night, but there was nervousness too. The number of hands that shot up when Obama asked undecided voters to identify themselves was surprisingly high – perhaps one in four of the attendees.

The next day, Obama did five events over 17 hours. At each stop, he gave the same speech, beseeched the undecideds and, in a nice piece of psychology, goaded young voters by telling them that 'the pundits' were predicting they were not going to turn out when it mattered.

'Are you gonna prove them wrong?' Obama would ask. No matter how loud the response, he would add: 'I can't hear you. Are you gonna show up or not?'

They did. Caucus sites across Iowa opened at 6.30 PM, and the voters came in a surge. The numbers were overwhelming. In a West Des Moines high school, Michelle Obama dropped in to rally her husband's supporters and ended up as just one more face lost in a large, chaotic crowd.

The story was the same all over the state. In the Ames precinct where Tom Harrington was managing things for Obama, more than 500 people turned out – more than twice as many as had ever shown up before. When the count began there, the result was soon clear.

'We'd count Obama supporters by getting everybody to shout out their number,' Harrington explained to me. 'So we'd go down each row of seats with people shouting out "48", "49", "50". In the end, the others had to watch us. We gave a big cheer when we got to 100, and then another when we got to 200.'

In the end, Obama got the support of 290 people, well over half the total. As soon as Harrington's caucus wrapped up, he opened his laptop to check the tallies coming in from elsewhere in the state. He was delighted by what he saw. 'We had a terrific party that night,' he remembered happily.

The celebrations were not confined to Iowa. The Obama volunteers up in New Hampshire had been watching every moment just as expectantly. Jennifer Tuttle, a 35-year-old film-maker, had travelled from her home in New York to canvass for Obama in the small town of Rochester.

Tuttle and her friends had tuned in to C-SPAN, a cable channel devoted to 24-hour coverage of public affairs. 'They didn't have any running commentary,' Tuttle later told me, 'and the camera they had in this caucus room in Des Moines was, I guess intentionally, pointing at the corner of the room where the other [minor] candidates like Dodd, Richardson and Biden had their supporters.'

Tuttle and her friends eventually discerned the voices of the organisers, who were counting up the people backing Clinton and John Edwards. Their numbers reached towards 100. 'But then it got to the point where there was just one group left counting, and it got up to 200, and we were ecstatic because we knew it was Obama. And we knew at that moment he'd won, because we knew the results in Des Moines were going to be pretty typical of the results across the state. It was euphoric; beyond amazing.'

*

Back at Obama's election night party in Des Moines, the air seemed charged. The audience in the same venue where Obama and Oprah had appeared the previous month was several thousand strong. They watched the results filtering through on massive video screens. The first returns showed a close, three-way race, but as the minutes ticked by, Obama opened up a small lead. Then the lead began growing.

Confirmation that Obama had won came about half an hour before any of the television networks had called the race. David Axelrod's demeanour told the story. He emerged as the hall was still filling up with Obama supporters touting placards and badges. Smiling broadly, he told me it was a 'great day' for the campaign. Asked directly if he was sure Obama had won, he glanced down at his Blackberry. 'All the reports we're hearing are very encouraging,' he said. Coming from the cautious Axelrod, this was high confidence indeed.

The turnout, Axelrod predicted, might even go above 200,000 – far beyond his campaign's best projections, and an outcome he described as 'fabulous'. In the end, even that was an underestimation. Fully 239,000 Iowans came out to caucus. The previous record, set four years before, was 124,000.

Terry Link, Obama's old friend from the Illinois state Senate, was holed up in the national campaign's 'war room' in Chicago that night. He and the other HQ staff had believed in advance that they were 'in good shape', he told me. Still, seeing their dreams realised was an intensely emotional experience.

'As we were getting the results in, we were turning to one another and saying: "We are making history tonight",' Link told me. 'This was not a flash in the pan. We knew it was the start of something big.'

The candidate, meanwhile, was as calm as ever. While the media and his supporters were tracking every shift in the returns, Obama was out for a seafood dinner with his family and some close advisors, including David Plouffe. It was there that he heard he had won the caucuses. After his convoy came back to central Des Moines, he read over his victory speech backstage, holding a wriggling Sasha in his lap as Michelle and Malia sat beside him.

Clinton appeared across town to concede at 9.26 PM. She urged Democrats to think about two questions: 'Who will be able to go the distance? And who will be the best president on Day One?' (Clinton eventually finished third in Iowa, behind Edwards as well as Obama.)

Obama took to the stage with his family soon afterwards. U2's 'City of Blinding Lights' accompanied his entrance. His first line was just about perfect: 'They said this day would never come.'

There he stood, a black man who had won a critical election in a white state in the middle of the farm belt. Such a thing had once been unthinkable. And now that it had happened, it seemed to say something not only about Obama but about a changing America.

The victory in Iowa was not just about race, however. 'This was the moment when the improbable beat what Washington said was inevitable,' Obama said. 'This was the moment when we finally beat back the politics of fear, and doubt, and cynicism; the politics where we tear each other down instead of lifting this country up. Years from now, you'll look back and you'll say this was the moment, this was the place, where America remembered what it means to hope.'

Obama's high-flown rhetoric could sometimes be thrown back to mock him. But that night in Iowa, his words matched the extraordinary mood in the hall.

Everything about the Clinton campaign, from the former First Lady's explanation of her war vote to the hackneyed sentiments strewn through her speeches, spoke of caution and calculation, and a joyless grind to outflank her opponents. Obama had drawn people together not because of the boldness of his policies but because he seemed so different – more authentic and sincere; looser and more civil.

That night, his campaign had changed too, as if at the flick of a switch. Up until the results came in, it had been powered by nebulous, abstract things like hope and faith. Now it was substantive and real. The idea that Obama could actually be the next president of the United States had become more than a quixotic daydream.

He thanked his volunteers and his campaign workers from the stage, giving another nod to his days as an organiser. 'I'll never forget that my journey began on the streets of Chicago, doing what so many of you have done for this campaign: organising and working and fighting to make people's lives just a little bit better. I know how hard it is. It comes with little sleep, little pay and a lot of sacrifice. There are days of disappointment. But sometimes, just sometimes, there are nights like this.'

I walked back to my hotel through the icy streets of Des Moines wondering what it was I had just witnessed. Plenty of others were struggling to comprehend the enormity of it all.

'You'd have to have a heart of stone not to feel moved by this,' David Brooks, a conservative columnist, wrote in the *New York Times*. 'Obama is changing the tone of American liberalism, and maybe American politics too.'

Peggy Noonan, a former speechwriter for Ronald Reagan and now a *Wall Street Journal* columnist, exulted: 'We wanted exciting, we got exciting. Barack Obama won. Hillary Clinton, the inevitable, the avatar of the machine, lost. It's huge. Even though people have been talking about this possibility for six weeks now, it's still huge. She had the money, she had the organisation, the party's stars . . . and the Clinton name in a base that loved Bill. And she lost.'

It was Joe Klein who captured what had happened best of all. Obama's victory, he posited, had been propelled by a new, young generation whose passions and energies had the capacity to transform the country. 'The Obama victory was not so much about his own generation but the kids two generations behind him, the college kids and recent graduates, blissfully colour-blind, who spent patient months as organisers out in the most rural counties,' Klein wrote in *Time*. 'And years from now, when they meet in the corridors of power or academia or at the inevitable reunions, they'll look at each other and smile, and they won't even have to say the words: We did something amazing back in Iowa, on January 3, 2008, didn't we?'

The leader of their movement had little time to dwell on such emotive ideas. The next contest loomed. The Obama and Clinton teams had dashed for the airport as soon as their respective election night events were over. Their campaign planes were airborne, New Hampshire-bound, shortly after midnight.

A reporter on board asked Obama how the race had changed. Tired and hoarse, he could only mutter, somewhat superfluously: 'We won the first caucus.' Then he asked the media to let him go to sleep. By 4.30 the next morning, he was on the ground in New Hampshire.

The wind was at his back. The nomination, it seemed, was there for the taking.

*

The next five days, which climaxed with the New Hampshire primary, felt unreal, almost dreamlike. The Iowa result had thrown everything up in the air. If Obama won New Hampshire, he would be a racing certainty to win the first southern primary, in South Carolina later in the month. Three wins in the first three major contests would make him virtually assured of the Democratic nomination.

Clinton looked for all the world like a busted flush – right up until election night, when she won the New Hampshire primary in one of the biggest upsets in American political history.

No one saw it coming – including Obama. 'I spoke with him on the phone several times and we talked about how happy he was feeling,' Terry Link told me. 'You could feel how pumped up he was.'

At Obama's first event after the late night flight from Iowa, in the coastal city of Portsmouth, New Hampshire, even Axelrod reached for soaring metaphors in an interview with two reporters from the *Huffington Post* website. 'You can build the plane,' he said, 'but last night we found out whether it could fly or not. And it flew beautifully. And I think it's going to continue to fly.'

All the indicators over the next few days suggested he was right. Everywhere Obama went, he was mobbed. I saw him on the eve of the primary in Rochester. Snow blanketed the streets of the 30,000-strong town. Two hours before the event was due to begin, a queue of 50 shivering people had already formed at the old Opera House, where he would speak.

By the time he arrived, the building was crammed full and about 200 people were locked outside. Obama addressed the overspill in the open air. Inside, organisers warned the audience not to stomp their feet, for fear they would cause the 100-year-old venue's floorboards to collapse.

Earlier that day, I had gone to a Clinton event 10 miles away in Dover. The atmosphere was flat and embattled. The New York senator's supporters were trying to put a brave face on things: 'She can win the White House and she very much reflects my values,' 49-year-old Ann Unitas told me.

Clinton's crowd was much smaller and less fervent than Obama's. When the former First Lady said from the stage that 150 people had turned up but could not be squeezed in, reporters exchanged puzzled glances. There was plenty of space towards the rear of the school gym where the event was being held.

The opinion polls in New Hampshire seemed to support the evidence before our eyes. Twenty-one major polls were conducted in the state after the Iowa caucuses. A grand total of one – taken immediately after Iowa and contradicted by other surveys carried out by the same organisation in the following days – gave Clinton the advantage. Eight indicated that Obama was leading by 10 points or more.

All of us – journalists, pollsters, the campaigns, the candidates themselves – obviously missed something. One error, perhaps, was to vest so much significance in the size of the crowds Obama was attracting. In the wake of his Iowa win, Obama's status had shifted from that of a prominent political hopeful. He was now a curious combination of social phenomenon, A-list celebrity and would-be history-maker. As a consequence, his events exerted a gravitational pull that brought people in from beyond the New Hampshire borders.

The line outside the Rochester Opera House meeting, for instance, was headed by Chris Riley, a 21-year-old student from the neighbouring state of Massachusetts. Riley told me that he had been won over by Obama's 2004 convention speech and that it was 'a dream come true' that the young senator's campaign had gone so well to date. He, a female friend, and his mother had come along to see Obama in person. For all their ardour, none of them would be eligible to vote in the primary.

There was another, more conventional factor behind Clinton's upset win, too: the sole televised debate between the Iowa caucuses and the New Hampshire primary, held on the Saturday night, was seen to have worked in her favour. Clinton performed competently rather than brilliantly. But two moments generated by her opponents proved powerful.

At one point, after she had criticised Obama, John Edwards waded in on the younger man's side. Claiming that both he and Obama were 'powerful voices for change', he asserted that any time such voices were raised, 'the forces of [the] status quo attack. . . . I didn't hear these kind of attacks from Senator Clinton when she was ahead. Now that she's not, we hear them.'

Edwards's move may have been as much a matter of strategy as sincerity – his only real hope, after the Iowa result, was to try to knock Clinton out of the race, then position himself as an alternative to Obama. Whatever his motivation, he helped create a sense that Clinton, down and bruised, was being set upon by her male rivals. Female voters, in particular, were likely to recoil from that.

Obama slipped up after one of the debate's moderators asked Clinton what she would say to those voters who respected her CV but simply liked Obama more. 'Well, that hurts my feelings, but I'll try to go on,' she replied with faux-fragility, drawing a laugh. When she agreed that Obama was indeed appealing, he unwisely interjected: 'You're likeable enough, Hillary.'

He said it with a sidelong glance. Whether the words bespoke a frustration at Clinton's tactics or simply came out wrong, his demeanour suggested dismissive condescension. The remark riled Clinton supporters for months afterwards. Other critics of Obama would refer to it often, offering it as evidence that he could be presumptuous, even arrogant.

In a debate less than two weeks later, Obama said: 'I absolutely regret' the comment. 'Folks were giving Hillary a hard time about likeability,' he explained, 'and my intention was to say: "I think you're plenty likeable."'

*

One other incident was widely held to have swung things at the last moment for Clinton. It was a remarkable occurrence that would bequeath the campaign one of its most enduring images.

On the eve of the election, Clinton made a campaign stop at a coffee shop in Portsmouth. The event included fewer than 20 voters. Clinton's aides had begun placing her in these 'round-table' formats because they believed she performed better in intimate settings than in front of large crowds.

A woman asked her to explain 'how you get out the door every day'. After a couple of mild generalisations, Clinton stopped abruptly. Her voice began to break and she cupped her chin in her hand. Tears started to well. 'I have [had] so many opportunities from this country, I just don't want to see us fall backwards, you know?' she said.

There was an awkward pause as she swallowed hard. Sympathetic applause burst forth. Then Clinton went on: 'This is very personal for me, it's not just political, it's not just public. I see what's happening; we have to reverse it. And some people think elections are a game, they think it's, like, who's up or who's down. It's about our country. . . . Some of us put ourselves out there and do this against some pretty difficult odds. And we do it, each one of us, because we care about our country. But some of us are right and some of us are wrong. Some of us are ready and some of us are not. Some of us know what we will do on Day One and some of us haven't really thought that through enough.'

Some observers felt that Clinton was contriving the moment, especially given the suspiciously rehearsed-sounding jabs at Obama with which the mini-speech concluded. Others, including Maureen Dowd of the *New York Times*, noted that, of all the things Clinton had confronted in her career – all the suffering she had witnessed and the people struck down by misfortune whom she had met – it was her own apparent impending defeat that had brought her close to tears. 'What was moving her so deeply was her recognition that the country was failing to grasp how much it needs her,' Dowd wrote. 'In a weirdly narcissistic way, she was crying for us. But it was grimly typical that what made her break down was the prospect of losing.'

Many people had a more sympathetic reaction. It was, in their eyes, a rare moment when Clinton allowed her feelings and vulnerabilities to show. (I lost a lot of respect for Clinton over the course of the primary season, but I thought the episode in the coffee shop was genuine. She seemed to me like someone teetering on the edge of humiliation and too bone-tired to conceal her hurt about it.)

Clinton's damp-eyed moment was accorded enormous significance in the end – not least by the candidate herself, who made a reference to it in her victory speech. 'I listened to you, and in the process I found my own voice,' she said.

There was toughness – even cynicism – behind Clinton's win too. The notion that she was propelled over the finish line by female voters who felt that 'one of their own' had been wronged was neat but inadequate. Some, not least in the Obama campaign, believed that the true roots of her comeback were much shadier, and lay in distorting Obama's position on abortion.

In the days immediately before polling, the former First Lady's campaign sent a controversial flyer out to homes across New Hampshire. The mailing alleged that Obama had been 'unwilling to take a stand on choice'. It added: 'Seven times, he had the opportunity to stand up against Republican anti-choice legislation in the Illinois state Senate. Seven times, he voted present – not yes or no, but present. Being there is not enough to protect choice.'

There was a problem with the attack: Obama's 'present' votes had been part of a strategy agreed upon by supporters of abortion rights. The tactical details were complex but essentially boiled down to this: Republicans, who were in the majority in the Illinois state Senate for most of Obama's time there, often put forth legislation aimed at limiting access to abortion. Democrats from socially conservative districts would be politically vulnerable in their re-election campaigns if they voted 'no'. But if enough members voted 'present', that would be sufficient to halt the proposed legislation, while not offering such an inviting target for anti-abortion attacks.

When Clinton had raised Obama's 'present' votes in milder, verbal form the previous month, the president and CEO of the Illinois Planned Parenthood Council, a group whose *raison d'être* was the protection of abortion rights, had come to Obama's defence. 'The poor guy is getting all this heat for a strategy that we, the pro-choice community, did,' Pam Sutherland told the *Chicago Sun-Times*. Sutherland's group had given Obama a 100 percent rating for his support of the issues they cared about.

When the mailing went out in New Hampshire, the Obama campaign did not have the people in place to rebut it effectively and quickly. Jennifer Tuttle, the Obama volunteer in Rochester, remains convinced that it swung the election.

As primary day approached, 'We were sure we had it', Tuttle told me. 'People were excited by him, really interested in him. I remember thinking: "He's going to win by 15 points."'

Then came the mailing, just before Tuesday's vote. 'It created a real ruckus,' Tuttle said, 'and I started to have some bad feelings. We campaigned vigorously on the day, and all I can tell you is that there was this sea change between Monday and Tuesday. I remember going to a house that even had an Obama yard sign. And I knocked on the door and the woman said: "Oh, I changed my mind and voted for Hillary." There were all these Democratic women who were pro-choice, and they were saying: "I didn't know he was soft on choice."'

It was only those as close to the ground as Tuttle who could discern how things were shifting. Obama and his advisors remained confident. The Clinton side was miserable. I watched Clinton visit a polling station with her daughter, Chelsea, on the morning of the election. She accepted the words of well-wishers like a widow accepting the sympathies of mourners at a funeral. On television, even the more measured analysts had begun talking about what Clinton would do when – not if – Obama won in New Hampshire.

The Obama election night rally was held in a large high school in the city of Nashua. The crowd that gathered expected a coronation. When the first exit polls, released just after 8 PM, showed a narrow lead for Clinton, some audience members began to worry – even if they found it difficult to grasp that their man might actually lose. Within the hour, their concern was deepening.

Dave Gourley, a 53-year-old computer programmer from the town of Rye, told me, as he glanced anxiously up at the video screens, that he was 'very surprised' and had 'expected it to be much more for Obama'.

There were to be no happy words from Axelrod, or anyone else, that night. No one from the Obama camp emerged. They stayed behind the scenes, stunned. 'The mood was obviously dejected,' Terry Link said.

Soon, it was over. Obama emerged with Michelle, who led him around to the front of the podium before he began his speech. One journalist observed that it was as if she wanted him to lift his spirits by absorbing the acclaim of the crowd.

Obama told his supporters that 'tonight belongs to you'. Clearly, it belonged to Clinton. But Obama's rhetorical skills salvaged something from the wreckage. 'We have been told we cannot do this by a chorus of cynics,' he said. 'They will only grow louder and more dissonant in the weeks and months to come. We've been asked to pause for a reality check. We've been warned against offering the people of this nation false hope. But in the unlikely story that is America, there has never been anything false about hope.'

He had never boiled down the rationale of his candidacy so powerfully, nor identified the differences between him and Clinton so crisply. He went on to invoke 'a simple creed that sums up the spirit of a people', just as he had way back in his Senate campaign: 'It was a creed written into the founding documents that declared the destiny of a nation: Yes, we can. It was whispered by slaves and abolitionists as they blazed a trail towards freedom through the darkest of nights: Yes, we can. It was sung by immigrants as they struck out from distant shores and pioneers who pushed westward against an unforgiving wilderness: Yes, we can. It was the call of workers who organised, women who reached for the ballot, a president who chose the moon as our new frontier, and a King who took us to the mountaintop and pointed the way to the promised land. Yes, we can, to justice and equality. Yes, we can, to opportunity and prosperity. Yes, we can heal this nation. Yes, we can repair this world. Yes, we can.'

But could they? The difference between the opinion polls and the final result in New Hampshire sparked dark whispers about the Bradley Effect. The label referred to one of the more dispiriting peculiarities of American politics: the tendency of African-American candidates to do worse in elections than opinion polls suggested. The disparity, it was assumed, came about because white voters told pollsters they would vote for a black candidate but did not actually do so. (The phenomenon was named for Tom Bradley, a popular Los Angeles mayor who was African-American. When Bradley contested the governorship of California in 1982, virtually every poll, including exit polls on the day, predicted he would comfortably defeat his white opponent, George Deukmejian. He lost.)

'I don't know if race played a part, but I do know there is a lot of evidence that that is the case,' Steve McMahon, a prominent Democratic strategist who was not working for any of the 2008 candidates, told me in the aftermath of the primary. 'The exit polls were right on the money in the Republican race [held the same day] but not in the Democratic race, where they showed Senator Obama winning by a fairly comfortable margin. So, clearly, someone was not telling the truth.' If the Bradley Effect was in play, it raised huge questions about Obama's viability.

There was also a broader issue. Could Obama's movement defeat the much more traditional politics favoured by Clinton? After Iowa, it seemed as though idealism and youthful energy could carry the day. Now, Clinton was again the frontrunner. Had Iowa been a fluke?

David Plouffe tried to buck up Obama's devastated team after the defeat. He laid out the plan for the states ahead, and then – startlingly, for he was normally polite and soft-spoken – insisted: 'Now let's go win this fucking thing.'

Jennifer Tuttle had watched the New Hampshire result come in that night, her and her Obama-backing comrades sitting side by side with Clinton supporters in a Rochester bar. 'There were a lot of [Washington] DC operatives who had come up to join Hillary's campaign, which wasn't like our side. At first, we were all trying to be, like, "Hey, we're all Democrats". So time went on, and they were celebrating with a few drinks. And by the end, they were saying, "Oh, you Obama people are so cute. You're so idealistic. But we know how to win elections. You've got to play dirty. You've got to get down in the dirt and fight there."'

What neither Tuttle nor anyone else realised that night was that the struggle would quickly get much dirtier. The Clintons were about to prise open the most explosive issue in America.

5

TRUMPING THE RACE CARD

The words had a façade of niceness, but a smack and a sneer lay just beneath.

'Jesse Jackson won South Carolina twice, in '84 and '88, and he ran a good campaign,' Bill Clinton said. 'And Senator Obama's run a good campaign here. He's run a good campaign everywhere.'

Clinton had just finished breakfast in Columbia, South Carolina. He had spent many days in the state, leading his wife's campaign when she wasn't there, playing second fiddle when she was. Primary day had finally rolled around, and Clinton, standing outside a diner, had been asked by a reporter what it said about Obama that 'it takes two of you to beat him'.

The former president, already seething about what he deemed to be unfair media coverage, laughed mirthlessly. Then he made the Jackson comment. That was the moment when the struggle between Obama and the Clintons turned toxic. Clinton had not been asked about Jackson, his exchanges with a group of reporters had included no previous reference to the civil rights leader, and, if he had merely been looking for an example of a plucky outsider winning a Democratic primary in the state, John Edwards, who had defeated John Kerry four years before, would have seemed a more obvious choice.

Clinton's comment therefore begged the question as to why he – the most brilliant and cunning political strategist of his generation –

88

had invoked Jackson's name. It was difficult to find a credible answer that did not centre on the colour of Obama's skin.

The popularity of the Clintons among the African-American community fell markedly during the primary campaign. There were several reasons for that. The former president's remark on that late January morning marked, for many blacks, a headlong tumble past the point of no return.

I was having breakfast elsewhere in Columbia when I first heard about Clinton's remarks, and I felt a visceral shock. When I returned to New York, a friend of mine, a white Republican who had previously held a sneaking regard for Clinton, told me that he had winced when he saw footage of the Jackson comment. 'That was hard to watch,' he said. 'He went right up to the edge there.'

Conversations with friends and colleagues in Ireland took a different shape. There seemed to be enormous resistance to the idea that the former president could behave in a racially insensitive manner. Part of this may have stemmed from the high esteem Clinton enjoyed as a consequence of his role in the Northern Ireland peace process; part of it may have been the general sense that he was left-of-centre and progressive on most issues; and a third element in the equation was a failure to take his comments at anything other than face value. Jesse Jackson had indeed won the elections Clinton said he had won, so what was the problem?

This third strand was the most important. Overseas audiences had grown accustomed to thinking of American racism as synonymous with the Ku Klux Klan and the occasional public figure, like Louisiana politician David Duke, who had emerged from the most lunatic fringes of the Right. But the America of 2008 no longer resembled the America of *Mississippi Burning*. Racial issues had not gone away, but they were now spoken about – at least in the public arena – in a coded, insidious way. The nuances of the code were easily perceptible to most Americans but often remained impenetrable, or simply invisible, to those across the oceans.

Clinton would bridle for months afterwards at criticisms of his comments. Yet he would often do so by defending himself against a charge that had not really been levelled. 'My office is in Harlem – and Harlem voted for Hillary, by the way,' he told a Philadelphia radio station in April. 'You really got to go some to try to portray me as a racist.' (As the interview ended, Clinton, apparently believing he was off-air, was heard to say: 'I don't think I should take any shit from anybody on that, do you?') In August, Clinton would tell Kate Snow of ABC News: '[I am] not a racist. I've never made a racist comment.'

But Clinton was not being accused of full-on racism. No one with any sense believed that he thought black people were inferior to whites or that he would have hesitated about situating his office in Harlem because so many African-Americans live there. What many people – including me – came to conclude after the Jackson comment was that his ferocious competitiveness respected no boundaries. If winning required exacerbating and exploiting racial divisions, he would do it. He was no bigot, but, if the situation looked dire enough, he was willing to throw a nod and a wink in the direction of those who were. It was, to put it mildly, a disappointing realisation.

(For the record, Clinton's claims about Harlem voting patterns were untrue. Despite considerable establishment support, including the hearty endorsement of the most prominent African-American politician in the area, Congressman Charles Rangel, Hillary Clinton did not win a plurality of the votes cast there in the New York Democratic primary. A tally of election results from the four state Assembly districts that include parts of Harlem showed that Obama received about 2,000 more votes than Clinton. In the heart of the neighbourhood – Assembly District 70 – Obama beat Clinton convincingly, winning 13,738 votes to her 9,124.)

Clinton's Jackson remarks were seen in a particularly dim light because they came on top of several other comments by him, his wife and their key supporters that had seemed to play upon racial stereotypes and fears.

The popularity of the Clintons among blacks had taken its first knock during the flap over Bill Shaheen's reference to Obama's drug use. The Clinton campaign co-chair in New Hampshire was a seasoned operator, and his wife Jeanne had been the state's governor from 1997 to 2003. That being so, when he said that Republicans would raise questions against Obama like 'Did you ever give drugs to anyone? Did you sell them to anyone?', the newsworthiness of his phrasing stood out.

To some, Shaheen's assessment was simply realistic. But many Obama supporters, as well as African-Americans who were not committed to either candidate, saw a disconcerting facet to the remark: an attempt to raise the stereotype of the black drug dealer and, however tangentially, to connect that stereotype to Obama.

The Clintons had ramped up the stakes just before the New Hampshire primary. On the eve of voting, with his wife's hopes of becoming the Democratic nominee apparently on the point of being extinguished, Bill Clinton spoke at the state's premier university, Dartmouth College. He embarked on a hoarse-voiced attack on Obama that attracted enormous attention.

The kerfuffle began when Clinton was asked a question regarding the issue of judgement. The body of his response was an attack on the media for having been, in his view, insufficiently rigorous in analysing Obama's claim to have consistently opposed the war.

Yet he began his answer by paraphrasing Obama's overall appeal: 'It doesn't matter that I started running for president less than a year after I got to the Senate. . . . I am a great speaker and a charismatic figure and I am the only one who had the judgement to oppose this war from the beginning.' Having then become angry while blasting the media, he concluded: 'Give me a break! This whole thing is the biggest fairytale I've ever seen.'

There was genuine confusion over Clinton's comments. What, precisely, was he referring to as a fairytale? You could certainly make the argument that he was referring only to Obama's position on the war. Or there was an alternative interpretation: that he was denigrating both Obama's campaign and those who believed in it. Black Obama supporters, in particular, detected in Clinton's words the suggestion that they were being naive in believing that the Illinois senator could reach the Oval Office. Was the former president suggesting that such a thing was impossible, they wondered; and if he was, what reason, other than ethnicity, could he be positing as the cause?

The controversy around the remarks picked up speed when Clinton was criticised on CNN the next day by political strategist Donna Brazile. Hardly anyone's idea of a black militant, Brazile had run Al Gore's cautiously centrist 2000 presidential campaign and was uncommitted in the battle between Obama and Clinton.

Believing, as almost everyone did at that point, that Hillary Clinton was about to lose the New Hampshire primary, she said the 'fairytale' remark sounded 'like sour grapes' from the former president. 'For him to go after Obama, using "fairytale", calling him a "kid", as he did last week, it's an insult. And I tell you, as an African-American, I find his words and his tone to be very depressing.'

At the end of the week, Clinton popped up on a radio show presented by Al Sharpton, the controversial African-American activist, to protest that he had been speaking only about Obama's record on the war. 'There's nothing fairytale about his campaign,' Clinton now insisted.

Further damage had already been done by the candidate herself, however. On the same day her husband made his 'fairytale' remark, the subject of the civil rights movement came up in an interview Hillary Clinton gave to Fox News. The interviewer told her that Obama, stressing the importance of hope and inspiration in bringing about change, had cited the example of Martin Luther King and his famous 1963 'I Have A Dream' speech. Clinton responded with an extremely clumsy formulation that seemed to downplay King's achievements. 'Dr King's dream began to be realised when President Lyndon Johnson passed the Civil Rights Act of 1964,' she said. 'It took a president to get it done.'

The comment was not factually incorrect. But the words were jarring and, even by the most benevolent reading, suggested a tone-deafness on Clinton's part. The notion of African-American inferiority – and the concomitant slur that blacks were not capable masters of their own destiny – had not died with the abolition of slavery. Its corrosive effect continued to be felt in the present day. Yet here was Clinton, firstly giving the lion's share of the credit for the advances made by the civil rights movement to a white man, and secondly, doing so in order to gain tactical advantage over the strongest-ever black candidate for the presidency.

Derrick Z. Jackson, a syndicated columnist and an African-American, accused Clinton of having 'fanned the fumes of patronisation when she reached clumsily for an analogy that appeared to link Obama and King to simplistic hopers and dreamers'. His was one of the calmer voices.

Peculiar comments from Clinton supporters and experienced politicians continued to emerge. The most incendiary of all came from Andrew Cuomo, the attorney general of the state of New York. Asked by a radio talk show host to explain Clinton's shock win in New Hampshire, he suggested that the fact that 'you can't shuck and jive at a press conference' might have had an impact. The use of the terms 'shuck and jive' in an implicit reference to an African-American presidential candidate was jaw-dropping.

Hillary Clinton was never one to shirk a fight. She upped the ante further, going on *Meet the Press* the Sunday after her New Hampshire win to accuse the Obama campaign of 'deliberately distorting' her remarks on King and Johnson. She called the criticism 'an unfortunate storyline that the Obama campaign has pushed very successfully'.

The tensions were threatening to spiral out of control by this point – to the horror of some unaligned Democrats. James Clyburn, the most senior African-American in the House of Representatives, was a native South Carolinian who had played a central role in getting the state's primary moved to such an early – and pivotal – point on the calendar. He had endorsed neither candidate and had pledged to remain neutral until his state voted. Nonetheless, he could not contain himself from expressing 'disappointment' regarding Clinton's remarks about King. As the 26 January primary approached, he was so concerned about the tone of the campaign that he publicly urged Bill Clinton to 'chill a little bit'.

The fact that a congressman would so openly chide a former president of his own party showed how febrile the atmosphere had become. And it was into this volatile setting that Bill Clinton sallied forth with his comparison of Jesse Jackson and Obama.

*

Jackson and Obama were very different politicians, in part because they had emerged from starkly contrasting milieus. Jackson was rooted in the civil rights movement. He had marched with King in the 1960s, and his rhetoric and worldview remained drenched in the concerns and confrontational politics of that era. In Jackson's two runs for the presidency, he had made some inroads with the most liberal whites, but his central appeal was clear to everyone, including himself. He was – first, foremost and proudly – the black candidate, the candidate who existed to give voice to the black community's grievances and sustenance to its dreams.

His most famous speech, to the 1988 Democratic convention, was an extraordinary piece of oratory, delivered just before delegates were given the chance to vote for him as their presidential nominee. He was sure to lose the vote – he had ultimately been defeated in the primaries by Massachusetts governor Michael Dukakis – but the placing of his name 'in nomination', as the official parlance had it, was a way of honouring his historic run.

Jackson's address reached out to many groups, from impoverished whites to those who had been struck down with AIDS, but there was no doubt who made up his core audience. The speech's opening was an extended homage to the civil rights movement; its climax was a call of empathic encouragement to those still struggling on the harsh streets from which Jackson, the son of a 16-year-old single mother, had himself come: 'Every one of these funny labels they put on you, those of you who are watching this broadcast tonight in the projects, on the corners, I understand. [They] call you outcast, lowdown, you can't make it, you're nothing, you're from nobody, subclass, underclass. When you see Jesse Jackson, when my name goes in nomination, your name goes in nomination. I was born in the slum, but the slum was not born in me. And it wasn't born in you, and you can make it.'

Jackson was the best-known black politician of his generation but there were many others – including Bobby Rush, the man who had handed Obama a drubbing in the congressional race – whose career had followed a similar template. Obama was cast from a different mould. Doug Muzzio, a professor of political science at New York's Baruch College, told me: 'Whereas Jesse Jackson was clearly a black candidate, Obama is more of a candidate who is black.' I asked Hermene Hartman, the *N'Digo* publisher who had declined to review Obama's first book, to contrast Obama's appeal with that of Rush. 'Bobby Rush is a race man; Barack is not a race man,' she replied.

Part of what set Obama apart was his time in elite, white-dominated institutions like Columbia University and Harvard Law School. His biracial background also played a big part: it had made him uncomfortable with swingeing racial generalisations since his earliest days. In *Dreams From My Father*, he recalled teenage conversations with other African-Americans who would complain about 'white folks' and their wiles.

'"White folks". The term itself was uncomfortable in my mouth at first,' Obama wrote. 'Sometimes I would find myself talking to Ray [a black friend] about "white folks" this or "white folks" that, and I would suddenly remember my mother's smile, and the words that I spoke would seem awkward and false.'

Obama, though he was singular in so many ways, was also part of at least one group: a new generation of black politicians who began emerging across the US around the turn of the millennium. Their names – Deval Patrick, governor of Massachusetts; Cory Booker, mayor of Newark, New Jersey; Artur Davis, US congressman from Alabama – were not especially well known beyond their own regions. But all had in common a keen awareness of the limitations of identity politics and an undisguised frustration with some of its more jaded practitioners.

This new breed of African-American leaders took full pride in their ethnicity – contrary to the aspersions cast by some of the old warhorses they were supplanting – but they focused on reaching beyond racial lines. They were more interested in building coalitions and making incremental progress than in chanting slogans and damning the system.

(Not coincidentally, they tended to be more politically moderate in general. Obama's early opposition to the Iraq war led some people to conclude that he was much more liberal than he actually was. On free trade, personal morality and the fundamentals of foreign policy, his positions were those of a centrist Democrat. Jesse Jackson, by contrast, was clearly on the left of the party.)

For Obama, the ability to transcend racial allegiances was a political necessity. Being seen as the black candidate was all very well in local politics, but it doomed you to defeat in almost any race beyond city or congressional level.

The fact of the matter was that if Obama were to be seen as a black candidate similar to Jackson, too many whites would baulk at supporting him, and he would lose the battle for the nomination. This, it was widely assumed, was why Bill Clinton was trying to bind him and Jackson together so closely – and why neither the former president nor his wife seemed overly concerned about raising the racial temperature.

The tactic was cynical in the extreme, but also potentially brilliant. Obama was relying in part on increased turnout from black voters to beat the Clinton machine. Those voters might stay away from the polls if they perceived him to be less than robust in his defence of the icons of black struggle. On the other hand, if in defending himself from attack he came to be seen as too fixated on racial issues, white support would seep away like water through a drain.

Clinton supporters insist that this is too conspiratorial an interpretation. But in the tense days of January 2008, even observers from distant ideological standpoints felt that it was the most convincing explanation for what was going on. 'The Clintons are reading the polls too,' Eugene Robinson, a columnist for the *Washington Post* wrote in the wake of the King-Johnson furore. 'They might well be resigned to the possibility that most black Democrats will vote for Obama. . . . Is it possible that accusing Obama and his campaign of playing the race card might create doubt in the minds of the moderate, independent, white voters who now seem so enamoured of the young, black senator? Might that be the idea? Yes, that's a cynical view. But history is history.'

Dick Morris, who disagreed with liberals like Robinson on more or less everything, was of the same mind on this issue. Morris was a pollster whom Bill Clinton had employed both in Arkansas and in the White House, despite his Republican leanings, though the two would end up permanently and bitterly estranged.

'Ultimately, the Clintons are playing a game of ju-jitsu with Obama, using his own strength against him,' Morris wrote in a syndicated column four days before the South Carolina primary. 'Block voting will trigger the white backlash Senator Clinton needs to win. Once whites see blacks voting en masse for a black man, they will figure that it is a racial game and line up for Hillary. The Clintons can well afford to lose South Carolina as long as the election is not seen as a bellwether of how the South will vote but as an indication of how African-Americans will go. It's a small price to pay for the racial polarisation they need to win.'

If that really was the plan, it suffered from some faulty assumptions. One was an underestimation of Obama's political skills and his ability to slide out of the corner in which the Clintons were seeking to entrap him. A second was a failure to recognise that, in a changing America, there was a larger cohort of white voters than ever before who would be so disgusted by race-baiting manoeuvres that they would make a point of sticking by Obama. The failure to understand those dynamics would wound the Clintons in the black community and leave a bitter taste in the mouths of progressives of every race.

*

I had never met a doctor who made a first impression quite like Brenda Williams. 'Earlier today, I had a speculum up a young woman's vagina and she said to me, "Dr Williams, why do you support Obama?" And I said to her: "Well, you just keep breathing in and out, and I will tell you what is so marvellous and splendid about this young man."'

So Williams told me in the town of Sumter, South Carolina, where she had made her home a quarter of a century before. We met three days before the primary. Williams had been asked to introduce Obama at an event in a community centre in the 43,000-strong city. She was one of Sumter's most respected Obama supporters, and also one of its most flamboyant.

Dressed in a striking, bright pink outfit, she had delivered an emphatic speech about Obama's integrity and wisdom, bringing the crowd to its feet before he even appeared. When Obama got to the microphone, he teased her gently. 'The only problem with Dr Williams is she's a little shy – doesn't like to speak up, let folks know what she's thinking,' he said with a chuckle.

The lives of many of the people in Sumter were no laughing matter. There was one major economic engine in the town – a sprawling air force base on its outskirts. Some streets were pleasant and well maintained, but most – especially those closest to where Obama spoke – were not. The shells of old shops, long since shuttered, stood ghost-like at the roadside. Houses were lapsing into ragged disrepair. I parked on the forecourt of a small garage close to the event. Groups of men sat in knots of four or five on a crumbling wall, watching the hubbub around the venue expressionlessly.

These were people for whom many of the grandiose promises of America had long rung hollow. Months later, after I got to know Brenda Williams better, she told me about the obstacles she had faced when she had first gone door-to-door in the poorest areas of town, trying to interest the residents in Obama's candidacy. 'With most of the people we encountered, it had been many years since they had voted,' she said. 'Many of them had never voted for anyone and felt there was no purpose in voting for anyone. If you are someone with little means, with little education, you don't matter in this country – in the courts, in society, on the job, in the workplace. So when we came to their door, asking them to come out and vote, they would say: "Why? Why is it important? Here I am, unemployed, with no insurance, living among rats and roaches."'

Having to confront and overcome that degree of disillusionment forced volunteers like the 56-year-old Williams to think more profoundly about their support for Obama. 'We had to be able to say to ourselves, "Well, why am I so charged up over this man?"' she told me.

The enthusiasm of those first volunteers might not have been enough to convert every erstwhile alienated citizen, but their efforts made a huge difference. And they were helped in a big way when Obama won Iowa, proving that he was a viable candidate.

The Obama rally in Sumter was crammed. African-Americans are the single biggest ethnic group in the city, making up about 50 percent of the population. The crowd for Obama was overwhelmingly black. A vocal group sang a Sam Cooke medley – including, appositely, 'A Change Is Gonna Come' – before Obama appeared.

His stump speech was honed and familiar by this stage. But, speaking to a black audience, his manner altered. The changes were subtle but unmistakable. Obama's demeanour was more casual, his attitude more playful. In the process of thanking various local dignitaries from the stage, he singled out a judge on the brink of old age, then turned his attention to the judge's wife. 'She's beautiful, so you just know he was smooth,' he said, drawing out the last word – *smooooth* – to cheers.

He seemed to revel in the boisterous call-and-response dynamics more common with black audiences than white ones, at one point leading a chant of: 'No Bush, No Cheney – No Sense'. Something else struck me, too: Obama's fondness for highlighting issues that were of particular interest to the black community without making any explicit reference to race. I had first noticed this in Harlem, where he had spoken about reforming the Justice Department but had not felt the need to spell out how that would benefit African-Americans. In Sumter, he drew roars of approval when he contrasted conditions in the state's schools with those in its jails. As part of his broader demand for change, he said that the US had to bring an end to the pattern whereby it was common to 'drive by a new prison and an old school. Kids aren't stupid. If they see a brand-spanking-new jail and an old, run-down school, that tells them something about our society.'

His point held, irrespective of the audience's race. But it had particular resonance in the African-American community, where disproportionate levels of incarceration and problems with the resourcing of education were persistent heartaches. Tellingly, I never heard Obama use the schools-and-jails riff anywhere else on the campaign trail, save for another venue in South Carolina where the audience was also heavily black.

(The way Obama presented himself to different ethnic audiences was a mightily touchy issue with his team. When writer Vanessa Grigoriadis, in the process of researching a broadly sympathetic profile of the Obamas' marriage for *New York* magazine, casually remarked on these differences to a campaign aide, the aide 'hit the roof'. Grigoriadis wrote that she soon 'received a call from Obama's "African-American outreach coordinator", who apparently clarifies race issues for reporters when they are perceived to have strayed'.)

The acclaim Obama received in Sumter was out of the ordinary, even by his standards. It seemed to be fuelled above all by a sense of pride. When Brenda Williams had gone door-to-door for Obama months before, she had carried a picture of the senator because many people had not even heard that an African-American was running. The doctor would ask the people she canvassed if they could ever remember a president 'who looked like this young man', adding mischievously: 'Go ahead: jog your memory, now.'

They all knew who he was by this stage. Obama's candidacy was celebrated in Sumter and other towns like it; places where causes for celebration were in short supply.

*

There was still the state's primary to be taken care of. Obama needed the fillip that a big win would provide. After New Hampshire, Clinton had gone on to win caucuses in Nevada. The state was seen as less important than others holding early contests, in part because it was not an established part of the election calendar. (In 2004, only about 10,000 people had shown up to caucus, despite the state's 2 million-plus population.)

Clinton's victory came in the face of an endorsement of Obama by the Culinary Workers Union, a key group whose members included many of the staff in Las Vegas's famous casinos. More importantly, it solidified the sense that the New York senator had righted her ship after the shock of New Hampshire.

The Clinton team held out some hope of an upset victory in South Carolina, a result which would almost certainly have ended Obama's campaign. The Clintons had targeted South Carolina early, in February 2007 going so far as to agree a $10,000-per-month contract with an influential black preacher and state senator, Darrell Jackson.

Jackson was the head of a 10,000-congregation 'megachurch' in Columbia. He endorsed Clinton six days after the lucrative consulting agreement was reached with his media and PR firm. The decision raised eyebrows, but Jackson forcefully defended his integrity.

Clinton was still promising to fight 'a very vigorous campaign' in the state in the last week before the election. I saw her speak in Rock Hill, a town on the state's northern edge, the day before the primary. 'I know how to find common ground, but I also know how to stand my ground,' she promised.

Later that night, I went back to Columbia for Obama's final pre-election event, an 11 PM rally in a large concert hall. It was one of those rare occasions when a candidate does not seem as confident as the crowd. Polls showed Obama leading by around 14 points, but that was not so very different from the projections that had been made just before the trauma of New Hampshire.

From the stage, Obama drew a clear parallel with his loss in the Granite State. After winning Iowa, he warned: 'I think people started thinking, "This is not hard." But you know that the status quo does not give up that easily. . . . The status quo resists.'

Before he took the stage, Michelle Obama – who tended to address racial issues more directly than her husband – had also seemed cautious. 'We can't take anything for granted,' she told the crowd. 'You all know folks who aren't ready for this.' Turning up at the voting booths, she said, was 'about ensuring that we change the dynamic in this country'.

The next day, the people of South Carolina answered the call. The polls were just as wrong as they had been in New Hampshire – but this time in the opposite direction. Obama defeated Clinton by almost 30 percent – roughly double the margin that had been predicted. It was a stunning performance.

The victory was powered by African-American support. In Sumter County, where Brenda Williams and her friends had toiled from dawn to dusk to turn out his backers, Obama won 10,765 votes and Clinton less than 3,000.

'I have arthritis in both knees, but when the result was announced that night, I was feeling no pain,' Williams told me. 'If anyone was passing this house, they would have thought something wild was going on. This was the same country where we were sold on slavery blocks.'

White Americans boosted the scale of Obama's victory. The polls had predicted he would receive only 10 percent of the white vote. In the end, he got 24 percent – a more impressive showing than it sounded, not just because it far outstripped expectations, but because John Edwards, born in the state and based in North Carolina, had always been assured of significant white support.

The result proved that Obama's cross-racial appeal was durable. It exploded the trap the Clintons had tried to set for him. At his victory rally in Columbia that night, I watched him drive home the point. He referred to a woman who had at one point worked for a white segregationist senator from the state, Strom Thurmond, but had canvassed on Obama's behalf in the 2008 campaign. 'So don't tell me we can't change. Yes we can, yes we can change,' he thundered.

He also noted pointedly that in campaigning through the state, he had not seen 'a white South Carolina or a black South Carolina. I saw South Carolina. I saw crumbling schools that are stealing the future of black children and white children alike. I saw shuttered mills and homes for sale that once belonged to Americans from all walks of life.'

The atmosphere seemed to me more loaded, more raw, than it had been in Iowa or New Hampshire. 'Race doesn't matter, race doesn't matter,' the crowd chanted at one point during Obama's speech. His victory, supporter Ava Boyd told me, 'proves that Obama is a candidate for all people, not for just black people'. Earlier, as the crowd watched the returns coming in on video screens tuned to CNN, the network cut to footage of Bill Clinton delivering a speech. The former president was instantly and lustily booed.

Even David Axelrod seemed more on edge than usual. At one point, he gloated that the result was 'a good old-fashioned butt-kicking'. When I asked him about the notion that Bill Clinton had tried to propagate – that Obama's victory was little more than a by-product of the state's large black population – he almost snorted. 'That's an attempt to marginalise what cannot be marginalised,' he said. Obama, he insisted, had 'galvanised people across the country'.

In the final hours of campaigning, presumably catching a sense of the prevailing political winds, the Clinton campaign had suggested that they had known all along that they could not win South Carolina and had therefore not put all that much effort into the campaign.

Axelrod was unimpressed. The idea was 'laughable', he told me. 'They spent about $8 million, they ran negative ads, they took this very seriously, and now they are trying to create the impression that they didn't.'

The race card had been played, and Obama had beaten it – for now. Many of his African-American supporters would not forget the remarks the Clintons had made. The duo's antics still rankled with Brenda Williams months afterwards. 'I felt then, and still feel now, that what Bill and Hillary Clinton did was done with the intent of bringing out race in a mean-spirited way, and to remind white folk: "This is a black man, now",' she told me in August 2008. 'They were talking to the rednecks, the racists, the same kind of people who killed Dr King.'

Hermene Hartman, the Chicago publisher, focused on Bill Clinton's Jesse Jackson remark. 'I was offended by it,' she said. 'It was a dismissal of the people who voted for Barack. It was: "If you don't vote for her, you don't count."'

The Clintons' travails on the race issue were not at an end. The former First Lady's conduct reached its nadir in May. First, she told *USA Today* that Obama's support was weak among 'hard-working Americans, white Americans' – a remark that provoked anger because of the way it conflated the two categories. Later that month, she was asked about the merit of continuing her candidacy, which by then seemed to have no realistic chance of prevailing. Astonishingly, she cited as one of her rationales the fact that 'We all remember Bobby Kennedy was assassinated in June in California'.

The possibility that Obama would be hurt or killed had been floating around in the ether since the start of his campaign. It had weighed on his and Michelle's minds as they considered whether he should enter the race. I had heard the issue discussed constantly by African-Americans from Texas to Harlem. For Clinton to raise it in the context she did – to come to the brink of seeming to welcome the possibility – left many people both stunned and incensed.

James Clyburn released a statement saying that her remarks were 'beyond the pale'. Television journalist Keith Olbermann, the presenter of MSNBC's *Countdown*, addressed a 'special comment' on that night's show to Clinton: 'This, senator, is too much,' Olbermann (who is white) said. 'A person who can let hang in mid-air the prospect that she might just be sticking around in part in case the other guy gets shot has no business being, and no capacity to be, the president of the United States.' Clinton had by then issued a half-baked apology, asserting that she had merely been referencing 'a historic fact' but expressing 'regret' if it had been deemed offensive.

It was too late for contrition – especially contrition expressed grudgingly. A month before the furore, a *Washington Post* poll had asked black Democrats about their views of the Clintons. The proportion with a strongly favourable view of the former First Lady had halved since January; her husband's popularity had suffered a comparable decline.

Some African-Americans continued to defend the Clintons, expressing a lack of concern about all the controversies. But others were deeply hurt. They were in no mood to give the couple a pass. They thought that the Clintons' behaviour had exposed as hollow their supposed solidarity with black America. They thought that, when the chips were down, the couple had embraced a strategy of breathtaking ruthlessness. They thought, in short, that the Clintons had sold them out.

I thought so too.

6

THE WARRIOR

One week before Barack Obama triumphed in the South Carolina Democratic primary, a 71-year-old Vietnam war veteran had stood onstage at the state's main military college and claimed his own sweet success.

'Mac is back!' the crowd at the Citadel in Charleston had chanted over and over again. John McCain was the object of their excitement. McCain, a senator from Arizona, had just won the state's Republican primary. The victory put to rest one of the most painful episodes of his political life.

Back in 2000, McCain had run a thrilling insurgent bid for the Republican nomination against the party establishment's favoured candidate, George W. Bush. Bush was avuncular but untested. His main asset was the enormous amount of money behind him.

For a while it had looked as though McCain might beat him. But it had all fallen apart in South Carolina, in the bitterest circumstances imaginable, and Bush had trundled on to the nomination.

Now, McCain stepped to the microphone and told the audience: 'You and I are aware that, for the last 28 years, the winner of the South Carolina primary has been the nominee of our party for president of the United States.'

The cheers were loud, and they took McCain aback. He was a pugnacious man who seemed more comfortable confronting opponents than accepting plaudits. So he stood there, smiling awkwardly, scratching self-consciously at the left side of his face, waiting for the noise to die down. 'We have a ways to go, my friends, and there are some tough contests ahead. But, my friends, we are well on our way tonight.'

He was indeed. When he finally clinched the Republican nomination only a few weeks later, he had completed one of the most astonishing comebacks in memory.

The previous summer, McCain's campaign had teetered on the verge of bankruptcy, several of his closest aides had departed, and even the media — often admiring of the maverick senator — had dismissed his chances.

He had fought on, stripping the campaign down to the bone. He travelled on commercial flights rather than the charter jets other candidates enjoyed. He embarked on a bus trip dubbed 'The No Surrender Tour'. He held town hall meetings and dealt with whatever questions were thrown at him. Ever so slowly, he came back from the dead, and he won.

Perhaps the outside world should not have been so shocked. John McCain had a long and intimate relationship with adversity.

*

Vietnam.

It was the centre of everything for McCain. It was the root of all that was compelling about his psyche, from the volcanic rages to the hunger for comradeship. It was where he had earned the label of hero. It was where his love of his country had become fierce and deep.

By 2008, virtually everyone with a passing interest in politics knew the outline of what had happened to McCain in south-east Asia. But the details never lost their power to shake you.

McCain had been a navy pilot. On 26 October 1967, he was shot out of the sky over Hanoi. A North Vietnamese missile blew off the right wing of his plane. McCain ejected from the spinning, diving aircraft and came down in a lake, both of his arms and his right leg broken. (A photograph of the moment is widely available on the internet, McCain's body limp and apparently insensate in the water as ten or so Vietnamese men gather around him.) He was dragged ashore, stripped, beaten and bayoneted in the ankle. Then he was dragged off to the infamous Hoa Lo Prison. The complex was better known by its ironic name, the Hanoi Hilton.

McCain lapsed in and out of consciousness for several days. His broken arms were never set. Even today, he cannot lift his arms above shoulder height. If his hair gets messed up, someone else must comb it for him. If his collar gets bunched behind his neck, someone else must straighten it out.

After about one year, McCain's captors offered to release him. They had discovered that he was the son of an admiral. McCain refused. American military code called for prisoners of war to be released in the order in which they had been captured. He would not breach it.

He would spend another four and a half years in the Hanoi Hilton. He was tortured repeatedly. One method employed by the Vietnamese was to tie his injured arms behind his back with ropes that were then tightened bit by bit through the night.

To his enduring shame, McCain broke. At one point, fearing that he could not keep his self-discipline for much longer, he tried to hang himself. Shortly afterwards, he signed a confession that included a reference to himself as an 'air pirate'. Though McCain would later write of coming to understand that everyone had a breaking point and that he had reached his, he never let go of a sense of guilt at the lapse. 'I failed in some ways,' he often said.

All except the most crazed anti-McCain partisans would consider that to be too harsh a judgement. McCain's time in Vietnam gave him a kind of moral heft. For those who would seek to disparage or oppose him, it was a big obstacle. His endurance and his refusal to accept early release just sat there, great craggy slabs of bravery and honour, unavoidable and irreducible.

I would come to appreciate from close quarters what a ferocious response lay in wait for those who would diminish McCain's sacrifice. In early March 2008, in the run-up to the Texas Democratic primary, I went to see the renowned feminist Gloria Steinem speak at an event organised by Hillary Clinton's campaign.

Steinem seemed to mock McCain's military service, suggesting that if a female pilot had been shot down, the media would have spent most of their time asking 'What did you do wrong to get captured?' Referring to McCain's time as a POW, Steinem added: 'I mean, hello? This is supposed to be a qualification to be president? I don't think so.'

After her speech, Steinem affably agreed to an interview. 'From George Washington to Jack Kennedy and PT-109 [the boat that Kennedy commanded during World War Two], we have behaved as if killing people is a qualification for ruling people,' she told me.

Filing my story for the *New York Observer* the next morning, I thought Steinem's remarks were interesting but, considering her ideological leanings, not especially shocking. Once the story appeared, it soon became apparent that others thought differently. The Clinton campaign hurried out a statement distancing the New York senator from Steinem. The offending quotes became a focal point for discussion on cable TV. Of the 600-plus comments on the issue posted on the *Observer*'s website, the overwhelming majority were hostile to Steinem, and a significant number were vigorously abusive. 'Let's put a hood over Gloria Steinem's head, take her to a Vietnamese prison, torture her . . . and see how she likes it,' wrote one reader.

McCain's time in Vietnam finally came to an end after the Paris Peace Accords of 1973. He was released on 15 March of that year. Footage of his homecoming shows a handsome but badly injured man, his gait ragged and halting as he salutes those who have lined up to greet him on the tarmac.

His re-entry into mainstream life was difficult. He remained in the navy, but he needed to go through a long and arduous period of physical rehabilitation. There were also marital difficulties. His wife, Carol, later suggested that many of the tensions sprang from 'John turning 40 and wanting to be 25 again'. The couple eventually divorced, and McCain went on to acknowledge in general terms the infidelities at which his wife's comment had hinted.

McCain met his second wife, Cindy Hensley, in 1979, while he was still married to Carol. Hensley was blonde, attractive and rich. Her father owned one of the biggest beer distributors in the American south-west and she was his sole heir. (Her net worth today is estimated at around $100 million.) At the time of the couple's first meeting – a cocktail party in Hawaii at which McCain, by his own account, tried his best to monopolise Cindy's attention – he was 42 and she was 24.

The future presidential candidate would propose only months after meeting Cindy. He was still married, though separated. He filed for divorce from Carol in February 1980 and married Cindy three months later.

There is nothing to suggest that McCain's attraction to Cindy was less than genuine. But it is indisputable that her family's prominence in Arizona gave him a valuable entrée into politics in the state. Retiring from the navy in the spring of 1981, he worked for a while for his father-in-law's business, all the time building up contacts. He was first elected to Congress in a safe Republican district the following year, and won re-election equally easily in 1984.

Two years later, Barry Goldwater, one of the two senators representing the state, decided to retire. Goldwater was a curious figure in modern American politics. He was militantly anti-communist, but he did not fit the standard template of a hard-right Republican: he was a libertarian at heart, leery of those who would use government to enforce their preferred moral code. In the mid-1990s, shortly before his death, he publicly condemned those who he claimed were 'trying to take the Republican Party and make a religious organisation out of it'.

This idiosyncratic bent was shared by the man who replaced him: John McCain. The war hero beat his Democratic opponent, Richard Kimball, by a margin of more than 20 percent in November 1986.

It would take time for McCain to acquire the maverick image that would prove such a boon to him. In his early years in the Senate, he was regarded as a conventional Reaganite Republican. Neither his speeches nor his votes displayed any great inclination to buck the party line.

If McCain was known for anything, it was the combustibility of his temper. His arguments, even with other senators, could degenerate into venomous personal abuse. It has been widely reported that he once told Senator Charles Grassley of Iowa that he was 'a fucking jerk'. After Cindy McCain lightly mocked him in public for losing his hair, he is alleged to have shot back that at least he did not 'plaster on the make-up like a trollop'. (McCain denies this, and also denies that he aimed a crude term for the female genitalia at his wife, as has been reported in some quarters.)

For the first eight years of McCain's time in the Senate, Dennis DeConcini, a Democrat, was the other senator representing Arizona. To say that there was no love lost between the two men would be an understatement. 'We did not work closely together,' DeConcini said drily when I spoke to him in the summer of 2008. 'He is a difficult man to work with because he insists on always being in charge, and that's not the way the United States Senate works.'

Those sentiments might be seen as the predictable carping of a partisan opponent. Yet DeConcini insisted that he had found plenty of common ground with Goldwater, McCain's Republican predecessor, and that 'any number of Republican senators' had also had 'really rough run-ins' with him.

DeConcini recalled that if legislation that would be to Arizona's benefit was being held up, he and McCain would sometimes go together to reason with whichever senators were being obstructive. If the other politicians refused to budge, he said, 'I witnessed McCain on a number of occasions absolutely explode. He had done that to me on a couple of occasions, but I had put that down to him being Republican and me being Democrat. Or I thought: "He's having a bad day." But after seeing him do that to other senators . . . I realised that there was something wrong with this guy, in my opinion.'

McCain and DeConcini had one thing in common: both became entangled in the so-called 'Keating Five' case of the late 1980s and early 1990s. The scandal would end DeConcini's political life and imperil McCain's.

The affair took its name from Charles Keating. A conservative stalwart – he had been centrally involved in several anti-pornography drives – and a leading property developer in Arizona, Keating had contributed to many of McCain's election campaigns. One of Keating's businesses, the Lincoln Savings and Loan Association, got into difficulties. (Savings-and-loan associations are the American equivalent of building societies.) In simple terms, Keating had used Lincoln's deposits to fund other ventures, those ventures had not turned out as he had hoped, and regulators empowered by the US government had begun to smell a rat.

McCain, apparently motivated by personal loyalty, wrote letters to the regulators on Keating's behalf. Then, in 1987, he and four other senators, including DeConcini, met in private with the officials who were putting pressure on Keating and urged them to back off. None of it did much good. Lincoln eventually collapsed and American taxpayers got stuck with the bill: a tidy $3.4 billion.

By 1991, the Senate Ethics Committee was investigating the series of events that had led to the fiasco. The other four senators involved were Democrats. McCain was judged less harshly than them, but he still faced criticism. The committee found that he had 'exercised poor judgement in intervening with the regulators'.

Controversy still festers over whether McCain's party affiliation helped or hurt him. DeConcini alleges that the committee went easier on him because of it. By contrast, Wes Gullett, an Arizona lobbyist and a close friend of McCain's, insisted to me that the Republican 'didn't do anything inappropriate' and that the committee had kept him in its sights only to preserve the appearance of bipartisanship.

Three of the other four senators retired after the scandal rather than face tough re-election battles. The imbroglio left its mark on McCain too. He compared the period with his imprisonment in Vietnam, noting that his sense of honour had never been questioned as a prisoner of war. In one of his books, *Worth the Fighting For*, he noted that his 'popularity in Arizona was in freefall' after his actions came to notice.

McCain was not about to go gentle into that good night, as his three colleagues had. He took the scandal as a forceful reminder that a senator must go the extra mile in order to ensure that his or her integrity is beyond reproach.

In 1994, he began working with a liberal Democratic senator, Russ Feingold of Wisconsin, to craft legislation aimed at reducing the influence of corporate money on the political system. The duo's efforts would be frustrated for almost a decade, but they ultimately prevailed when the McCain-Feingold Act was passed in 2002. In apparent proof of the dictum that no good deed goes unpunished, McCain's work on the issue fuelled the distrust with which many supporters of his own party came to regard him.

*

McCain's new-found willingness to breach the party line continued throughout the 1990s, and, in September 1999, he officially declared himself a candidate for the presidency. He did so with a promise to enact reform. 'If we are to meet the challenges of our time, we must take the corrupting influence of special-interest money out of politics,' he said in his announcement speech in Nashua, New Hampshire. 'I want to return our government back to whom it belongs – the people – so that Americans can believe once again that public service is a summons to duty and not a lifetime of privilege.'

The phrase 'lifetime of privilege' neatly captured the background of George W. Bush at that point. McCain knew that he could not come close to raising the kind of money Bush had at his disposal. But he also knew that the voters of New Hampshire had a gnarly, independent streak. He held over 100 town hall meetings the length and breadth of the state. His message began to resonate.

McCain's outsider image was burnished by his decision to give the media almost unfettered access to him. He travelled on a bus christened *The Straight Talk Express* and held court, often for hours at a time.

Eve-of-election polls in New Hampshire showed McCain with a narrow lead. In the end, he hammered Bush. His margin of victory was almost 20 percentage points. 'Today the Republican Party has recovered its heritage of reform,' he told his boisterous victory party that night. He added that a 'great national crusade has just begun'.

Except it hadn't.

Bush's brains trust, led by the Machiavellian, Texas-based strategist Karl Rove, was appalled by the scale of their man's loss in New Hampshire. They knew that if McCain beat Bush again in the next major contest, which was to take place in South Carolina eighteen days later, the jig might well be up. That could not be allowed to happen. They decided to hit McCain hard. What happened next made South Carolina synonymous with dirty politics of the most sulphurous kind.

McCain, his wife and his children were systematically slandered. When he spoke at rallies, flyers would be found on audience members' windscreens afterwards suggesting that he was mentally unstable as a result of his experiences in Vietnam. Or that he was gay. Or that his forced confession in Vietnam made him a traitor. Cindy, who had admitted to a period of addiction to legal painkillers years before, was labelled a drug addict.

In the most reprehensible of all the attacks, McCain was said to have had an illegitimate child with an African-American prostitute. The bogus 'proof' for that allegation came in the shape of photographs of McCain's family, which includes an adopted daughter, Bridget, who is Bangladeshi and was brought back to the United States from an orphanage by Cindy. At the time of the South Carolina primary, Bridget McCain was not quite 10 years old.

In 2008, Cindy would tell *Newsweek* that it took her much longer than her husband to get over the tactics used that February. 'It was my daughter,' she said. 'I think any mother would agree with me. You can go after me, but stay away from my children.'

Adding to the general chaos, no one could track down who was spreading the rumours. A local politician, James Merrill, recalled that he had chased after some people whom he had seen handing out the noxious flyers. Merrill told the *New York Times* that when he had asked the young men where they had got the material, they had said: 'Some guy in a red pick-up truck said, "Hey, do you wanna make $100?"'

'It was a rough campaign,' Wes Gullett, who worked on McCain's bid for the nomination that year, told me with studied understatement.

'It went beyond the normal rough-and-tumble that we've become accustomed to.'

Virtually everyone suspected that the Bush team had given covert approval for at least some of the attacks. They denied it, and their culpability was never proven. This didn't matter to McCain. *Time* magazine reported that when a Republican TV debate was held in the state, Bush went over to McCain during a commercial break, put his hand on his arm and told him that he had nothing to do with the smears. 'Don't give me that shit,' McCain responded, 'and take your hands off me.'

The most depressing aspect of all was that the smears worked – not merely because some of the mud stuck but because the way it was flung knocked McCain off his game. One instance came when he got himself embroiled in a strange row over a flag.

The flag of the Confederacy – the de facto pro-slavery side in the American civil war – still flew above the South Carolina statehouse in 2000. Most other southern states had, in the face of protests, ceased flying the divisive ensign. McCain, asked about the flag on a national political talk show, said that it was 'offensive in many, many ways, as we all know. It's a symbol of racism and slavery.' He was being both honest and accurate. But his advisors panicked, convinced that the answer would doom him among the trenchant conservatives who made up a large part of the Republican electorate in the state.

Faced with their objections, McCain fell back on one of his less appealing traits: a kind of juvenile churlishness. When he was asked about the flag from then on, he would ostentatiously take a piece of paper out of his pocket and, in a flat monotone, begin reading a statement that began: 'As to how I view the flag, I understand both sides . . . .'

It was a move that was too clever by half, as McCain would later admit. 'By the time I was asked the question for the fourth or fifth time, I could have delivered the response from memory,' he wrote in one of his memoirs. 'But I persisted with the theatrics of reading it as if I were making a hostage statement. I think that made the offence worse. Acknowledging my dishonesty with a wink didn't make it less a lie. It compounded the offence by revealing how wilful it had been.

You either have the guts to tell the truth or you don't.'

If that farrago was not enough, McCain made another error of judgement when he OK-ed a TV ad that said Bush 'twists the truth like Clinton'. McCain's comparison seemed excessive to many of the state's Republicans; more to the point, he gave up his one big advantage over Bush – a supposed ethical superiority – the moment the ad ran.

In the end, Bush beat McCain by 11 percent in South Carolina. McCain won a few states later in the primary season but they were the political equivalent of consolation goals in a one-sided football match. Bush won nine of the thirteen states voting on Super Tuesday in early March, and the contest was as good as over.

*

The anger engendered by the defeat stayed with McCain for a long time. His backing of Bush in the 2000 presidential election was every bit as tepid and contrived as his ability to 'see both sides' of the Confederate flag issue. 'I endorse George Bush, I endorse George Bush, I endorse George Bush,' he told reporters robotically.

In the years that followed, McCain's disenchantment with the Republican Party was well known throughout Washington. Democrats, including Edward Kennedy, sought to persuade him to change parties, or at least declare himself an independent. His advisors examined whether it was realistic for him to mount an independent bid for the White House. In 2004, John Kerry's campaign made serious overtures to McCain, hoping to persuade him to become the vice-presidential nominee on a 'unity' ticket. McCain was reportedly offered control of foreign policy if he accepted. Following several conversations, he declined.

After all that, he surprised many observers by campaigning vigorously for Bush in the final months before the 2004 election. He figuratively – and, in one awkward instance, literally – embraced his old nemesis. McCain seemed to have accepted that there was only one viable route to the White House left open for him. If he were to stand a chance in 2008, he would have to reconcile himself with the mainstream of the Republican Party. Perhaps he could never become a candidate beloved of his party's grassroots supporters, but he would at least try to soften their dislike of him.

It was, presumably, this notion that led him to speak at a graduation ceremony at Liberty University, a Christian college in Virginia founded by the ultra-right-wing fundamentalist preacher Jerry Falwell. Back in 2000, McCain had denounced Falwell as one of the 'agents of intolerance' bedevilling America. Now he seemed to be giving him his blessing.

There were other moves to placate the Right. McCain had previously opposed Bush's 2001 and 2003 tax cuts for the richest Americans. Now he supported them. Having spent years complaining that ethanol subsidies were wasteful, he came around to the idea as he began positioning himself for a presidential run. (Ethanol is a big issue in Iowa, where many farmers are dependent upon the associated subsidies.)

These U-turns badly tarnished McCain's independent-minded image. But his maverick streak could not be entirely suffocated. He came together with Edward Kennedy to draw up a Senate bill aimed at immigration reform. The proposal had some security safeguards, but the Republican Right was horrified that it included a pathway by which illegal immigrants could become American citizens.

In July 2006, I saw McCain address an Irish-American event in New York. 'We shouldn't be impugning those who come here for the same reasons our forefathers came here: because we wanted a better life for ourselves and our families,' he said. McCain's reference to Kennedy as 'a lion in winter' whose 'word is good' was met with appreciation by the Irish-American audience. It was hardly likely to endear him to conservatives, for whom the Massachusetts senator was a *bête noire*.

Despite his ongoing detours from Republican orthodoxy, McCain's advisors believed – much as Hillary Clinton's did on the other side – that they could present him as the inevitable choice for the party's presidential nomination in 2008.

In the summer of 2006, key McCain strategist John Weaver told the *Washington Post* about the awesome political machine they intended to build. 'We'll be in good shape,' Weaver said. 'We'll have a 50-state structure by early next year, as opposed to a three-state structure last time.'

McCain's team had badly misjudged the mood of the party, and the strengths and weaknesses of their candidate. They underestimated the virulence with which a large part of the base opposed his immigration proposal and they overestimated his capacity to raise money. (McCain simply didn't like making phone calls to solicit donations – a trait that stood to his credit as a human being but was a dangerous demerit for him as a politician.)

It gradually became clear that the campaign was in a cavernous hole. In the first quarter of 2007, it raised an unimpressive $12.5 million, while Mitt Romney, one of McCain's chief rivals, raised $21 million. The results for the next quarter were even worse: McCain raised only $11 million. More to the point, his team, intent upon building their 50-state structure, had run through the funds with abandon. McCain had only $2 million left. The candidate, who had railed against reckless spending on the part of government for years, now faced the reality that his campaign had been as undisciplined as any federal department.

Drastic action was called for. He cut his staff numbers in half, but even that did not lance the boil. At a meeting in Washington, he ranted at Weaver and campaign manager Terry Nelson. Weaver stormed out. McCain accepted Nelson's resignation. When Weaver found out the news, he too departed.

It was July 2007, and McCain had gone from first place to fourth place in the polls. One anonymous Republican told the *Politico* website that 'at this rate the senator's going to be driving *The Straight Talk Express* himself'. Another predicted that his campaign 'could dissolve pretty quickly'.

McCain's recovery from that seemingly hopeless position had a great deal to do with resilience. He also backed away from his support for immigration reform, soothing right-wing nerves. There was one other factor, and it was even more crucial: he was lucky in the enemies

117

he faced. Every Republican candidate had a fundamental flaw when it came to appealing to the party's base.

Romney had serious shortcomings in the eyes of social conservatives. He was a Mormon, which disquieted some. He was also a vastly wealthy businessman who had served as governor of Massachusetts from 2003 to 2007. Competing in that strongly liberal state, he had presented himself as pro-choice, pro-gay rights and pro-gun control. He reversed himself on every one of those issues as he prepared to run for the presidency.

Romney's perceived phoniness went deeper than his mutable positions. Part of it was his appearance: a rather wooden-looking man with a pure-white smile and Brylcreemed dark hair, he resembled a political candidate from central casting rather than the genuine article.

His efforts to prove himself at one with the people could also seem hapless. Currying favour with opponents of gun control in New Hampshire, Romney said he had been 'a hunter pretty much all my life'. Under pressure, his campaign later admitted that his lifetime experience amounted to two actual hunting trips.

Romney tried to clarify the matter, but his way of doing so only hurt him more. 'I'm not a big-game hunter. I've made that very clear. I've always been a rodent and rabbit hunter. Small varmints, if you will.' The phrase 'small varmints, if you will' somehow captured everything that was wrong with Romney's candidacy.

The other candidate thought to be in with a real chance at the start of the nomination process was former New York City mayor Rudolph Giuliani. 'Rudy' had become a national hero through his response to the attacks of September 11 – in the process almost erasing memories of how his popularity had dwindled in the city until those attacks took place.

Giuliani's celebrity did not entirely cloak his weaknesses. He had never run anything bigger than a city – albeit one of the world's largest. He was moderate, relatively speaking, on social issues like abortion and gun control, and went to less bother to hide it than Romney. His oleaginous personality was not a great help either. The polls in New

Hampshire suggested that he became less popular with voters the more he visited there.

Of the other candidates, libertarian gadfly Ron Paul and two congressmen, Tom Tancredo and Duncan Hunter, were no-hopers. Excitement flared briefly around Fred Thompson, a former senator from Tennessee who by 2007 was best known as an actor on the hit TV series *Law & Order*. Thompson entered the race in September, but his lack of enthusiasm for the rigours of the campaign trail was conspicuous. His bid went nowhere.

American presidential politics was about to prove that it still had the capacity to throw up dark-horse candidates. In 2000, McCain himself had played that role; in 2008, it was filled by Mike Huckabee.

Huckabee was a former Baptist minister who had become governor of Arkansas. He was far to the right on social and religious issues (he indicated during one debate that he did not believe in evolution), but his personality was infinitely more agreeable than that of many of the leaders who had previously emerged from the evangelical community. 'I'm a conservative but I'm not angry about it' became one of his signature lines.

Huckabee played bass guitar in a rock band, had become something of a diet guru (he had shed more than 100 pounds while governor) and had the best sense of humour of any presidential candidate in either party.

His appeal wasn't purely superficial. He was the perfect electoral vehicle for something the other candidates had ignored: a sense of resentment among poorer conservatives. The night before the Iowa caucuses, he appeared on *The Tonight Show* and told host Jay Leno: 'People are looking for a presidential candidate who reminds them more of the guy they work with, rather than the guy that laid them off.'

The Republican Party had been successful in several elections by painting Democrats as being out of touch with 'regular' Americans. Yet for all the talk about mainstream values and love of the heartland, the party itself was dominated by a wealthy elite. Washington careerists and their friends in big business held the levers of power. The social class from which Huckabee had emerged — he

119

was the son of a car mechanic – was regarded by these people with disdain.

(I was reminded of this in June 2008, in the unlikely environs of a Cape Cod country club. I found myself in conversation with a former CEO of a one-time Fortune 500 corporation. The man was a large and frequent donor to Republican causes. 'Huckabee?' he spluttered, seemingly appalled at the memory of the Arkansan's strong primary performance. 'We just pat those kinds of people on the head and take their money.')

Huckabee's unimpeachable conservative credentials, his plain-speaking style, and his instinctive feel for the concerns of lower-income voters combined to create electoral rocket fuel. One poll in September 2007 had given him just 4 percent support in Iowa. By the end of November, he was at 28 percent, and leading the field.

Huckabee's rise delighted the so-called McCainiacs for several reasons. Prime among these was his potential to thwart Romney, whom McCain's people considered a much more dangerous long-term threat.

Romney's strategy involved sinking vast sums of money into Iowa. A victory there would make him more or less invincible in New Hampshire, which adjoined his home state. He had always been a strong favourite to win the third contest, in Michigan, because of family connections: his late father had been a popular governor there. If all those things happened, Romney could realistically expect the party to fall in behind him as its nominee.

Everything looked good for Romney – until voters started thinking seriously about the choices before them. Then, his opinion poll leads in Iowa and New Hampshire melted away. In the former, Huckabee surged; in the latter, McCain came on strong.

McCain had largely given up on Iowa, but on the eve of polling he made a final, brief trip to the state. I saw him speak at a small hall on the outskirts of Des Moines. The puny size of the venue and the rather chaotic way the event was organised offered a sharp and unfavourable contrast to the scale of the Obama and Clinton rallies happening elsewhere at the same time. But, though McCain spoke only briefly, he was clearly energised.

As he left, the BBC's Katty Kay asked him if a third-place finish in Iowa would constitute success for him. McCain responded that whether he came 'third, fourth, fifth or sixth', he would be heading on to New Hampshire.

It was a politic response. McCain finished fourth in Iowa. His bid could have died that night. Instead, Huckabee saved him by walloping Romney. The mechanic's son beat the multimillionaire by more than nine points. 'People really are more important than the purse,' Huckabee said in his victory speech.

The McCain team was jubilant. Romney's aura of inevitability had been destroyed. And Huckabee had no chance of winning New Hampshire, a much more liberal state than Iowa. If McCain could win the Granite State, he would be back in the race.

New Hampshire had catapulted McCain into serious contention in 2000. Now, it did it again. He won by five points. 'I always told you the truth, as best as I can see the truth,' he told voters, 'and you did me the great honour of listening.'

(McCain's personal popularity in New Hampshire was inescapable. News of McCain's victory came through during the Obama election-night rally I attended. It was met with warm, sincere applause from the overwhelmingly Democratic audience.)

Romney managed to win both the Michigan primary and the Nevada caucuses shortly afterwards, but his victories did little to change the dynamic of the race.

South Carolina was up next. The McCain campaign was determined not to leave the same vulnerabilities that Bush's supporters had capitalised on eight years before. Rapid-response phone banks were set up to rebut any murky allegations. McCain also had the support of much of the state's Republican establishment. He edged out Huckabee by three points, essentially putting paid to any outside chance the former preacher had of winning the nomination. Romney got only half as many votes as McCain.

In the meantime, Rudy Giuliani's campaign had drifted. His initial plan had been to win in New Hampshire, but he abandoned that state as his poll ratings sagged. He settled upon an all-or-nothing strategy pinned on winning Florida, a state to which many older people from New York and the states around it retire. Florida was to vote immediately after South Carolina.

By that stage, however, Giuliani had been out of the headlines for weeks. The former mayor got trounced, receiving only 14 percent of the vote. Romney did better, but McCain won fairly comfortably in the end. When he also won most of the big states voting on Super Tuesday, including New York and California, the nomination was effectively wrapped up. The process had resembled a demolition derby more than a conventional Republican primary.

'You can never count John McCain out,' Wes Gullett reflected. 'He outworked everybody in the field. He is the same person who wore out three pairs of shoes knocking on 50,000 doors when he first ran for Congress. He is a tenacious campaigner.'

The question of who McCain would face in the general election was, at that point, still an open one. He genuinely preferred Hillary Clinton on a personal level. In 2004, they had got into a vodka-drinking contest during a trip to Estonia, apparently at Clinton's instigation. In early 2007, he had told *Vanity Fair*'s Todd Purdum: 'I like her. I know you're not supposed to say that, but I do.'

McCain shared another piece of common ground with Clinton. Both of them seemed to regard Obama as an upstart. McCain's most high-profile interaction with the Illinois senator prior to the presidential race had been a bizarre one. In February 2006, McCain believed that Obama had back-pedalled on a commitment he had made during negotiations on the issue of ethics reform. The older man's temper flared, and he made public a sarcastic letter he had sent to Obama.

'I would like to apologise to you for assuming that your private assurances to me were sincere,' McCain wrote. 'Sorry for the confusion, but please be assured I won't make the same mistake again.'

Obama wrote back, professing himself 'puzzled'. He added that he had 'no idea what has prompted your response'.

That particular flap went no further. But the seeds of McCain's dislike of Obama had germinated. They would come into full bloom soon enough.

7

ELATION AND FRUSTRATION

The news hit like a piledriver. Edward Kennedy would endorse Barack Obama.

The story broke the day after the South Carolina Democratic primary. It was the most powerful single example of how the tremors from the Clintons' conduct were continuing to reverberate.

Kennedy had felt driven into the fray in part by Bill Clinton's behaviour. The older man had called Clinton more than once to ask him to take greater care not to exacerbate ethnic divisions. The conversations had been tense. The last one had almost degenerated into a shouting match. There had been some final pleas by the Clinton team for Kennedy to remain neutral in the race, but he had proven impervious to them.

The ageing Irish-American's backing of Obama was of profound symbolic importance. It showed that the heavyweights of the Democratic Party were beginning to move towards him. It also seemed like a passing of the torch.

Kennedy's name, and even his physiognomy, nudged forth memories of his two dead brothers and of what they had represented. John had seemed to usher in a new era of American idealism as the 1960s began; Robert was in the process of reviving it when he was shot dead in the kitchens of a Los Angeles hotel. Now, the sole surviving brother seemed to be giving the clan's imprimatur to a senator almost 30 years his junior who looked like he could resuscitate that same optimistic spirit.

Obama and Kennedy appeared together for the first time the next day, at an event at American University in Washington. The Massachusetts senator described Obama as 'a new national leader who has given America a different kind of campaign – not just about himself, but about all of us'.

In another line, which many took as an implicit criticism of the Clintons, Kennedy insisted that Obama would 'turn the page on the old politics of misrepresentation and distortion'.

*

Kennedy's words could not have come at a better time for Obama. The biggest single day in the primary calendar was looming. The fifth of February was 'Super Tuesday', when 22 states would hold Democratic primaries and caucuses. Huge prizes like New York, California and Illinois were up for grabs.

With so many people in so many places due to go to the polls, the kind of intense, localised campaigning that had marked the previous contests had to go by the wayside. The biggest states might receive one or two visits from the candidates leading up to polling day, but for the most part the battle would be fought through competing television ads and other forms of mass media.

The move on to a larger canvas was – at the outset – assumed to favour Clinton. She had a significant head start across the board because of her name recognition and personal history. Obama, the sceptics said, had only been able to close the gap in the earlier states by visiting again and again, building enthusiasm through town-by-town appearances. They argued that, stripped of this opportunity, he would meet his Waterloo.

The ground began to shift after Obama's South Carolina victory, at least according to the opinion polls. Several surveys showed Obama narrowing the lead that Clinton had long held in California, and even moving ahead there. Swings of significant magnitude were also seen in key states like New Jersey, Missouri and Massachusetts.

The sense of momentum would prove to be a double-edged sword for Obama. It shifted expectations for his performance on Super Tuesday. His supporters had once aspired only to staying in the game on 5 February; now they wondered if this would be the day when he would vanquish Clinton.

Obama, certain of a big victory in Illinois, spent the night of Super Tuesday in Chicago, where he watched the results come in with Michelle and the girls. The several thousand supporters who gathered in the city's Riverside Center to hear him speak had to cope with an initial feeling of anticlimax.

In Massachusetts, despite Kennedy's endorsement, Clinton held on very comfortably, winning by more than 15 percent. In New Jersey, the final polls had predicted a Clinton victory in the region of 5 percent; she won by double that margin. Most critically of all, when the action swung westwards across the continent, Clinton easily bested Obama in California. Five of the last seven opinion polls had shown him with a narrow lead; in the event, Clinton won by more than 8 percent.

The outcome in those states was yet another reminder of the dangers of putting too much faith in the opinions of pollsters. As with the New Hampshire result, it was also a wake-up call for those who believed that Obama's ability to draw crowds and create a buzz would automatically translate into votes.

*

Obama's most fervent supporters may have been disappointed at first, when their highest hopes had gone unfulfilled on Super Tuesday. But as the results sank in, they soon began to see things in a more positive light. Obama had essentially shared the honours with Clinton. He had won more states than the former First Lady, thirteen to nine. He had beaten Clinton in Connecticut, which borders New York and where she had been highly fancied. While several of his victories were in sparsely populated or Republican-dominated places like Utah, North Dakota and Idaho, others came in large states such as Georgia and Missouri.

There was one factor above all that was working in Obama's favour. Having endured Super Tuesday, he was now facing a succession of contests where the odds tilted towards him in a big way.

'Winning Massachusetts, winning New Jersey, was never part of any nomination scenario for us,' David Plouffe said. 'We like where we stand right now.'

Plouffe's confidence was borne of hard-headed demographic analysis. Obama's pillars of strength were younger voters, better-educated and more affluent Democrats, and African-Americans. Older voters, Hispanics and less-well-off whites, by contrast, tended to go heavily for Clinton, with women in all those categories more favourably disposed towards her than their male counterparts.

There were all sorts of hypotheses for why those segments of the voting population behaved as they did. For instance, there had traditionally been rivalry between Hispanics and African-Americans for political power – something which was said to contribute to Obama's weakness with the former group. His elevated rhetoric, and his call for a new kind of politics, seemed certain to appeal to idealistic young voters more than to older people, who may have learnt from experience to be wary of lofty promises. And some women voted for Clinton in the same way as some blacks voted for Obama: with a keen pride that 'one of their own' was a serious contender for the nation's highest office.

The 11 contests scheduled during the rest of February were due to include several places with large African-American populations (notably Louisiana, Maryland and the District of Columbia) and other states where younger, more affluent and more liberal Democrats were in plentiful supply.

In the end, Obama swept the board, winning every one of those battles. In retrospect, it was the decisive phase of the primary campaign. Clinton would never again get back on level terms.

Perhaps the most striking thing of all was that, for those few weeks, Obama made it look easy. He drew huge crowds, and their excitement was irrepressible. (It was during this period that I saw him address the rally in Baltimore mentioned in the Preface.) The results were emphatic. On 9 February, he took Louisiana, Nebraska, Washington State and the US Virgin Islands. The closest of the four was Louisiana – and there he won by 21 percent.

The Clinton team, in briefings with reporters, kept tentatively offering examples of states in which the former First Lady might at least hold down Obama's margin of victory. Every time they did so, he proved them wrong. A respectable performance in Maine might be possible, the Clintonites suggested – and Obama won by almost 20 percent. On 12 February, the Clinton people held out some hope of a decent showing in Virginia, one of three primaries to be held that day in and around Washington, DC. Obama won by 29 percent in Virginia, by 25 percent in Maryland and by 52 percent in the District of Columbia itself.

On 19 February, another Clinton firewall fell. Several polls in the closing days before the Wisconsin primary had shown Obama grinding out a win of around four points. He won by 17.

His aides were exultant. Axelrod, trying to maintain realistic expectations for the more challenging contests to come, told reporters: 'I'd be lying if I told you we won't miss February.'

The Clinton camp, meanwhile, was in disarray. Immediately after Super Tuesday, it had revealed that the senator had been obliged to lend her campaign $5 million of her own money. Clinton's campaign manager, Patti Solis Doyle, stepped down on 10 February, amid complaints that she had never come to grips with the job. Doyle apparently said that if she was going, so too should Mark Penn. The chief strategist's brusque manner and Machiavellian tendencies fuelled distrust among the rest of the staff, but he stayed in place.

Penn had been similarly unpopular within Bill Clinton's administration, and many of the former president's old lieutenants were furious about the job he was doing on Hillary's campaign. Murmurs of discontent had been growing for some time. Late in February, Leon Panetta, who had been Bill Clinton's White House chief of staff from June 1994 to January 1997, broke ranks to tell me about his dissatisfaction in an interview for the *New York Observer*.

Panetta lashed Penn, saying that he was 'a political pollster from the past. I never considered him someone who would run a national campaign for the presidency.' Panetta also compared Penn to Karl Rove – a high insult in Democratic circles – saying that both men believed that winning elections was 'all about dividing people into smaller groups rather than taking the broader approach that was needed'.

Finally, and just as devastatingly, Panetta condemned the lack of planning on the part of the campaign as a whole. 'It seems to me like they rolled the dice on Super Tuesday, thinking that would end it,' he said, 'and when it didn't end it, they didn't have a plan. And when it came to the caucus states, they did have a plan – which was to ignore them. I think those were serious mistakes.'

The former First Lady, for her part, seemed to decide that her best bet was to take an ever-harder line against Obama. Solis Doyle was replaced by an older aide, Maggie Williams. Shortly afterwards, a photograph of Obama in African clothing during a visit to Kenya appeared on the *Drudge Report*, the influential, conservative-leaning website.

The publication of the photo was clearly intended to fuel the false rumour that Obama was secretly a Muslim – a smear that had been doing the rounds of the right-wing blogosphere for months. Alas for Clinton's aides, Matt Drudge, the website's semi-reclusive owner, made it known that it was they who had supplied the picture.

Plouffe described the move as 'shameful, offensive fear-mongering'. Williams shot back that the Obama campaign should be 'ashamed' for characterising the photo as divisive. 'Hillary Clinton has worn the traditional clothing of countries she has visited and had those photos published widely,' Williams added. It was a ridiculous defence. No one was suggesting that Clinton had any fealty with Islam.

*

The next big date on the election calendar was fast approaching. Texas, Ohio, Vermont and Rhode Island would vote on 4 March. Even Bill

Urging that 'the ways of Washington must change', Senator Barack Obama
launches his presidential candidacy in Springfield, Illinois, on 10 February 2007.
(Photo by Ted Schurter/WireImage)

Obama with Oprah Winfrey, whose support gave him a crucial boost as the
race for the Democratic nomination
began to heat up.
(Photo by Jemal Countess/WireImage)

With Bono in Washington, DC, 2006.

(Photo by Dennis Brack-Pool/Getty Images)

St Patrick's Day Parade, Chicago, 2005. Although willing to pay some lip-service to America's many ethnic lobbies, Obama was less inclined than most politicians to pander to them.

(Photo by Tim Boyle/Getty Images)

Obama and Hillary Clinton at a crucial TV debate just before the New Hampshire primary.
(Photo by Chip Somodevilla/Getty Images)

Obama and his wife, Michelle, have breakfast with Obama's running mate, Senator Joe Biden, and his wife, Jill, at the Yankee Kitchen Family Restaurant in Boardman, Ohio, on their second day of campaigning together after the Democratic National Convention.   (Photo by Saul Loeb/AFP/Getty Images)

Senator John McCain accepts the Republican Party's presidential nomination, with Governor Sarah Palin of Alaska alongside him. The choice of the untested Palin as his running mate helped McCain initially but hurt him more and more as the campaign went on.   (Photo by Ethan Miller/Getty Images)

Obama's chief strategist, David Axelrod (right), with his counterpart on the McCain team, Steve Schmidt.

(Photo by Alex Wong/Getty Images for Meet the Press)

Obama campaign manager David Plouffe speaks to the media in the spin room after the vice-presidential debate in St Louis on 2 October 2008.

(Photo by Chip Somodevilla/Getty Images)

Mama Sarah Obama, Barack Obama's step-grandmother, receives congratulatory messages at her home in Kogelo, Kenya, shortly after the senator became the first African-American presidential nominee of a major party.

(Photo by Simon Maina/AFP/Getty Images)

Reverend Jeremiah Wright, former pastor of the Trinity United Church of Christ in Chicago, addresses the National Press Club in Washington, DC.

(Photo by Chip Somodevilla/Getty Images)

Obama walks towards his daughters Malia (left) and Sasha and his wife, Michelle,
after accepting the Democratic nomination in front of a crowd of 80,000 people in
Denver.   (Photo by Win McNamee/Getty Images)

President-elect Barack Obama gives his victory speech to supporters during an election night gathering in Grant Park, Chicago, on 4 November 2008.

(Photo by Anthony Jacobs/Getty Images)

Clinton had acknowledged that if his wife lost either of the two biggest states, Texas and Ohio, she would be out of the race.

Clinton was strong in Ohio. In Texas, it seemed like a different story. She had once held a lead there, but it had never been as commanding as in strongholds like California. Obama was once again whittling away her advantage – to the point where, of seven polls conducted in the last days of February, five gave Obama a small lead and two suggested a tie.

On 27 February, I saw Obama speak at a rally at Texas State University in San Marcos. He assailed John McCain as much as Clinton – a move intended to present him as the inevitable Democratic nominee. He accused McCain of having followed George W. Bush 'into the quagmire' of Iraq.

The crowd was around 10,000-strong in a college town with approximately 50,000 residents. Yet though the setting was undeniably dramatic – Obama spoke under floodlights in an open-air arena – the candidate sounded slightly flat. And many members of the crowd were there to experience the sense of occasion rather than out of any strong sense of loyalty to Obama.

Twenty-two-year-old Samantha Manley told me that although she found Obama 'very inspirational', she was unsure whom she would vote for if he ended up facing McCain in the presidential election. Her enthusiasm for Obama had a single root. 'I don't like Hillary at all,' she said.

Another student, Kaitlin Murphy, was emphatically in Obama's corner, however. 'I'm tired of old, white men running the country – people whose lives don't reflect how most of us live,' the 21-year-old told me. 'He just draws you in,' she added of Obama's speech. 'It seemed like everybody could relate to one part or another.'

Facing political peril once again, Clinton released her most cutting TV commercial yet, a 30-second message that became known as 'the 3 AM ad'. Its purpose was to assert that Obama was unprepared to be commander-in-chief – and to do so as dramatically as possible without inciting a negative counter-reaction.

'It's 3 AM, and your children are safe and asleep,' a sinister-voiced narrator said over tinted footage of a sleeping child. 'But there's a phone in the White House, and it's ringing. Something's happening in the world. Your vote will decide who answers that call.' The ad went on to argue that Clinton alone was 'tested and ready to lead in a dangerous world'.

By historical standards, it wasn't an especially harsh spot. Nonetheless, its tone discomfited some Democrats. Obama was now the strong favourite to become the party's presidential candidate and such attacks ran the risk of weakening him in the general election, they thought.

The morning the ad came out, I was with the press pack trailing Obama to a small, invitation-only meeting with war veterans at an American Legion hall on the outskirts of Houston. An old fighter jet stood on the parched grass outside. Inside, a few men were already clustered around the bar. They eyed the reporters, campaign aides and secret service agents who make up the human paraphernalia of a presidential campaign with a combination of wryness and displeasure.

Obama spoke in a room that held perhaps 100 veterans. He looked even skinnier than usual and spoke cautiously, calling Clinton's ad 'an attempt to play on people's fears'.

He added: 'The question is not who will pick up the phone, the question is what kind of judgement you will show when you pick up the phone.' He called the decision over whether to go to war in Iraq 'a red-phone moment' and added that Clinton, Bush and McCain had all given 'the wrong answer'.

That all sounded calm and measured. But his demeanour told a different story. Obama's irritation was becoming more difficult to hide.

Despite his efforts, the 3 AM ad seemed to have some bite. Adding to his woes, a Chicago property developer, Tony Rezko, went on trial on bribery, fraud and money-laundering charges at around the same time. (In June, Rezko would be found guilty on 16 of the 24 counts he faced.)

Rezko had been an early fundraiser for Obama, and the two men had known each other socially. Obama had even been involved in a real-estate deal with the developer, a decision he later referred to as 'bone-headed'. Obama was not implicated in Rezko's offences but the timing of the trial did him no favours.

On election night itself, Clinton departed for Ohio, where she was almost certain of a win. Obama stayed in Texas. It wasn't to be his night. In the end, the former First Lady edged him out by 3 percent, or 100,000 votes. She won Ohio by a comfortable eight points and also claimed the tiny state of Rhode Island. Obama's sole win came in Vermont. (He was later declared the winner of the caucuses in Texas, which, confusingly, took place the same day as the primary and were much less important in shaping public perceptions.)

Frustration and fatigue lay over Obama's election night rally in San Antonio like a blanket. Never before or since have I seen him so listless in public. Adding to the feeling of ennui, the crowd that showed up was much smaller than usual. About 1,500 people were in attendance. Obama had become used to attracting audiences ten times that size.

He congratulated Clinton, emphasised that he remained in the lead, and insisted: 'We are on our way to winning this nomination.' He spoke, as he often did, about the importance of inspiring new voters and the possibility of 'writing a new chapter in the American story'. But it all had a perfunctory feel.

Axelrod was not happy either. Irked that the negative tone of the Clinton campaign had worked, he now had to solve a conundrum: how to defend his candidate from attack while also remaining true to Obama's promise to practise a new kind of politics. The chief strategist seemed, at that point, more interested in taking Clinton down than in worrying about the niceties of the methods.

After Obama had left the stage and the camera crews had begun packing up, I asked him about Clinton's tactics. 'If Senator Clinton wants to take the debate to various places, we'll join that debate,' he said ominously. 'We'll do it on our own terms and we'll do it in our own way. But if she wants to make issues like ethics and disclosure and law firms and real-estate deals and all that sort of stuff issues . . . I don't know why they'd want to go there.'

That sounded to me like an allusion to the Whitewater imbroglio that had proven to be a distracting sideshow during Bill Clinton's years in the Oval Office. Axelrod instead focused on the reluctance of the Clintons to release their tax returns – something which candidates for high public office in the US customarily do. 'For all their yammering about how unfairly they have been treated, they haven't really been pursued at all by the media on some of these questions,' he said.

Axelrod was also growing impatient with Hillary Clinton's argument that her experience offered a stark contrast with Obama's alleged callowness. 'You hear Senator Clinton talk, and you would think that she was Lyndon Johnson in the US Senate,' he said. 'But I don't know what her major legislative achievements are.'

The defeats in Texas and Ohio were only part of the difficulty. Two other states, Wyoming and Mississippi, would vote within the next week. Yet even if Obama won both convincingly – which he duly did – he would not deliver a knockout blow, since neither state was seen as especially significant. (Wyoming is the least populous state in the union, and Mississippi's large African-American population meant that an Obama victory there was a foregone conclusion.) Mississippi voted on 11 March. The next primary would not be held until six weeks later, on 22 April, when Democratic voters would go to the polls in Pennsylvania.

The same night as Obama's desultory Texas event, McCain had made mathematically certain what had long been a de facto reality: he would be the Republican Party's nominee for the presidency. Axelrod told me that Obama had called McCain to congratulate him. What the strategist didn't need to say – because he and I and everyone else knew it – was that McCain would be rubbing his hands in delight at the prospect of the two most prominent Democrats in the nation attacking each other for almost two months while he had the Republican pulpit to himself.

The weeks ahead held dangers. But no one, that night in Texas, realised how quickly Obama would be engulfed by a tempest.

*

The words would haunt Obama throughout his bid for the White House. They came in an angry torrent. They weren't even his own.

'The government . . . wants us to sing "God Bless America". No, no, no! Not God bless America. God damn America! . . . God damn America for treating our citizens as less than human. God damn America for as long as she acts like she is God and she is supreme.'

The speaker – the shouter, actually – was Reverend Jeremiah Wright, Obama's erstwhile pastor from Chicago's Trinity United Church of Christ. Wright's fondness for incendiary sermonising would come to threaten his congregant's electoral viability more than any single comment by Hillary Clinton or John McCain.

Wright's 'God Damn America!' outburst became the most famous soundbite associated with him, but there were others – a lot of others. In one instance, protesting continued white domination of the United States, Wright invoked the Ku Klux Klan, calling the country 'the US of K-K-K-A.' In another, he suggested that the American government had created the HIV virus to kill black people. In yet another, he addressed the presidential campaign, saying in a hoarse, escalating roar: 'Barack knows what it means to be a black man living in a country and a culture that is controlled by rich white people. Hillary can never know that. Hillary ain't never been called a nigger!'

Next to 'God Damn America,' the Wright sermon that most outraged mainstream opinion had come the Sunday after the September 11 attacks. Having run through a long litany of American misdeeds in foreign climes, Wright said: 'The stuff we have done overseas is now brought right back into our own front yards. America's chickens are coming home to roost.'

There may have been a time and a place to raise questions about American foreign policy. In the judgement of most of Wright's compatriots, a pulpit the weekend after the worst terrorist attack in the nation's history was not it. Exacerbating the offence, Wright delivered the 'chickens are coming home to roost' line with flapping hand gestures and a tone that sounded suspiciously like glee.

The Wright furore raged like a wildfire. Excerpts from the preacher's sermons were shown constantly on the 24-hour cable news channels. Pundits weighed in from every quarter, predicting doom for Obama. On the day the Wright videos were first broadcast, a Gallup tracking poll had Obama six percentage points ahead of Clinton among Democrats across the US. Less than a week later, the same organisation had him five points behind.

Obama's own feelings could only be guessed at or learned second-hand. The candidate's oratory often moved audiences to tears; his memoirs revealed strong currents churning inside him; but he was not given to vivid outward displays of emotion. His unusual equanimity would be remarked upon more and more as the campaign went on.

It was left to his closest friends to acknowledge, albeit obliquely, the extent to which the Wright episode had affected him. Obama 'didn't show his moods too much at that time,' Terry Link told me in the summer of 2008. 'He was trying to keep up the positive face. He wasn't going to show anything about being down, and he wanted to keep his eye on the ultimate goal, which was to win the primary. But obviously in his heart there was disappointment.'

One of the many difficulties the Obama camp faced was that it was almost impossible to distance the candidate from Wright in a credible way. Obama had been a member of the church for 20 years. Wright had married him and Michelle on 18 October 1992, and he had baptised Malia and Sasha.

The controversy also tarnished what had previously been some of Obama's most popular moments. The phrase 'the audacity of hope' – the climactic line of the 2004 convention speech before it had become the title of his second book – had its provenance in the title of a Wright sermon. In *Dreams From My Father*, Obama had explicitly credited Wright, and that sermon in particular, with awakening his sense of Christianity.

Obama and his advisors had been aware for some time that Wright could prove unpalatable to the nationwide audience the young senator was trying to reach. When Obama had launched his campaign on that cold day in Springfield in early 2007, Wright had been due to deliver the invocation.

The night before, Obama had called Wright to withdraw the

invitation. Wright was hurt by the snub and ascribed it to the influence of an unnamed Obama advisor widely believed to be Axelrod. ('Axe' had considerable experience helping African-American candidates win races in which the majority of the electorate was white. As such, he may have been more attuned than most to the dangers Wright posed.)

Problematically, Wright had prayed with the Obama family before they had walked out to launch Barack's presidential bid. When the Springfield episode had come to light, an Obama spokesperson had reiterated that 'Senator Obama is proud of his pastor and his church'.

Everything about Wright spelt trouble. He buttressed the arguments of those who contended that Obama was something different from what he claimed to be: more threatening, more angry and more entrenched in old-style racial politics.

The flap also removed an important shield from Obama's armoury. Prior to Wright's emergence, he had been able to rebut the Muslim smears through deliberate references to his Christianity. I had seen him in South Carolina, for instance, note with exaggerated emphasis: 'I have been a member of the same church for the past 20 years. Praying to Jesus. With my Bible.' Now, such references were to all intents and purposes off-limits, since they served not to reassure voters of his God-fearing ways but to remind them of the rants of his preacher.

The Obama campaign was on the brink of panic about the affair. So close to claiming the nomination after what he himself called his 'unlikely journey', Obama could be undone at the last moment.

Excerpts from Wright's sermons had first been broadcast on a Thursday morning. By Friday night, the row had built to such a pitch that Obama, who had otherwise become increasingly distant from the media, gave interviews to CNN, Fox News and MSNBC, the three main cable news channels. His performances, though competent, were inevitably defensive, and insufficient to staunch the damage.

He had arrived at a moment of truth. He told his aides that he would give a major speech on race in Philadelphia the following Tuesday. Some of those closest to him thought it was a bad idea. They feared that once he had opened the Pandora's box, there would be no way to close it. 'There wasn't a discussion,' Robert Gibbs told *Time* magazine. 'He made a decision.'

Obama wrote the speech himself, over two days and two nights. According to Axelrod, he finished it at 2 AM on the morning on which it was to be delivered.

He stepped to the podium at the National Constitution Centre shortly before 11 AM. The stage was festooned with American flags. Obama's tone was serious, even sombre. In contrast to the celebratory atmosphere that usually attended his addresses, he spoke for 15 minutes before the first burst of applause rang out.

He began with a reference to the signing of the Constitution, which had occurred just across the street from where he now spoke. He went on to retell the story of his biracial background. Then he took a jab at Wright, who, he said, had used 'incendiary language to express views that have the potential not only to widen the racial divide, but views that denigrate both the greatness and the goodness of our nation; that rightly offend white and black alike'.

Yet Obama would not – at least on this occasion – repudiate Wright. While admitting that he would be offended if he had just seen the snippets from Wright's sermons that had played on cable news, he asserted that such brief glimpses produced only 'caricatures' of his church.

In what became the speech's most frequently quoted passage, Obama said of Wright: 'As imperfect as he may be, he has been like family to me. . . . I can no more disown him than I can disown the black community. I can no more disown him than I can my white grandmother – a woman who helped raise me, a woman who sacrificed again and again for me, a woman who loves me as much as she loves anything in this world, but a woman who once confessed her fear of black men who passed by her on the street, and who on more than one occasion has uttered racial or ethnic stereotypes that made me cringe. These people are a part of me. And they are a part of America, this country that I love.'

Obama went on to talk frankly about the challenges that faced the black community, and the lingering, corrosive legacy of slavery. But the speech also acknowledged the resentments of white Americans who, as Obama put it, 'don't feel that they have been particularly privileged by their race'.

He closed with a moving story of the common bond that had been forged between a young white woman and an old black man, both of whom had volunteered for his campaign in South Carolina. When he left the stage, he stepped into the embrace of Michelle. She was weeping.

To many Americans of all races, the speech, which acquired the title 'A More Perfect Union', struck a deep chord that echoed long after the primary campaign had ended. Terry Link told me that he thought that it was 'one of the finest speeches I have ever heard on the racial issue in the United States'. It is available in its entirety on YouTube. By November 2008, it had been viewed almost 7 million times.

The media reaction to the address was forcefully positive. 'Politically ambitious, intellectually impressive and emotionally compelling,' David Broder asserted in the *Washington Post*. 'Pitch-perfect,' said Roger Cohen in the *New York Times*. James Carney, in *Time*, called the speech 'profound, one of the most remarkable by a public figure in decades'.

To my ears, some of the praise seemed a bit extravagant. The speech had much to recommend it, including sophistication and, most notably of all, a respect for the intelligence of the audience. Impressive though it was, however, I was not convinced that Obama had done enough to cut himself free of Wright. In particular, the description of the preacher as 'like family to me' seemed ill-advised and over-generous. (Usually, I thought that the Clinton campaign's complaints of media bias were exaggerated. Yet I could not help but wonder what the press reaction would have been had the former First Lady used such a fond phrase to describe such an antagonistic associate.) Nonetheless, Obama's poll ratings climbed steadily in the days after his speech, and the candidate used his public appearances to move the discussion on to other, less combustible issues.

Some questions still lingered, but Obama had provided a potent answer to one charge that had long been thrown at him by his critics.

They had suggested that he couldn't take a punch. The first real crisis he faced would be enough to sink him, they predicted. No one would say that any longer.

*

If Obama needed respite after the lurching drama of the Wright episode, he soon received it – from the most unlikely source, and in the strangest way.

Hillary Clinton had made a peculiar comment on St Patrick's Day, 24 hours before 'A More Perfect Union.' At the time, the anticipation of Obama's big speech was sucking up all the oxygen in the media atmosphere. Once that was out of the way, the press turned their attention back to the Clinton oddity.

The former First Lady had for some time been making trenchant assertions of her superiority when it came to foreign policy experience. During a speech at George Washington University, she referred to a trip she had made to Bosnia almost exactly 12 years before. 'I remember landing under sniper fire,' she said. 'There was supposed to be some kind of a greeting ceremony at the airport, but instead we just ran with our heads down to get into the vehicles to get to our base.'

This was not merely untrue; it could be proven to be so in graphic terms. Video footage of the landing duly emerged. It showed Clinton calmly speaking to a welcoming party on the tarmac at Tuzla as her daughter, Chelsea, stood by. There was no sniper fire and no apparent hurry to get the two female Clintons to a less exposed location.

The media mockery was intense. The *Washington Post*, which had begun to run a feature called 'The Fact Checker' to settle the more contentious claims made by candidates, awarded Clinton its maximum 'Four Pinnochios' rating for mendacity.

The controversy lingered into the following week, when I joined other reporters on a conference call with Clinton's chief spokesman, Howard Wolfson. We could almost feel Wolfson squirming on the other end of the telephone line. There wasn't anything he could say to defend Clinton's account. He tried valiantly, emphasising that she had been going into a combat zone, and saying that she 'misspoke'. Unfortunately for him, he also said that Clinton had given an erroneous version of the events in question only 'on one occasion'.

That message seemed to have come down from his boss. The senator had told a Philadelphia newspaper that she had given 'contemporaneous accounts' of her Bosnia trip that were accurate and characterised her drift into fantasy as 'a minor blip'.

That wasn't true either – which gave the story a new burst of life. She had given similar accounts of having to run for cover under sniper fire on at least two other occasions. A reporter now asked Clinton how she would respond to Republican claims that this was part of 'a pattern of exaggeration'.

'I just disagree with that,' a brittle Clinton responded. 'I made a mistake. That happens. It proves I'm human – which, you know, for some people is a revelation.'

Far from being a reminder of Clinton's humanity – as, say, the teary moment in New Hampshire had been – the Bosnia episode seemed to intensify the whiff of weirdness that clung to her. Had Clinton over the years actually convinced herself that her landing in Bosnia had been a life-and-death, bullet-dodging drama? There did not seem to be any other explanation as to why she would publicly, and repeatedly, make a claim that could be disproven by any television network that bothered to search its vaults.

The controversy died down over time – until Bill Clinton interjected once again. More than three weeks after the row had erupted, Clinton meandered off-script to give yet another finger-wagging denunciation of the media. 'A lot of the way this whole campaign has been covered has amused me,' Clinton said in Indiana, not sounding even faintly amused. 'But there was a lot of fulminating because Hillary, one time late at night when she was exhausted, misstated – and immediately apologised for it – what happened to her in Bosnia in 1995.' He added, of journalists: 'When they're 60, they'll forget something when they're tired at 11 o'clock at night too.'

This compressed a veritable feast of fibs and distortions into two sentences. As has been noted, Hillary Clinton had not misstated her

Bosnian adventures only once but had done so at least three times; she did not make the remarks late at night on any occasion; she did not immediately apologise for them, doing so only after coming under pressure later; and she was in Bosnia in 1996, not 1995. Most inexplicable of all, perhaps, was the suggestion by the former president that Hillary's slip-up was a consequence of her age.

Soon afterwards, Clinton made it known that his wife had called to tell him to butt out of the Bosnia flap. 'I said, "Yes, ma'am",' he added, somewhat sheepishly.

*

There was one more swing of the pendulum left. In what was becoming a season of gaffes, on Friday 11 April the *Huffington Post* website published comments that Obama had made at a fundraiser in San Francisco the previous Sunday.

Referring to industrial decline in America's Rust Belt, and the scepticism that he believed had been engendered among its people by years of unfulfilled government promises, Obama said: 'So it's not surprising then that they get bitter, they cling to guns or religion or antipathy to people who aren't like them, or anti-immigrant sentiment or anti-trade sentiment, as a way to explain their frustrations.'

In many liberal circles, the remark, and the idea behind it, seemed unremarkable. Obama's point – that when people's lives do not work out as they would like economically, they take their self-esteem and identity from other things – seemed irrefutable.

There was outrage nevertheless. The nub of the political problem was his juxtaposition of the words 'cling' and 'religion', a formulation which some took as a suggestion that their religious faith was shallow and simply a by-product of failure in other areas. The reference to guns did not help either. Democrats had suffered in the past when Republicans had painted them as out of step on gun control, an emotive issue among rural voters who regarded hunting as an integral part of their cultural tradition.

The comments were particularly dangerous for Obama because they fed into the sense that had long lurked in some voters' minds that he was not quite in tune with them; that, despite the modest circumstances of his upbringing, he now bore the stamp of the elite institutions where he had been educated, and looked down on church-going, gun-loving Americans in the heartlands.

Hillary Clinton, naturally enough, pounced on the remarks. The former First Lady described them as 'elitist, out of touch and frankly patronising' when the candidates addressed a forum on faith in Pennsylvania the day after the *Huffington Post* story appeared. Obama countered that he would never, and could never, be 'demeaning of a faith that I myself embrace'.

In a televised debate days afterwards, Obama would protest: 'The problem that we have in our politics, which is fairly typical, is that you take one person's statement, if it's not properly phrased, and you just beat it to death. And that's what Senator Clinton's been doing over the last four days.' But the damage had been done. Obama had been knocked off-balance yet again.

He did not even stay in Pennsylvania on the night the results were announced. He headed for Indiana, which was due to vote in two weeks' time. I walked the streets of Philadelphia on primary day. The spring sunshine was a reminder of how long the campaign had already dragged on since the snows of Iowa. Obama volunteers in the city centre were giving out professionally printed versions of the 'More Perfect Union' speech and waiting for the surge of voters that they still hoped might deliver victory. They told me that turnout was above average, but they could not hide their concern. The tidal wave they had hoped for was not swelling.

I went to Clinton's rally that evening. She won by 10 points. For the fourth time, her bid had come to the edge of defeat and she had survived. 'She has won eight of the nine largest states,' Chris Doherty, the Irish-American mayor of the proudly working-class city of Scranton, told me. 'If you don't win Pennsylvania or Ohio, you can't be president. Just ask "President" Kerry or "President" Gore.' Doherty added that Clinton had 'really identified with the regular people of Pennsylvania' – and he made clear that Obama, in his view, had not. Jon Corzine, a key Clinton supporter and the governor of the neighbouring state of New Jersey, noted happily that the Obama 'bandwagon' had been 'slowed down'.

The increasing bitterness of the primary fight was obvious to everyone now. On the way in to the Clinton event, I had watched groups of her supporters and backers of Obama taunt each other. The media were being sucked in to the strife as well. Inside the hall, as the results came in and it became obvious that Clinton had prevailed, one woman leaned across the barriers that separated the media from the rest of the crowd. 'Tell me why this doesn't really matter,' she asked sarcastically. 'Tell me why she didn't really win.'

In Indiana, Obama insisted, somewhat listlessly, that he would 'wrap up this nomination as quickly as possible'. But just how quickly would that be? North Carolina, as well as Indiana, would vote in two weeks. Clinton might push Obama close in the former and she was heavily favoured to win the latter. The contests from there to the end of the primacy process in June would be held in places like Kentucky and West Virginia – states that Clinton was expected to win comfortably for many reasons, including racial ones.

Obama was still in the driving seat, but the ride was far from smooth. The prize of his party's nomination had been within sight for months, yet it remained infuriatingly elusive. Sometimes, on the longest, most miserable nights on the campaign trail, it seemed to be drifting further away.

8

An End and a Beginning

Then, suddenly, it was over.

On 6 May, on a warm spring evening in the handsome city of Raleigh, North Carolina, Obama sealed a victory to which there could be no reply. He won the state's primary by a thumping 14 percent margin. Just as importantly – perhaps more so – Clinton could only eke out a 2 percent victory in Indiana. It was the first time in months that Obama had outperformed expectations.

His triumphal day had not begun well. He had got knocked flat on his back.

The scene of the crime was a basketball court. Obama loved the sport, to the point where Michelle – whose brother, Craig, was a professional coach – had been known to roll her eyes when he talked about it. He had been a handy player in his schooldays. Old TV footage can still be found of him representing Punahou Academy, where his skills earned him a nickname that had fortuitously been jettisoned long before he thought of a political career: Barry O'Bomber.

Basketball was also at the core of Obama's most notable campaign trail superstition. On the morning of the Iowa caucuses, he had recruited aides and secret service agents to join him in a game. Five days later, in New Hampshire, they had foregone the same pleasure. Look how that turned out, Obama would note archly. From then on, he played a game on the morning of every election day.

Alexi Giannoulias was among those regularly drafted in for these matches. Giannoulias was the treasurer of the state of Illinois and had played professional basketball for a year in Greece, from where his parents had emigrated to the US. As he surged towards the basket on the morning of the two primaries, he speared Obama in the chest with his shoulder, laying him out flat. Axelrod, another regular on the court, ended up having to explain to Lynn Sweet of the *Chicago Sun-Times* that the overly zealous treasurer had 'bashed the ribs of the next president of the United States'. Obama, Axelrod clarified, had been bruised but had not needed to see a doctor.

Things could only improve from there – and they did. The TV networks projected Obama as the winner in North Carolina as soon as voting had ended. When he took the stage at the Reynolds Coliseum, a huge sports hall belonging to the local university, he immediately shot a rhetorical dart in Clinton's direction. 'Some were saying North Carolina would be a game-changer in this election. But today, what North Carolina decided is that the only game that needs changing is the one in Washington, DC.' That may have sounded cocky to some, but it was little more than an acknowledgement that Clinton's final hopes had fizzled out.

The former First Lady had needed the results that night to be very different. Her big wins in Texas and Pennsylvania had created the impression that Obama might be losing altitude. If she kept bringing him down, she could have a chance.

The Democratic nominee would be chosen by delegates sent to the party's convention in August in Denver. The vast majority of them – about 80 percent – would be so-called 'pledged delegates', who had been awarded to one candidate or another on the basis of the state-by-state results. The remainder, labelled 'superdelegates', were elected officials and party apparatchiks who could throw their support behind whomever they liked.

Even before North Carolina and Indiana, it was unlikely that Obama's pledged-delegate lead, run up in part through his succession of wins back in February, could be erased. Clinton's only hope was that she could continue to rack up wide margins of victory in the remaining primaries. She would then be able to make the case that Obama's electability had been fatally punctured by the Jeremiah Wright and 'cling to religion' controversies. This, in turn, would enable her to go to the superdelegates and argue that they needed to back her en masse if the party was to have any hope of retaking the White House.

Clinton was stronger in Indiana, where the demographics favoured her, than in North Carolina. But she had said four days before the primary that 'the entire country – probably even a lot of the world – is looking to see what North Carolina decides'.

Now, North Carolina had decided that it preferred Obama after all. More depressingly still for Clinton, she had to wait until after one o'clock in the morning before being declared the winner in Indiana. (One of the difficulties in determining the result had been late returns from one Indiana county. The *New York Times* later reported that a small-town mayor there, Thomas McDermott Jr, had received an irate phone call from a Clinton aide during the evening. 'I've got an angry president here and a candidate who wants to know whether or not she won,' the campaign worker told him. In the background, McDermott could hear Bill Clinton complaining furiously about the delay in the results. There was nothing McDermott could do. 'It's not very often you basically have a former president yelling at you to get the numbers out,' he told the newspaper.)

Clinton eventually won Indiana by about 14,000 votes out of almost 1.3 million cast. She had spoken to her supporters in the state earlier that night, promising them that it was 'full speed on to the White House', but it seemed unlikely that even she believed it. Obama had proven his durability once again, with decisive consequences. 'We now know who the Democratic nominee's going to be, and no one's going to dispute it,' Tim Russert said on MSNBC that night.

Back in North Carolina, I watched Axelrod walk from volunteer to volunteer, pumping hands and slapping backs. He looked like a man who had been sprung from purgatory. 'We feel really great about the position we're in, despite the tortured constructions we're getting from the Clinton side,' he told a group of reporters. 'We believe the momentum and the superdelegates will continue to go our way and we will be where we need to be before the convention.'

Renee Edwards, a 33-year-old African-American in the crowd, told me she was thrilled by Obama's capacity to bind up the racial wounds that had lain open for so long. 'I think Barack is bridging that [racial] gap. Look at what he has done tonight – and this is in a Southern state,' she said. There was, she added, something about Obama that 'just makes you trust him'.

Those sentiments were hardly universal. Exit polls indicated that 29 percent of voters said that Obama did not share their values. Still, Edwards was right in noting Obama's cross-racial appeal – an appeal that was strongest among younger voters. Among white voters aged 29 or younger, Obama defeated Clinton by 16 percent. Although Clinton did much better with white women overall, besting Obama by a margin of almost two to one, his share of the white male vote (42 percent) was unprecedented for a black candidate in the South.

The 6 May results were remarkable for another reason. On previous nights when the nomination seemed close at hand, Obama had come up short despite having the momentum with him. The big win in North Carolina and the moral victory in Indiana had come, by contrast, in the teeth of a storm. Jeremiah Wright had strode back into the spotlight.

*

No one expected Wright to fade into obscurity. The pastor was a canny and tenacious operator – qualities without which he could not have expanded his church from the 87 members it had when he took over in 1972 to its 2008 size of more than 6,000.

Wright had been on a long-planned holiday when Obama had given the 'More Perfect Union' speech and had avoided journalists since. Obama and he had spoken shortly after that address but, when reporters had asked him about the conversation, Obama had clammed up, declining to describe it.

The preacher decided to reintroduce himself to the public slap in the middle of the period between the Pennsylvania and North

Carolina primaries. His first appearance was innocuous enough. Bill Moyers was a well-respected veteran TV journalist who had once served as Lyndon Johnson's White House press secretary. He was also a member of the same denomination as Wright – something that may have played a part in persuading the preacher to appear on his show rather than on one of the countless others that were seeking to book him.

With Moyers, Wright spoke thoughtfully about his roots in the ministry. He had been persuaded when still a young man that churches too often seemed to exist in 'a fantasy world' disconnected from the troubles outside their door; he did not want that pattern to afflict his church, he said. He made calm, valid points about the way in which black culture had, in the West, often been dismissed or sidelined, even by those who would never have considered themselves racist. And perhaps most importantly, he gave an explanation of his view of religion, shorn of the kind of abrasive sentiments that had marked his sermons.

'We serve a God who comes into history on the side of the oppressed. . . . We serve a God who cares about the poor. . . . Because that same God says, "I'm with you, and I'm with you in the struggle,"' Wright said. 'The God of the people who [are] riding on the decks of the slave ship is not the God of the people who are riding underneath the decks as slaves in chains.'

Yet Wright did not keep his pride or his prickliness entirely in check. When Moyers mildly suggested that the 'chickens are coming home to roost' sermon in the wake of September 11 might have represented a failure to communicate, Wright responded: 'The persons who have heard the entire sermon understand the communication perfectly.'

Wright's feelings about Obama also seemed complex. At first, he paid tribute to the senator's Philadelphia speech. But as Moyers probed deeper into how he felt about being criticised by Obama, Wright fell back on an explanation which was at best unhelpful. 'He's a politician, I'm a pastor. We speak to two different audiences. And he says what he has to say as a politician. . . . He does what politicians do.' This was hardly likely to reassure anyone who had begun to doubt Obama's sincerity or character when Wright had first hit the headlines.

Much worse was to come. On the Sunday night when the pre-taped Moyers show was broadcast, Wright appeared at a meeting of the NAACP in Detroit. His demeanour was entirely different – more confrontational and defiant – and his speech was rambling and strange. He careered through a peculiar theory that black and white children learn using different sides of the brain, imitated the accents of John Kennedy and Lyndon Johnson by way of arguing that African-American children were unjustly mocked for poor English, and embarked on a lengthy thesis as to why black and white people clap in different ways.

(Much of this was absurd, but I was curious about Wright's theory on racial-based brain and learning differences. I called Martin Kozloff, a professor of education at the University of North Carolina, to ask him whether there was anything to the idea. The response I received was pretty unusual, especially by the standards of academia. 'That's horseshit!' the professor said with a guffaw. 'It's utter nonsense. That theory has been around for about 20 years and has been completely discredited by people who are actual neuroscientists. But in the field of education, there is no idea so stupid that some people won't accept it.')

Wright's nadir was reached the following day when he appeared at the National Press Club in Washington. His performance was off the wall. The problem was less with his prepared remarks than with the question-and-answer session that followed them. Wright suggested that Louis Farrakhan – the ultra-controversial leader of the Nation of Islam who had once described Adolf Hitler as 'a very great man' – was 'one of the most important voices in the 20th and 21st century'. He declined to back away from his claim that the US government had created AIDS, saying: 'I believe our government is capable of doing anything.'

As at the NAACP, Wright's mien was even more damaging to Obama than his words. The moderator of the question-and-answer session was a young woman who could not quite disguise her nervousness. Wright seemed to pick up on that, and he responded with boorishness. He rounded off one answer by staring at her and asking:

'Understand that? Capiche?' When she raised his 'chickens are coming home to roost' comment, he asked her whether she had heard the whole sermon. She replied that she had heard most of it, to which Wright shot back: 'No, no, the whole sermon, yes or no? No, you haven't heard the whole sermon?' He preened himself and announced: 'That nullifies that question.'

Even some of those who had been defenders of Wright during the earlier furore were appalled. Kimberly Lightford, the state senator from Illinois who was a friend of Obama's, had attended services in Wright's church in the past, and told me she would have become a member had the building not been so far from her home.

Months after Wright's press club outing, I asked her what she thought had motivated him to act in the way he had. 'I have no idea,' she replied sadly. 'I'm still trying to figure it out. I think part of it was maybe ego. I saw him as offended [by Obama's earlier distancing of himself from him] and wanting to let Barack know: "You know, it's not appreciated." Jeremiah's own selfishness came out because he was offended.'

Obama did not immediately realise the full import of the fiasco. He heard a summary of his former preacher's remarks shortly after they were made, but decided to hold a press conference in front of his campaign plane before he had seen Wright's antics or read a full transcript of his comments.

Obama's words were clear enough in a literal sense. 'He does not speak for me. He does not speak for the campaign,' he said. Yet there was also a hint of wryness about Obama's reaction that was ill-suited to the circumstances. 'I think certainly what the last three days indicate is that we're not coordinating with him, right?' Obama told reporters.

Much later that night, in his hotel room in the city of Chapel Hill, North Carolina, Obama got to see the footage of Wright's Washington appearance for the first time. According to a *New York Times* report, it was only then that he realised the severity of the damage Wright was capable of inflicting.

The next day, grim-faced, he called another press conference. 'I am outraged by the comments that were made and saddened over the spectacle that we saw yesterday,' he began.

The Philadelphia speech had focused on grand issues of racial injustice and misunderstanding. Now, Obama's condemnation of Wright had a personal bite. The candidate at one point accused the pastor of having 'caricatured himself' – something which he said 'made me angry but also made me sad'.

Obama noted bitterly: 'I don't think he showed much concern for me' – and then, almost as if catching himself lapsing into solipsism, added: 'More importantly, I don't think he showed much concern for what we are trying to do in this campaign.'

Later, Obama would charge Wright with 'a show of disrespect to me' because the preacher had again suggested that Obama's denunciation of his sermons had more to do with political expediency than conviction.

At the very least, Wright had played into the hands of Obama's enemies. Those foes were barely able to disguise their joy. During this period, I found myself in a debate on the right-leaning Fox News Channel with a conservative political strategist and author, Angela McGlowan.

McGlowan accused Obama of having used his church membership for purely political purposes, stating in characteristically colourful fashion: 'He pimped that church.' McGlowan added happily: 'This is the first time I will give Reverend Wright respect . . . because he told the truth: Obama is a politician and he is out to get votes.'

The candidate's new, forceful rejection of Wright raised its own questions. How did it tally with his earlier insistence, in Philadelphia, that he could no more renounce Wright than he could his own grandmother?

Voters seemed to give Obama a pass on that point, presumably feeling that the sheer belligerence of Wright's appearance in Washington had left the candidate with no choice but to cut him off.

Obama's performance in the 6 May primaries was nonetheless remarkable in the circumstances. The threat posed by Wright had been neutralised for a second time.

*

Just how vital Obama's North Carolina win had been became obvious in the weeks that followed. Clinton now had virtually no chance of becoming the party's presidential nominee, yet she still handed him drubbings in several states. She beat him by more than 40 points in West Virginia on 13 May; a week after that, she won by 35 points in Kentucky. When the island territory of Puerto Rico went to the polls on 1 June, Clinton won 68 percent of the vote to Obama's 32 percent.

Some of these victories could be attributed to the older, less affluent demographic profile of the places in question. Racial bias also played a depressing part. In exit polls in Kentucky and West Virginia, about one in five voters said that race had been an important factor in determining whom they would back. More than 80 percent of those voters pulled the lever for Clinton.

It was assumed – as it always was when racial attitudes were surveyed – that there were many more people who did in fact vote along ethnic lines but would not admit it to pollsters. And this, it bears emphasising, was in a Democratic primary.

The patterns were enough to knot the stomach of anyone hoping for an Obama victory in the November election.

It was not until 3 June, the final day of the primaries, that Obama made the nomination secure. Though Clinton beat him by 10 points in South Dakota, he defeated her by 16 percent in Montana. While he flew to St Paul to give his victory speech – the location chosen in part because the city would host the Republican convention later in the year – much of the media gathered in New York. Clinton had scheduled an evening rally in the city. A concession speech was widely expected.

It didn't come. The night turned into one of the oddest in an odd campaign. Critics had long charged that Clinton's most impassioned supporters – those who, even now, believed that she could still become the Democratic nominee – were only able to cling to their beliefs through a wilful shutting-out of reality.

The New York event seemed to prove their point. The video screens that were usually set up at such events to broadcast TV coverage of the results were absent. The hall was deep underground in the bowels of Baruch College, so there was no mobile-phone coverage or internet access available, and hence no way of finding out that Obama had clinched the prize.

When it came time for the New York senator to speak, she was introduced by the chairman of her campaign, Terry McAuliffe, who absurdly continued to insist that she would be 'the next president of the United States'.

Clinton's speech was notable for all the things it didn't say. There was no explicit acknowledgement that Obama had won, only a pro-forma, vague tribute to 'him and his supporters for all they have accomplished'.

Lanny Davis, a special counsel to Bill Clinton during his years in the White House, had been among the most aggressive media surrogates for the former First Lady. In a corridor outside the gym where Clinton spoke, he told me that Obama 'still has a major problem. He doesn't talk to people who are working class, he talks above them. He has basically written them off and he thinks he can win without them.'

To have such close allies of Clinton arguing that Obama was, at root, an elitist who lived in some rarefied atmosphere was not only troubling in itself; it also added heft to the attempts by the McCain campaign to push the same line.

During her speech, Clinton had posed the question: 'Where do we go from here?' She had not hinted at an answer. There were only two possible justifications for keeping her campaign alive: a hope that some new development would immolate Obama before the Democratic convention, or a belief that, by refusing to leave the battlefield, she could put pressure on him to offer her a slot as his running mate.

The next day, even erstwhile Clinton loyalists began to peel off, stating that neither rationale was acceptable. Charles Rangel, the Harlem congressman who had long backed her, and Walter Mondale, the party's 1984 presidential nominee, were among those who let it be known that the former First Lady had nowhere left to go but the exit.

The New York rally had happened on a Tuesday. About 24 hours later, Clinton sent out an email to supporters. She would announce her support for Obama on Saturday, she wrote.

On the Thursday, she and Obama met privately at the Washington home of a fellow senator, Dianne Feinstein of California. No details of their conversation emerged. Feinstein, who was present but retired to another room, good-humouredly told reporters she had heard no shouting and that 'they got along very well'.

On Saturday 7 June, Clinton's rally took place in Washington's National Building Museum. Bill, Chelsea, and Dorothy Rodham – Hillary's mother – joined her on stage.

This time, Clinton avoided the kind of equivocations that had marred the New York event. 'I congratulate him on the victory he has won and the extraordinary race he has run,' she said of Obama. 'I endorse him and throw my full support behind him. And I ask all of you to join me in working as hard for Barack Obama as you have for me.' She also sought to remind voters about the policy issues that should, at least in theory, prove a powerful enough glue to hold Democrats together, irrespective of personal tensions.

There were no guarantees that things would work out as she was suggesting. A CBS News poll released on June 4 had indicated that 22 percent of Clinton's supporters intended to vote for John McCain in the presidential election. A further 8 percent claimed they would stay at home rather than support Obama.

While Clinton was in Washington, the Obama team was in Chicago, contemplating their strategy for the fight against McCain, while also getting some rest. The need to ease the tensions with Clinton supporters continued to be a distraction.

A set-piece event was needed, they thought – one that would act as a kind of full stop, breaking the enmity of the primary and providing a pivot point into the general election campaign.

*

The coming together took place at the end of June in the small town of Unity, New Hampshire. The location had more than its name to recommend it. In the January primary, it had given exactly the same number of votes, 107, to Obama and to Clinton. The symbolism was

153

so perfect that Axelrod told me he expected to be accused of 'inventing' it.

The day was warm and sunny. The smell of hot dogs and hamburgers hung in the air. Axelrod was in characteristically droll form. When I asked him what he expected to come out of the event, his moustache twitched upwards into a smile. 'Unity, man!' he exulted in faux-hippie tones. 'That's what it's all about.'

The sardonic reply reflected a realistic acceptance that his candidate and the Clintons were not on the verge of becoming bosom buddies. But the Unity event went better than most people had expected, in part because Hillary Clinton delivered another emphatic endorsement of Obama.

She expressed her pride that she and Obama had had 'a spirited dialogue' during the primaries and then added, to laughter: 'That was the nicest way I could think of phrasing it.' Clinton also said that she would 'strongly urge' supporters of hers who were tempted to migrate to the McCain camp to rethink their plans.

As for Obama, he paid extensive tribute to Clinton, talking about the 'honour' of sharing a stage with her and describing her as 'one of the finest senators that New York has ever seen'. As Obama continued with his respectful, rather formal, homily, a raucous female voice in the crowd shouted out: 'Hillary rocks!' Obama went with the flow. 'She rocks. She rocks. That's the point I'm trying to make.'

That day, at least, there seemed to be nothing to divide the duo. Even the body language between them was surprisingly relaxed.

Their supporters were not all ready to fall into lockstep, however. As Clinton spoke, a middle-aged woman in the crowd began shouting: 'We want Hillary!' Her angry tone revealed what she really meant: we don't want Obama. Axelrod, who was standing in the press enclosure only yards away, returned to his default look of melancholy. A few others joined in with the woman's chant, only to be counter-heckled by Obama supporters shouting: 'It's over!'

Maureen Dowd of the *New York Times* ventured forth to find the leader of the anti-Obama group, who identified herself as Carmella Lewis, a 57-year-old retired ad saleswoman. 'I have a gut feeling,' Lewis told Dowd darkly, 'that something is going to happen so that she becomes the nominee.'

Those two threads – the drive to heal the party and the difficulty of doing so – would continue to unspool long after the crowds at Unity had dispersed. About two weeks later, I saw Obama appear at a fundraiser in a Manhattan hotel. He was supposed to ask the high rollers in attendance to donate to Clinton's campaign, helping to erase her debts. (She owed around $20 million by the time her campaign finally ended.) There was even a donor form placed beneath every seat before Obama appeared.

He instead delivered what was to all intents and purposes his standard stump speech – and forgot to mention Clinton's debts. One of his press aides, Jen Psaki, happened to be standing beside me as he left the stage, and I saw her eyes widen in alarm. Told of his error shortly after stepping off the podium, Obama returned to do his duty, and apologised for his forgetfulness.

The moment hardly eased the glumness of Clinton supporters. Nor did it suggest that thoughts of helping the former First Lady were to the fore in Obama's mind.

In fairness, he had more important things to worry about. Past primary contests had mostly been over by early spring, giving the winner some time to rest before the general election campaign began in earnest. Obama was not afforded that opportunity. His final primary victory had come five months after Iowa – and just five months before the nation would elect its next president. There was work to do.

*

On 7 June, as Clinton's supporters gathered in Washington to mark her departure from the race, Obama had addressed his troops in a very different setting. He turned up at his Chicago headquarters to give a speech to any staff member who wanted to hear him. The youthfulness of the workers and the open-plan layout of the offices created an ambience that had more in common with an internet start-up company than an old-style political campaign. Obama stepped up to the microphone with many of the staff sitting atop their desks or cross-legged on the floor in front of him.

The speech showed the candidate at his best, mixing earnestness with a light touch of self-deprecation. Shortly after he began speaking, it became obvious that there was a technical glitch which was preventing his remarks from being streamed to workers in other locations. When Obama asked if he should stop, the woman who was trying to repair matters encouraged him to continue. 'Yeah, but I might have something really inspiring to say,' he responded with mock-pomposity, 'and they'll miss the whole thing.'

Technical issues resolved, he turned to pay tribute to his audience. 'Everybody thought that at some point this thing was all going to be a flash in the pan,' he said, referring to the campaign. 'And collectively, you – all of you, most of whom are . . . I'm not even sure [you're] of drinking age – you've created the best political organisation in America and probably the best political organisation that we've seen in the last 30, 40 years. That's a pretty big deal, that's pretty remarkable. And so I hope that all of you understand your achievement.

'I owe thanks to you,' he continued, 'and I'm grateful to you, and you've inspired me. And what you've done is something that continually restores my faith – in people, in America, in the world, in what's possible. And that is a great gift that you've given to me.'

Obama's intention was not just to spread a feel-good atmosphere. He encouraged the staff to take a day or two to savour their victory in the primary and to unwind. 'Get your ya-yas out,' Obama urged them. When a perplexed silence settled over the room, he added, with mild embarrassment: 'That's an old sixties expression.' But the break would have to be short, he insisted.

'Understand that, coming back, we are going to have to work twice as hard as we have been working. We are going to have to be smarter, we are going to have to be tougher, our game is going to have to be tighter, we are going to be attacked more viciously, we are going to have to respond more rapidly.'

For the first time, Obama explicitly admitted that, had he lost the Iowa caucuses back in January, he would also have lost the nomination. In that scenario, he said, 'It would have been OK. One of the other Democrats would have emerged, and they would have carried the banner, and we would have joined their campaign. Because we've won, we now have no choice. We have to win. . . . If we screw this up, all those people that I've met who really need help, they're not going to get help.' Obama was girding his people as they filed onto a new battlefield.

The policy differences between him and Clinton had been small. Both wanted more affordable health care, a prompt end to the war in Iraq, greater environmental protections and at least a partial reversal of the tax cuts Bush had enacted for the richest Americans. The voters for whose support they were competing in the primary subscribed to the same tenets.

All of that, it seemed to me, had played its part in fuelling the bitterness of the primary fight. The contrasts between Obama and Clinton on the issues had been so slight that the election was at some level inherently, unavoidably personal. Voters were being asked not who had the better policies but who was the better person.

The battle against McCain would be more issue-driven and therefore in some senses more predictable. McCain's move away from his maverick positions during the primary had left him astride a more-or-less-conventional Republican platform going into the general election. He opposed a timetable for withdrawal of US forces from Iraq and criticised Obama for not having supported the so-called 'troop surge' that had begun in early 2007. He argued that the kind of health care reform Democrats wanted would lead to increased bureaucracy and government meddling. The 1973 Supreme Court ruling in the *Roe* v. *Wade* case – which guaranteed a right to abortion for American women – should be overruled, he said. And he hewed close to perhaps the most central Republican nostrum of all: that economic growth is best promoted by keeping taxes low.

To the relief of Democrats, McCain had made little apparent headway in shaping public opinion since clinching the Republican nomination. In early June, polls showed Obama leading him by about six points. Conservative strategists who were unaligned with McCain's campaign were appalled by its lapses into amateurishness. The contrast offered on the night Obama sealed his victory in the battle for the Democratic nomination was especially striking. McCain spoke, haltingly and in front of a sickly-green backdrop, to a crowd in Louisiana that could be measured in the hundreds. Obama's event in St Paul was customarily slick and attracted an audience of about 20,000 people.

Soon afterwards, McCain made a decision that would come to be seen as much more important than it appeared to be at the time. Day-to-day control of his campaign was taken away from Rick Davis, an urbane lobbyist, and handed over to Steve Schmidt. Schmidt, a bulky and shaven-headed prodigy of Karl Rove who had worked on George W. Bush's 2004 re-election campaign, immediately began imposing some discipline. 'Sergeant Schmidt', McCain called him.

From then on, the press would be granted less access to McCain. The freewheeling sessions that had begun eight years earlier on *The Straight Talk Express* found no favour with Schmidt, who regarded them as too risky. The Bush veteran's combative approach would intensify in the autumn as, with the election on the line, the McCain campaign unloaded attacks of startling ferocity – and dubious accuracy – against both Obama and the media.

If McCain had got off to a sluggish start in his general election campaign, Obama did not exactly set his supporters ablaze with excitement either. One of the most time-honoured, if unimpressive, traditions in American politics is the alacrity with which candidates who have just won their party nominations tend to tack towards the political centre ground.

For all his claims to be different, Obama did much the same. In June, he announced that he would support a bill that gave telecom companies immunity from prosecution for participating in the Bush administration's contentious surveillance efforts. He had vowed to oppose an earlier, but barely different, version of the legislation.

Days later, the Supreme Court struck down a District of Columbia ban on handguns, calling it unconstitutional. Obama's response was almost incomprehensible in its vagueness, but it seemed to support the Court's decision. In a statement given to the *Chicago Tribune* the previous November, an unnamed aide had said that Obama believed the opposite: that the ban was constitutional and so should be upheld. Now, spokesman Bill Burton said that the earlier statement was 'inartful'.

Both of these actions antagonised liberals, less for their specifics than because they seemed to suggest that Obama was going soft on civil liberties and gun control.

Controversy – perhaps unwarranted – erupted again at the beginning of July. Obama, speaking in North Dakota, stated the obvious: that his view of Iraq would take into account the situation on the ground if and when he took office. In so doing, he said he would be prepared to 'refine' his policy – a word that seemed to reek of compromise.

He called another press conference later the same day. 'We're going to try this again,' he announced. 'Let me be as clear as I can be: I intend to end this war. My first day in office, I will bring the Joint Chiefs of Staff in, and I will give them a new mission – and that is to end this war, responsibly, deliberately but decisively.'

The early skirmishes were closely followed by political obsessives but, after the melodramas of the previous six months, the broader American public found other things to occupy its mind as summer rolled on.

Even the candidates seemed to be operating in the human equivalent of standby mode. In July, I went to see McCain on a swing he was making through New Hampshire and Maine. His performance was mediocre at best. In Maine, he ploughed his way through his stump speech without nuance or passion. He sounded like a man who was seeking the Oval Office because he saw it as a fitting way to cap his career, rather than because he had any strong ideas about what to do once he got there.

In New Hampshire, at a town hall meeting, he was only marginally better. His more likeable side still peeked through on occasion, as when a young woman from the floor attacked him harshly for his support of the Iraq war. McCain hushed members of the audience who tried to heckle her and, after he had given his answer, asked that the microphone be passed back to the protester so that she could have the last word.

Yet even the New Hampshire meeting was not gaffe-free – McCain referred to Czechoslovakia rather than the Czech Republic, an error he made with surprising frequency for a supposed foreign policy expert – and it, too, failed to answer the basic question of why he wanted the presidency.

The crowds for McCain were much smaller than those which typically turned up to see Obama. Some of their views were just as emphatic, if disconcerting. As rain began to fall at the conclusion of McCain's event in Maine, I asked one woman, Sue Brunner, why she supported the Arizona senator. She replied that she believed Obama to be 'evil' and distrusted his 'Muslim connections'.

The Sue Brunners of the world would self-evidently remain outside Obama's reach. But there were millions of Americans who were open to voting for him if their doubts could be assuaged.

The opinion polls indicated that Obama was still suffering by comparison with McCain on foreign policy. That was not so surprising. He had, after all, been an obscure Illinois state senator just four years before. How would he cope as the leader of the free world?

At the height of summer, Obama and his aides decided he should try to answer that question. It was time for the man who had captured America's imagination to make his grand entrance onto the world stage.

9

OBAMA, IRELAND AND THE WORLD

All the familiar elements were in place: the big, buoyant crowd; the confident candidate; the well-crafted, uplifting speech. But 24 July 2008 wasn't like any other day on the Obama campaign.

Obama was speaking in Berlin. A crowd estimated at 200,000 had turned up to see him. It was the most spectacular event of a week-long foreign trip that had already taken him to Afghanistan, Kuwait, Iraq, Jordan, Israel and the West Bank. Stops in France and in London beckoned before his campaign plane would transport him back to Chicago.

It was not Obama's policies or oratory alone that had brought out the crowd. It had been less than seven years since the French newspaper *Le Monde* had run a famous headline proclaiming 'WE ARE ALL AMERICANS NOW' in the wake of the September 11 attacks. That sentiment had all but expired in the face of the Bush administration's bullheadedness. Obama seemed to hold out the possibility of renewing a transatlantic trust that had been violated.

The speech he delivered in the once-divided city was not among his finest – it was too general and hazily drawn for that – but it was good enough. The core of his argument was that as borders became more porous and the world more interdependent, it was more important than ever for nations that held common values to work together.

'Poorly secured nuclear material in the former Soviet Union, or secrets from a scientist in Pakistan, could help build a bomb that detonates in Paris,' he said. 'The poppies in Afghanistan come to Berlin in the form of heroin. The poverty and violence in Somalia breeds the terror of tomorrow. The genocide in Darfur shames the conscience of us all. In this new world, such dangerous currents have swept along faster than our efforts to contain them. That is why we cannot afford to be divided.'

Much of the rest of the speech was predictable, some of it platitudinous. As Chuck Todd, the respected political director of MSNBC, commented to the domestic audience back in the US: 'The speech, frankly, could have been given by John McCain.'

That was no accident. One of the dangers Obama faced was the scepticism, even hostility, with which many Americans continued to regard Europe. (During the 2004 presidential campaign, Republican operatives had sneered that John Kerry 'looks French', a juvenile jibe that was nevertheless thought to have helped caricature the Democratic nominee as effete and untrustworthy.)

If Obama said anything in the shadow of Berlin's Victory Column that could be perceived as offering support for so-called 'anti-American' theories, it would be political poison at home. But the need for the speech to be both robustly patriotic and respectful of European sensibilities left Obama with a fine line to walk. 'If we're honest with each other, we know that sometimes, on both sides of the Atlantic, we have drifted apart, and forgotten our shared destiny,' he told the crowd. 'In Europe, the view that America is part of what has gone wrong in our world, rather than a force to help us make it right, has become all too common. In America, there are voices that deride and deny the importance of Europe's role in our security and our future. Both views miss the truth: that Europeans today are bearing new burdens and taking more responsibility in critical parts of the world; and that just as American bases built in the last century still help to defend the security of this continent, so does our country still sacrifice greatly for freedom around the globe.'

London's *Daily Telegraph* noted the next day: 'For all the morality, it was hard to detect a single moment when Mr Obama exposed himself to the charge of being a wet and weedy liberal.'

Prior to Berlin, the most important leg of Obama's journey had been in Iraq. He had met with Prime Minister Nouri Al-Maliki and David Petraeus, the commander of US forces. Petraeus and Obama took a helicopter tour over the country, in the process producing TV footage that must have delighted the campaign.

Shortly before Obama had arrived, Maliki had caused a stir when a German magazine quoted him as endorsing the Democrat's proposal to withdraw American troops over a 16-month period. According to the English-language version of *Der Spiegel*, the Iraqi leader referenced Obama's plan and called it 'the right timeframe for a withdrawal, with the possibility of slight changes'.

This undercut McCain on two points: first, the policy issue itself, because he had insisted that any timetable for withdrawal was akin to admitting defeat, and, second, the broader point of readiness to lead. He had sought to present Obama as insufficiently seasoned to take the reins as commander-in-chief. Now, here was Maliki appearing to agree with Obama and disagree with McCain, a move that mocked the Republican.

In the ensuing rumpus, a spokesman for Maliki said that his words had been mistranslated in the interview, though he conspicuously failed to take back the withdrawal idea. McCain's chief foreign policy aide, Randy Scheunemann, tried to make the best of the situation, putting out a statement arguing that the difference between the two candidates was that Obama advocated an 'unconditional withdrawal', whereas McCain believed that 'withdrawal must be based on conditions on the ground'. Scheunemann asserted that Maliki's comments amounted to an endorsement of the McCain position – a claim that almost no one believed.

Episodes like that gladdened the hearts of the Obama team. A *Washington Post* poll published just before his trip had indicated that only 48 percent of Americans believed that he would do a good job as commander-in-chief, whereas 72 percent believed that McCain was up to the task. The Maliki story was the sort of thing they hoped would help erase the deficit.

*

Obama's relative youth, and the breakneck speed of his political climb, had left many Americans unsure of how he viewed the world.

Semi-paradoxically, his best-known public pronouncement on foreign affairs had come while he was still a peripheral figure. The 2002 speech he had given in Chicago opposing the push to war in Iraq had been delivered before he had even declared himself as a candidate for the US Senate. It had become famous in retrospect during the 2008 primary campaign. It was the bedrock on which Obama based his claim to have better judgement than some of his opponents, notably Hillary Clinton. Since it had been delivered when the case against the war was politically perilous to make, it also buttressed the sense that he had the courage of his convictions.

'I know that even a successful war against Iraq will require a US occupation of undetermined length, at undetermined cost, with undetermined consequences,' he had said. 'I know that an invasion of Iraq without a clear rationale and without strong international support will only fan the flames of the Middle East and encourage the worst, rather than the best, impulses of the Arab world, and strengthen the recruitment arm of al-Qaeda.'

The passage made Obama sound much more perspicacious than the bulk of the political establishment. During the same speech, he stressed how far removed he was from the far leftists and pacifists in attendance. He stated six times that he was opposed only to 'dumb wars', not to all wars. For good measure, he added that he supported the war in Afghanistan, and noted that the American civil war and the Second World War were necessary fights in the name of justice and freedom.

Obama put more flesh on the bones of his foreign policy ideas as the campaign wore on. On 15 July 2008, I saw him deliver a considered, if not especially surprising, speech in Washington. In it, he ran through a list of specific policy proposals in relation to Iraq, Afghanistan and Pakistan.

On Iraq, he not only proposed a troop withdrawal; he also committed to providing $2 billion in aid to help support the 4 million displaced Iraqis, and said he would emphasise that the US sought no permanent bases in the country. He stated that another two combat brigades would be sent to Afghanistan and that greater efforts would be put into training the Afghan security forces and judiciary. He cautioned against uncritical US support for the then-president of Pakistan, Pervez Musharraf. 'We must offer more than a blank cheque to a general who has lost the confidence of his people,' he said. 'It's time to strengthen stability by standing up for the aspirations of the Pakistani people.'

All of these proposals were wrapped up in a promise of a deeper, attitudinal change. Calling for 'a new era of international co-operation', he stated: 'This must be the moment when we answer the call of history. For eight years, we have paid the price for a foreign policy that lectures without listening; that divides us from one another – and from the world – instead of calling us to a common purpose; that focuses on our tactics in fighting a war without end in Iraq instead of forging a new strategy to face down the true threats that we face. We cannot afford four more years of a strategy that is out of balance and out of step with this defining moment.'

Comments like those were part of the reason Obama was so popular beyond America's shores. A poll published by the *Daily Telegraph* in June 2008 found that he was favoured over McCain by enormous margins in Europe. Asked whom they would vote for if they had the chance, German respondents went for Obama by 67 percent to 6 percent, Italians by 70 percent to 15 percent, French by 65 percent to 8 percent and Britons by 49 percent to 14 percent. (Ireland was not among the countries surveyed.)

Several of Obama's policies were not the stuff that European liberal dreams were made of. He favoured an expansion of the US military and had indicated in his Berlin speech that, if elected, he would want a greater commitment from Europe towards the NATO mission in Afghanistan. He had also become a more trenchant supporter of Israel over the course of his career. Yet his offer of a break from the unilateralist impulses of the Bush administration seemed to trump any European misgivings.

At the beginning of 2008, as Obama's candidacy was beginning to take off, I had asked the author and *Guardian* columnist Jonathan Freedland if he believed that Britons were ready to take a positive view of America once again. 'I would say they are not just ready, they are almost yearning to take a more positive view,' he replied. Obama, he added, could be just the man to provoke a re-examination of the US, even among those who had bought into the most hostile sentiments about the nation.

'The United States of Abu Ghraib, of Iraq, of hubris, simply wouldn't have a black First Family. It would not have a man whose name is Barack Hussein Obama as its president,' Freedland said. 'So if that were to happen, the cognitive dissonance there would force people to reassess their ideas about America.'

There was still plenty of rough terrain to cross before Obama reached that destination, though. For all the European excitement about Obama's visit – and for all the exhaustive coverage it received in the American media – the trip seemed to have little immediate impact on the domestic electorate. While Obama accepted plaudits overseas, McCain hewed close to the bread-and-butter concerns of the general public.

With Obama in the Middle East, McCain journeyed to Bethlehem, a medium-sized, struggling steel town in Pennsylvania, where he went into a supermarket to help a woman and her two young daughters do their shopping. On the day of the Berlin speech, McCain ate bratwurst with local businesspeople in a German restaurant in Ohio.

At the second engagement, McCain said he would 'love' to give a speech in Germany, but added: 'I would much prefer to do it as president of the United States rather than as a candidate for the office of the presidency.'

The suggestion that Obama was presumptuous was already being levelled with increasing frequency by the Republicans. Sometimes, the Democrat played into his opponents' hands. In June, his campaign had taken to adorning the lectern from which he spoke with a presidential-looking seal. The seal even featured a Latin phrase, *Vero Possumus*, that roughly approximated to 'Yes, We Can'. The seal, which was met with instant and widespread ridicule, was soon retired.

It could not be proven one way or another whether the American public viewed Obama's foreign sojourn as similarly hubristic. But the small opinion poll boost Obama received when the media focus on his adventure was at its height vanished instantly. By the week after his trip, the two major national tracking polls, by Gallup and Rasmussen, had him ahead of McCain by a margin so small (typically 1 to 2 percent) as to be statistically insignificant. That was exactly how the race had looked before he departed.

The Obama team, though, still believed the trip had been worthwhile. 'The value to me of this trip is, hopefully, it gives voters a sense that I can in fact – and do – operate effectively on the international stage,' Obama told Dan Balz of the *Washington Post* as he prepared to leave Paris for his final stop in London. 'That may not be decisive for the average voter right now, given our economic troubles, but it's knowledge they can store in the back of their minds for when they go into the polling place later.'

On the same short flight, he also told Jeff Zeleny of the *New York Times* that he would not be surprised to see his poll ratings dip in the immediate aftermath of his tour. 'People at home are worried about gas prices, they're worried about mortgage foreclosures – and for a week they're seeing me traipse around the world? It's easy to paint that as somehow being removed from people's day-to-day problems.' Obama added: 'We thought it was worth the risk.'

Time would tell.

*

You didn't have to be among the crowd of 200,000 in Berlin to detect the intensity of support welling behind Obama in Europe. You might just as easily have gone to Ollie Hayes' pub in Moneygall, County Offaly.

The small, red-fronted lounge on the village's main street had become an unofficial Irish headquarters for Obama. On 5 January, the bar had held a special event to mark his victory in the Iowa caucuses two days before. Expat Americans joined the regulars to celebrate his achievement, and a camera crew from RTÉ came along to witness the

167

festivities. On Super Tuesday, there had been almost no media, but even more locals. Henry Healy, the 24-year-old nephew of the bar's owner, told me that around 200 people had crammed in to see the first results come through.

They had gathered to cheer on a man they had come to define – tenuously, it must be said – as a local hero. Genealogists had discovered that Obama's great-great-great-grandfather, Falmouth Kearney, had been a native of the village and had emigrated to the US in 1850. (Some records rendered Kearney's first name as 'Fulmuth' or other, similar variants.)

Research by a Trinity College-based company, Eneclann, found that in previous generations the Kearneys had been involved in wig-making. One distant ancestor had even opposed gerrymandering in Dublin City Council elections in the 1750s, the researchers claimed.

Ireland was hardly alone in wanting to claim Obama for itself. He seemed to have achieved the status of a demigod in Kenya, given his direct connection to that nation through his father. A *Chicago Sun-Times* investigation traced other ancestors to England, Scotland, France, Germany and the Netherlands.

The number of branches on Obama's exotic family tree did not distract the residents of Moneygall from insisting that it was there, on the Offaly–Tipperary border, that his true roots lay. Stephen Neill, a Church of Ireland minister in nearby Cloughjordan who had helped with the genealogical research, told me that Obama's connection to the village was 'a huge talking point' for months after it was first discovered. Neill had been taken aback by the press interest in the story: he had fielded calls from Australia, Germany and the US, as well as from the Irish and British media.

Henry Healy told a similar story. 'There is only a population of about 300 or so in the village,' he said, 'so it's amazing to think there could be this relationship with the next president of America.'

*

The denizens of Hayes' bar provided Obama with moral support on Super Tuesday, but Ireland had also helped him in a more concrete way. The Democratic Party made it convenient for American expatriates to exercise their franchise by allowing them to vote in their country of residence during the week-long Democrats Abroad primary, which began on Super Tuesday. Over 23,000 votes were cast in 164 countries and territories. In Ireland, where Americans could cast a ballot in O'Neill's pub on Dublin's Suffolk Street as an alternative to voting by mail or online, Obama received 243 votes to Hillary Clinton's 142. Around the globe, he won a 65 percent share of the vote. The Democrats Abroad organisation would send a total of 22 delegates to the Denver convention (including eight superdelegates), though they had only half the voting power of delegates from the states.

One of the group's superdelegates was Irish-based. Liv Gibbons had moved to Ireland in 1985, having met her future husband while she was a student in California. The couple set up home in the north Dublin suburb of Sutton. Gibbons declared her allegiance to Obama while the battle with Clinton was still ongoing. When I spoke to her in April 2008, she said that a brief conversation with him at a meeting of the Democratic National Committee the previous year had played a key role in making up her mind.

'It wasn't any big policy discussion, but he just gave me his full attention,' she said. 'I wanted him to sign some books so I could raffle them off to raise money for our organisation. And he was very nice, very courteous. As he was talking to me, people tried to cut in on us and he kind of sent them to the back, saying he was helping his party. I thought that was very respectful of me and what I was there to do.'

Gibbons had intended to stay uncommitted for as long as possible, but what she regarded as negativity from the Clinton camp changed her mind. She had worried about how the Clintons' tactics might affect Obama. 'The Clinton campaign – not her personally, but the people close to her – were the ones to start throwing stones,' she said. 'And that is very difficult for him to respond to, because he is trying to be a healer and a uniter.'

On the far side of the Atlantic, most of the high-profile figures in the Irish-American community had leaned heavily the other way. Their scepticism about Obama said more about them than it did about the candidate.

*

I had lived in the United States for just over five years by the time of the 2008 election, covering the country's politics throughout that time for the *Sunday Business Post*. Every foreign correspondent periodically runs up against misconceptions that have a frustratingly strong hold at home. The single most persistent myth that I grappled with was the belief that Irish America plays an important role in American electoral politics. That may have been true half a century ago, when John F. Kennedy became president, but it had been a fantasy for at least 20 years.

The delusion had lingered, so far as I could tell, because too many people had a vested interest in maintaining it. The hunger of editors and producers back in Ireland for local 'angles' on American political stories led coverage down spurious paths. (During the Democratic primary process, I read with astonishment one daily newspaper's story about how the Irish-American vote would all but determine not just the party's nominee but the identity of the next occupant of the White House – a viewpoint so preposterous that it would have been laughed out of the room in any American newspaper office or TV studio.)

It was easy to find sources willing to propagate the chimera of Irish-American power, however. A small cadre of New York-based Irish-American activists had built public profiles disproportionate to their actual political heft by pushing the fairytale with vigour and persistence.

The reality was very different. For an ethnic group to hold genuine sway in American politics, it needs at least two of three things: serious numerical strength; a capacity to deliver some semblance of a bloc vote; and a set of issues, discrete from the mainstream political debate, that play a pivotal role in determining where those votes go. African-Americans, Hispanic-Americans and Jewish-Americans meet those criteria. Most other ethnic groups, including the Irish, do not.

Advocates within the Irish-American community assert its importance by pointing to the huge number of Americans, some 43 million, who lay claim to Irish heritage. But the proportion of that total which has a real interest in Ireland is minuscule. As Dr Feargal Cochrane, a

Belfast-born academic at Britain's Lancaster University, puts it, the superficial impressiveness of the 43 million figure 'obscure[s] a great shallowness of interest for the vast majority'.

Most Irish-Americans are now culturally and politically indistinguishable from the American mainstream and, as a consequence, experts scoff at the idea that an Irish-American vote even exists. 'Is there really a sense of Irish-American-ness when it comes to voting?' Doug Muzzio, the political science professor at New York's Baruch College, asked me rhetorically in a 2007 interview. 'I would imagine that the only time a lot of those [43 million] people consciously think of themselves as Irish is when they drink to excess' on St Patrick's Day.

Jolly Emrey, a professor at the University of Wisconsin-Whitewater who teaches a course in ethnic politics, made a similar point – if more gently – about the loss of a distinct Irish-American political identity. 'The first wave of Irish immigrants were mistreated, and looked down upon by other groups,' she told me in September 2008. 'But over time they became integrated. I think it is almost a full blend. Certainly, they would be considered by most people just as mainstream Americans.'

*

Irish America has always had two strands: the US-born descendants of Irish immigrants and Irish-born people now resident in the US. If the first group had more or less dissolved into the figurative American melting pot, the second was also facing serious challenges to its relevance as the 21st century began.

The first and most basic problem was diminishing numbers. According to Ireland's Central Statistics Office, every year between 2001 and 2007, migrants coming to Ireland from the United States outnumbered those going in the other direction. (Preliminary figures suggest that the same will be true for 2008.) In none of those years did more than 5,000 Irish people move to the US; 2002 was the only year in which more than 4,000 did so.

This offered a striking contrast to just a decade and a half earlier. Between 1986 and 1990, there had been a net 'outflow' of 160,000 people from Ireland; in total, as many as 200,000 are believed to have gone to America.

Niall O'Dowd, the publisher of the *Irish Voice* newspaper and one of the chief cheerleaders for Irish America, admitted in a 2007 interview with me that he was worried about the community's waning influence. O'Dowd told me its political power was 'declining'. He added that one manifestation of the health or otherwise of New York's immigrant population, the city's GAA organisation, seemed to be nearing the point of extinction. 'I am absolutely certain that within five years the GAA to all intents and purposes will be dead in New York – which I think will be a dreadful situation,' he said.

Another factor also disconcerted the activists. For all the human misery engendered by the armed conflict in the North of Ireland, it had at least provided a cause around which Irish-born activists in the US and Americans of Irish descent could rally. This had been particularly true at times of great crisis (the 1981 H-Block hunger strikes) and of great opportunity (the early stages of the peace process). As the Troubles faded from the headlines and the peace process rolled on, the conflict lost its power to energise.

By the time of the 2004 US presidential election, an aura of pointlessness had begun to hang over everything. 'This time, there is nothing I could point to that would energise the base,' O'Dowd told Feargal Cochrane that year. 'As an activist issue, Northern Ireland is still there, but in terms of how we deal with it politically . . . it is not the same issue at all. . . . I don't see a battle this time, I just don't see one.'

Over the course of Bush's second term, the activists fixed onto another cause: immigration reform. Their basic aim was to create a pathway for those who had come to the US illegally to regularise their status and become American citizens. A pressure group named the Irish Lobby for Immigration Reform (ILIR) was set up in December 2005. O'Dowd and his brother-in-law, Manhattan businessman Ciaran Staunton, were co-founders, and O'Dowd's wife, journalist Debbie McGoldrick, sat on the advisory board – a testament less to nepotism (Staunton and McGoldrick each had a track record on the immigration issue) than to how small the pool of New York activists really was.

The Irish were always destined to remain marginal to the American debate on immigration. The ILIR contended that there were as many as 50,000 Irish illegal immigrants in the US. Other estimates put the number closer to 20,000. Either way, they were a small fraction of the approximately 12 million illegal immigrants in the US as a whole.

In spring 2006, when immigration reform briefly looked as though it might win passage in the US Senate, the ILIR congratulated itself on turning out 2,400 people for a demonstration in Washington. It was an impressive feat, so far as it went, but the real centre of power in the movement for immigration reform was Latin-American. Around the same time as the ILIR event, half a million people, primarily Hispanic, turned out in Dallas, with roughly the same number in Los Angeles, 100,000 in New York and in Phoenix, and 50,000 in Atlanta and in Houston. Those numbers didn't mean that the ILIR's efforts were without merit, but it did put them in perspective.

*

As the presidential race began to take shape, there was never any doubt whom the New York Irish lobby would back. 'There was hardly any-one in the primary who was supporting Senator Obama over Senator Clinton,' one of their number, attorney Brian O'Dwyer, told me in October 2008.

There were substantive reasons for the activists to favour Clinton, the most obvious being her husband's engagement in the Irish peace process. Clinton was as well-versed as any politician in the Senate on issues pertaining to Ireland. Just as much to the point for those activists for whom personal access to power seemed to be the be-all and end-all, she could be relied upon to make the right noises, wearing green on St Patrick's Day, showing up at events, and paying lip service to Irish goals.

A 2007 ILIR meeting in Washington that I attended was a perfect example of Clinton's willingness to tick the right boxes. She insisted that 'America would not be America without Irish immigration' – a point that was undeniable but could have been applied just as easily to any other immigrant group – and allied herself as closely as possible with Edward Kennedy, referring to him as 'our leader'.

Clinton was far too shrewd to get boxed into any commitment from which she could not extricate herself. She promised that she was dedicated to achieving 'comprehensive immigration reform', a phrase used by many on Capitol Hill (including Obama) in part because it sounded good but provided several acres of wriggle room.

The limit of the Irish lobby's supposed influence with Clinton was vividly illustrated later that year. As already mentioned, Clinton got herself into a twist on the issue of drivers' licences for illegal immigrants during a televised debate in October. This was one of the few issues I had heard mentioned by rank-and-file Irish 'illegals', many of whom worked in construction, needed to drive vans in the course of their jobs, and were worried that a routine traffic stop could lead to them being deported.

In the wake of the confused debate performance, Clinton was faced with a choice. She could follow through on the positive noises she had made to the liberal reformist lobby, or she could throw the illegals over the side. To no one's great surprise, she chose the latter course. 'As president, I will not support drivers' licences for undocumented people,' she said in a statement.

Obama was not some kind of unbending idealist who floated above all political posturing: he was as likely to don a green tie on St Patrick's Day as any other candidate. But he seemed, at least at first, less keen than Clinton to go through the usual back-slapping and back-scratching with the various ethnic lobbies, including the Irish.

He did not bother to show up at any ILIR events – a perfectly defensible decision, given the peripheral nature of the group, but one that rankled with its leaders. Nor did he commit to attending the Irish-American Presidential Forum, a grandly titled event run in large part by Manhattan attorney John Dearie where candidates were invited to state their views on a laundry list of issues that the activists had deemed to be of concern to the Irish community.

Most tellingly of all, in a January 2008 interview with my *Sunday*

Business Post colleague Martha Kearns, one of Obama's key foreign policy advisors, the author and academic Samantha Power, suggested that the Illinois senator had little patience for the whole ethnic-lobby game.

Kearns wrote: 'When asked about Obama's relationship with the Irish, Power said that Obama did not want to peel off groups – such as the Irish and women – and start pandering to them. She said he preferred to deal with the issues as they affected everyone in the country, and not pigeonhole them into categories.'

That sounded promising, I thought. It put the noses of the New York Irish circle badly out of joint, though. Power's remark was cited negatively on at least three occasions in O'Dowd's newspaper.

Given the Irish lobby's investment of its limited political capital in Clinton, her defeat came as an unpleasant shock. 'People were very disappointed – including myself – that she lost,' Brian O'Dwyer told me. 'We continue to believe she would have been a magnificent president. But you have to make a choice between "A" and "B" [in the presidential election]. "C" is not on the ballot.'

Whether to go for 'A' or 'B' appeared to be a more difficult decision than one might have imagined for the Irish-American New York activists, who were predominantly Democratic in their affiliation. The problem seemed to be that Obama still displayed no great interest in stroking their egos. Ciaran Staunton made the sense of pique obvious in an interview with the *Irish Voice* in June. 'We're disappointed with the lack of reaction from the Obama campaign to date. We invited them to our rally in Washington, and I'm not sure if they're getting no advice or bad advice, but clearly whoever wants to be in the White House next year should reach out to the Irish-American community.'

Staunton's reference to 'no advice or bad advice' was seen by some as a jibe at Trina Vargo, Obama's main advisor on Irish issues. (The fact that the senator had such an advisor should not be taken to denote an unusually high level of interest in Ireland; he had around 300 such experts on call, covering every aspect of international relations.) Vargo was a very different kind of activist: she was not herself Irish; she was based in Washington, where she had previously worked on Edward Kennedy's foreign policy staff, rather than New York; and the organisation of which she was president and founder, the US-Ireland Alliance, was focused on building transatlantic links among influential figures and rising stars in politics, culture and academia.

Vargo was, in my view, a more substantive and forward-looking figure than any member of the New York set, but she had fallen into disfavour with them by coming out against the idea of a special deal for illegal Irish immigrants. A phrase she had used to describe attempts to pretty up their proposal – she had written in the *Irish Times* that it was akin to 'putting lipstick on a pig' – had infuriated them. The commonly used phrase led, absurdly, to her being accused by Staunton and others of comparing Irish illegal immigrants to pigs. (The same unfair fate would befall Obama later in the campaign, when he used the same saying in a very different context.)

The steady drip of stories hostile to Obama continued to appear in the *Irish Voice*. A July article in the paper's anonymous 'Intelligencer' column referenced his overseas trip and asserted that 'there was considerable disappointment that his campaign decided to skip over Ireland on this visit – a strange decision given the reality of the ethnic vote in America'.

It wasn't a strange decision at all, given that the 'reality' of the ethnic Irish vote was that it was effectively non-existent. The number of Americans who would be more inclined to vote for Obama because he had touched down in Ireland for a few hours was negligible.

*

John McCain, meanwhile, had commended himself to the Irish lobby through his support for immigration reform, even though he had done little to push the issue after the 2006 bill had petered out in the Senate. McCain had also proven more willing than Obama to pay obeisance to the Irish lobby's sensitivities, for instance by attending a 2006 event run by another of O'Dowd's publications, *Irish America* magazine.

O'Dowd (who had sat on Hillary Clinton's finance committee and was customarily described in the Irish media as a Clinton supporter) and John Dearie both gave money to McCain's presidential campaign, according to Federal Election Commission records. In June 2007, O'Dowd had given $2,300, the maximum individual donation for the primaries, to McCain. Dearie gave the same amount in three instalments between May 2007 and January 2008.

'I'm detecting a move toward McCain from some of the activists in the immigration reform community,' Terry Golway, a history professor at Kean University and the author of several books on Irish-American themes, told me in autumn 2008. 'It's pretty clear where they're going, and they're going there for a very specific reason. I think they see an avenue to power, or access to power, with him, and maybe they weren't going to get that with Obama.'

The flirtation between the Irish-American activists and the Republican reached an even more advanced stage after Obama released a statement on Irish issues over the summer. In late August, Obama called into question whether a special envoy to Northern Ireland was really required. The statement said that Obama 'recognises that the crisis period for Northern Ireland has passed, and that the people of Northern Ireland are now in charge of their own destiny. He will consult with the Taoiseach, the British prime minister, and party leaders in Northern Ireland to determine whether a special US envoy for Northern Ireland continues to be necessary, or a senior administration official, serving as point person for Northern Ireland, would be most effective.'

Obama's statement struck me as sensible. Ten years on from the Good Friday Agreement, it seemed past time that the parties in the North were told that other governments would no longer be permanently available to hold their hands. It was faintly ridiculous to suggest that an Obama administration trying to extract itself from an epochal war in Iraq, struggling to make sustainable progress in Afghanistan, and facing a multitude of other threats and challenges, should be spending much time on the increasingly petty squabbles between politicians in the North of Ireland.

Obama's decision merely to raise the question of whether a special envoy was needed – he had not said he would not appoint one – caused another bout of near-apoplexy among the New York Irish set. O'Dowd told the *Irish Times* that any weakening of US input into Northern Ireland would be 'completely unacceptable'. Brian O'Dwyer professed himself 'shocked' in the pages of the *Irish Echo*, adding: 'It is hard for me to fathom how anyone who knows anything about Ireland would say this.'

The McCain campaign knew an opportunity for mischief-making when it saw one. The Arizona senator had been harshly critical of the peace process in its initial stages. In a 1996 article in *Foreign Policy*, he described those who argued in favour of granting a US visa to Sinn Féin president Gerry Adams as being 'motivated by romantic, anachronistic notions of Irish republicanism'.

Now, McCain claimed to believe that Bill Clinton's decision to appoint a special envoy had been 'critical to fostering peace and recon- ciliation in Northern Ireland'. The statement about the envoy, he asserted, showed Obama's 'total lack of experience and profoundly poor judgement on matters of foreign policy'.

Obama might have stuck to his guns. Instead, with just two months left before the presidential election, his campaign judged that there was no point in leaving room for any distraction, however trivial. On 1 September, the campaign announced the setting up of an advisory panel on Irish issues. It was comprised of seven politicians who had been conspicuous by their past level of engagement with Ireland, including Edward Kennedy, former senator George Mitchell, who had chaired the 1998 peace talks, and two Irish-American congressmen, Joe Crowley of New York and Richard Neal of Massachusetts.

The panel seemed like a classic – and somewhat dispiriting – exer- cise in political cosmetics. No one believed that its formation bespoke a realisation on Obama's part that Northern Ireland was more impor- tant than he had hitherto thought. It was a convenient way to blunt the Irish lobby's capacity to cause a ruckus in the media – which was, by this point, the only type of muscle it had left. The advisory panel also gave cover to a later declaration, made on 18 September, that Obama would appoint a 'senior envoy' to Ireland.

McCain made one more attempt to revitalise the issue. A campaign rally in Scranton, Pennsylvania, in mid-September had the banner of Dearie's Irish-American Presidential Forum appended to it. After making a corny Irish drinking joke, McCain spoke about the economy before insisting that he would do nothing to weaken America's commitment to Northern Ireland. 'I'll maintain the special US envoy,' he reiterated.

The extraneousness of Ireland to the main American political debate was revealed afterwards. As Denis Staunton noted in the next day's *Irish Times*: 'Almost one third of Scranton's population is of Irish descent, but few of those who came to the city's wood-panelled, Victorian Gothic cultural centre yesterday appeared to be preoccupied by Irish issues. When the meeting was opened to the floor, nobody asked Mr McCain about Ireland, focusing instead on jobs, health care and his running mate, Sarah Palin.'

The US media paid virtually no attention to McCain's comments about Ireland. Nor did they pay much heed to the conference call held by the Obama advisory panel that same morning. It had been unre-markable and flat, consisting largely of the politicians complimenting the Clinton administration for its support of the Irish peace process and drawing attention to McCain's opposition to those policies at the time.

Ireland never surfaced again in a meaningful way during the campaign. There was one further, inadvertently revealing, vignette, however. In a 10 October editorial in the *Irish Voice*, O'Dowd again complained that 'the question of where Senator Barack Obama stands on Irish issues is still up in the air'. In making that criticism, he unfavourably contrasted Obama's approach with that of Al Gore during his bid for the presidency in 2000. O'Dowd wrote: 'Gore in 2000 won many Irish-American votes, in part because he appeared at a forum and made his commitments known on Irish issues.'

In an *Irish Times* column less than two months before, O'Dowd had

179

written: 'The Obama camp seems reluctant to engage the ethnic vote, in a manner eerily similar to Al Gore in 2000, who threw away countless opportunities to engage ethnic communities such as Irish-Americans in the full-throated way that the Clintons did.'

Even someone so involved as O'Dowd could not seem to work out whether Gore had engaged with Irish America or neglected it. That, in turn, said all that needed to be said about how little Irish issues really mattered in American politics.

For the candidates, there were bigger things to worry about.

10

Unconventional Conventions

Sometimes the biggest moments are best illuminated by the small details.

On a summer night in Denver, Colorado, I bumped into two women. They were friends, both African-American. One was noticeably taller and older than the other, and tears coursed freely down her cheeks.

'I am ecstatic,' she told me, 'and I can't stop crying. What happened tonight shows that this is my country. When I was little, this country was segregated. I did not think something like this was possible. This is a miraculous thing.'

Her name was Karren Pope-Onwukwe. She had grown up in the heart of the American South, in Georgia, in the 1950s. Racism ran deep there, and it was suffocating.

So it was no wonder that Pope-Onwukwe was crying on that night of 28 August 2008. We were standing in the middle of an enormous sports stadium under a cloudless, starry sky. She wanted her photo taken in front of the stage where, only moments before, Barack Obama had formally accepted the presidential nomination of the Democratic Party in front of 80,000 people. She gave up trying to wipe the tears away.

Pope-Onwukwe's friend was Karen Toles. 'For the first time, you can really say to a young African-American: "You can be president of the United States,"' Toles told me. 'To have someone like [Obama] for those young people to look up to is amazing.'

Obama's speech in the Invesco Field stadium, home of the Denver Broncos American football team, was the culmination of the four-day Democratic National Convention – and the culmination of something infinitely bigger, too. It took place 45 years to the day after Martin Luther King had delivered his 'I Have a Dream' address. The scene in Denver seemed to suggest that one of King's most central aspirations – that future generations would be judged 'not by the colour of their skin but by the content of their character' – was on the cusp of being fulfilled.

The massive crowd was comprised of Americans of every race and age group. Many of them had begun lining up in the early morning for a speech that was not due to start until after 8 PM. In the hours before the main event, political celebrities strolled around among the media, the state delegates and other invited guests at pitch level. Jesse Jackson was among them. He and Obama had a complicated relationship, friendly but wary. (This relationship had taken another lurch in July, when Jackson had been caught on a live microphone telling a fellow guest before a television interview: 'I want to cut [Obama's] nuts off.' The candidate's crime, in Jackson's eyes, was talking down to African-Americans.)

In Denver, however, Jackson professed himself moved by the moment. His praise for Obama seemed sincere. 'This has been a 54-year journey,' he said of the civil rights movement. 'It has been a long relay but Barack is the great runner running the last lap.'

(Jackson was apparently taking the 1954 Supreme Court case, *Brown* v. *Board of Education*, which had declared segregated schooling in the US to be unconstitutional, as the starting point of that journey.)

He told me that he had seen a fundamental change in America during the primary season. He had been in Mississippi when the state's Democratic primary (which Obama had won easily) had been held. 'I saw men voting for Hillary and I saw whites voting for Barack, and I said to myself: "This is a new day."' He added: 'You have never seen a day like this in America. Nineteen sixty-three was a season of fear; this is a season of celebration.'

On another part of the pitch, I found Mayor Cory Booker of Newark, New Jersey, one of the new breed of black politicians of which Obama was the most celebrated example. When I asked Booker about the day, he answered not with an office-holder's usual clichés but with more personal thoughts.

'There are two different feelings,' he told me. 'Tactically, of course I am excited about the election and about getting the Democratic candidate elected. And the second part is, for this to be happening on today of all days: I am just overcome with emotion, really. You will have to excuse me if I start misting up a bit.

'We are afforded opportunities that the earlier generation [of African-Americans] was never afforded. I am thinking of my mother today. She gave up her whole summer to work for the Urban League organising the March on Washington [where King gave his famous speech].

'We are not beyond bigotry in America but we have grappled with this so much and we are moving in the right direction,' Booker concluded. 'And it proves once again that ordinary people can do extraordinary things.'

The occasion was so swollen with meaning that the candidate did not have to labour the point. Obama's speech alluded to King only glancingly – though emotively – at its climax, when he sought to link the slain civil rights leader to the broader and deeper promise of America.

'It is that promise that, 45 years ago today, brought Americans from every corner of this land to stand together on a Mall in Washington, before Lincoln's Memorial, and hear a young preacher from Georgia speak of his dream,' he said.

'The men and women who gathered there could've heard many things. They could've heard words of anger and discord. They could've been told to succumb to the fear and frustrations of so many dreams deferred. But what the people heard instead – people of every creed and colour, from every walk of life – is that, in America, our destiny is inextricably linked, that together our dreams can be one. "We cannot walk alone," the preacher cried. "And as we walk, we must make

183

the pledge that we shall always march ahead. We cannot turn back."

'America, we cannot turn back . . . .'

Obama seemed to be suggesting that he and King were linked not primarily by the colour of their skin but by their ability to summon Americans towards a recognition of their common interests and common humanity. Obama was, once again, trying to speak not to a sense of racial grievance, but to a much grander notion of the US and its possibilities.

'This country of ours has more wealth than any nation, but that's not what makes us rich,' he said in the speech's most lyrical passage. 'We have the most powerful military on earth, but that's not what makes us strong. Our universities and our culture are the envy of the world, but that's not what keeps the world coming to our shores.

'Instead, it is that American spirit, that American promise, that pushes us forward even when the path is uncertain; that binds us together in spite of our differences; that makes us fix our eye not on what is seen, but what is unseen, that better place around the bend. That promise is our greatest inheritance.'

The sheer size of the crowd made for an astonishing sight. Many of those in the seated tiers above the field stamped their feet in approval as well as applauding when Obama hit a good line. From where I was standing, about 100 yards from the candidate, it sounded like thunder.

Kimberly Lightford, the state senator from Illinois who had become friendly with Obama during their time in the legislature in Springfield, was also watching close by. Telling me about her reaction weeks afterwards, her voice trembled with pride. 'It's hard to describe what I was feeling – it was just joy,' she said. 'The closest thing I've ever felt to that feeling was when I gave birth.' Lightford used her mobile phone to call her mother from her seat in the football stadium, but found herself unable to find words to describe the sight before her.

'I was so proud to be his friend,' she said. 'He struck me as the same guy he had always been. I just felt overwhelmed.'

Such highly pitched emotional moments tended to bring a sense of foreboding in their wake. All the promise that Obama spoke about could be snuffed out in an instant, just as it had been in King's case. As the evening sun sank low in the sky in the hours before his speech began, it silhouetted the police marksmen, rifles at the ready, surveying the crowd through binoculars from the roof of the stadium. Threats against Obama's life had been made so frequently that he had been obliged to have secret service protection since May of the previous year. (During the time he was in Denver, three men were arrested and held under suspicion of plotting to kill him. Despite the fact that the men had two rifles fitted with telescopic sights, the police eventually came to believe that they were fantasists who had no real capability to carry out the threats they had allegedly been heard making.)

The most poetic moments of Obama's speech were also its most memorable; overall, the oration was more prosaic than his convention address in Boston four years before. In Denver, he sought to do two things: connect with the day-to-day concerns of Americans in a time of economic uncertainty, and demonstrate that he would not be pushed around.

'He's going to lay out what "change we can believe in" means to everyday lives,' Obama's deputy communications director, Josh Earnest, had told me that afternoon, alluding to the campaign slogan. 'This is really an opportunity for him to drill down into the specifics of where he wants to take the country and how it relates to the problems people are experiencing every day. By the end of the speech, people are really going to understand that.'

After it was over, I wasn't sure that they would. The supposedly specific elements of the speech were really broad brushstrokes rather than concrete policy prescriptions. More successful, if less noble-sounding, were his attempts to take the fight to McCain. Democratic presidential candidates of the recent past had proven shockingly vul-nerable to aggressive Republican attacks – with the sole exception of Bill Clinton, whose 1992 campaign had included a fierce 'war room', set up to drive back such assaults. Obama used the night in Denver to show that he would not wilt.

He even assailed McCain on national security, an issue on which Republican candidates had traditionally held an advantage over

185

Democrats. Citing McCain's peculiar 2003 comment that the US could 'muddle through' in Afghanistan while concentrating its main efforts on Iraq, Obama tried to turn one of his opponent's signature lines against him: 'John McCain likes to say he'll follow bin Laden to the gates of hell, but he won't even follow him to the cave where he lives,' he said.

Obama also tackled the 'country first' slogan that the McCain campaign had, by then, adopted – a slogan that many assumed was intended to impugn Obama's patriotism. 'Let us agree that patriotism has no party. I love this country, and so do you, and so does John McCain,' he told the audience. 'So I've got news for you, John McCain: we all put our country first.'

Those words were yet another example of Obama's toughness, a quality which had been in evidence – but often overlooked – throughout his career. In the final phase of the 2008 election campaign, he would tell *Rolling Stone* magazine: 'Because I tend to be a pretty courteous person and I don't lose my temper, I think people underestimate my willingness to mix it up. I don't know if they'll continue to underestimate that after this campaign.'

When the journalist asked him if he liked being underestimated in that way, Obama – in an unusually revealing moment, since most of his interviews tended to be disciplined, rather bland affairs – replied: 'Yeah. No point in having them see you coming.'

Obama's performance in Denver was good enough to win grudging plaudits even from some ideological opponents. As we filed off the pitch that night, I spoke to Mike Murphy, a Republican political consultant. Murphy, a good friend of McCain's, had been the senior strategist during the Arizonan's 2000 run for the presidency and had remained an informal advisor to him.

'I thought it was very impressive,' Murphy told me. 'It was the strongest Democratic acceptance speech in a long time.'

I asked Murphy why he had such a high opinion of the address.

'It showed strength,' he replied, 'and it was also intensely focused on the groups he needs to win – older voters and blue-collar voters. The whole package was very good. Now the spotlight shifts to McCain, and he will be very good too. But the battle has been joined.'

The same sense – of the speech as the first shot in the war for the White House – was reinforced by Michael Dukakis. He was 74 now, but save for some slowness of movement and the grey that was advancing through his once-dark hair, he was almost indistinguishable from the man who had lost the 1988 presidential race. He was insistent that Obama should not make the same mistakes he had.

Obama's speech was terrific, he told me. But he added: 'Now we have to go out and work, and win this thing. We have to work in every state and in every precinct.'

The fight was on.

*

It had taken a while for things to heat up. The sense of ennui that had crept into the campaign shortly after Hillary Clinton withdrew from the race in June had lingered. In early August, I had journeyed to Ohio to hear Obama at a couple of rallies. The first event was in Youngstown, a place that had once thrived as a home to several major steelworks but had become synonymous with the industrial decline that had afflicted so much of the American Rust Belt. (Its downward economic trajectory had even inspired a song, 'Youngstown', by Bruce Springsteen.)

Obama spoke at a school there, his focus on the importance of developing alternative sources of energy. It was a worthy speech, awash in specifics, but it was not especially exciting. The same was true of a later engagement on the outskirts of Cleveland. The intensity seen in both the candidate and the crowds during the primary season had gone, and it would not return for many weeks.

The McCain campaign had become noticeably more aggressive under Steve Schmidt's direction, however. One of the most talked-about examples of its new tone was a TV ad that had been released at the very end of July, just after Obama's foreign trip. It spliced footage of the Democrat together with images of Britney Spears and Paris

Hilton. 'He's the biggest celebrity in the world,' the female narrator said, 'but is he ready to lead?'

This was straight from the Karl Rove school of politics. Most strategists before Rove had searched for the weak spot of an opposing candidate and sought to exploit it. Rove believed that if you could transform an opponent's main asset into a liability, the results would be even more crippling. He had proven his point when John Kerry's gallant war record in Vietnam had been questioned and undermined by operatives both within and outside the official Bush campaign in 2004. Now, Schmidt and McCain were trying to make Obama's signature strength – the ability to generate excitement – into a weakness by suggesting that it was nothing more than a kind of ditzy star-power.

In Cedar Rapids, Iowa, Obama shot back that 'you'd think we'd be having a serious debate. But so far all we've been hearing about is Paris Hilton and Britney Spears. I do have to ask my opponent: "Is that the best you can come up with?"'

Robert Gibbs told MSNBC: 'We'll let them take the low road. It's a place they feel very comfortable in.'

Concern began to spread among Democrats as their convention neared. Many could hardly believe that a Republican, even one with McCain's unconventional qualities, stood a chance after eight years of the Bush administration and in such a hostile political climate. Yet the polls showed Obama clinging to a narrow, statistically insignificant lead.

Even John Kerry professed himself concerned: 'Viscerally, my feeling is they've got to come back at [McCain] hard,' Kerry told the *New York Times*. 'And they've got to do more to complete the task of definition — both definition of him [Obama] as well as definition of John McCain.'

The convention loomed as the obvious opportunity for Obama to assert himself. But there was something else to be taken care of first: who would be his running mate?

*

Prospective vice presidents are a bit like football referees: only the worst become big news; the best tend to fade into the background. There are exceptions to the rule, but the last one cropped up almost half a century ago. Lyndon Johnson was by general consent the last vice-presidential selection who made the difference between winning and losing. John F. Kennedy would probably have lost Texas – and with it the 1960 election – to his Republican opponent, Richard Nixon, had Johnson, a Texan icon, not been his running mate.

Still, if the vice-presidential candidate seldom determined the election result, that was no reason to make a rash choice. Obama ultimately picked Joe Biden, a US senator representing Delaware. Biden was, at one level, the epitome of the seasoned hand. Aged 65 at the time Obama selected him, he had been first elected as a senator at 29 (an achievement that was only possible because he would reach the age of 30, the minimum age for senators as stipulated in the US Constitution, between the election and his inauguration). His short-lived 2008 presidential candidacy had actually been his second White House run. He had made a much stronger effort 20 years before, only to be undone when he plagiarised language which had first been used by the then-leader of the British Labour Party, Neil Kinnock. He had also chaired two major Senate committees, on the judiciary and foreign relations. Biden, the Obama campaign hoped, might go some way to mollifying voters who were still concerned about the presidential candidate's youth.

Importantly, though, Biden also commended himself to the Obama team because he had gained his experience without coming to be seen as a fully paid-up Capitol Hill insider. He commuted to Washington from his Delaware home every day on the national railway service, Amtrak, and he had always been one of the least wealthy members of the Senate. (Obama, he later recalled, teased him for this during the vetting process that all potential vice-presidential candidates had to undergo. 'All these years and you still have no money,' Biden said a smiling Obama told him.)

There were rumours that Obama had been strongly tempted by two other possibilities besides Biden – Kathleen Sebelius, the governor of Kansas, and Tim Kaine, the governor of Virginia. He had eventually concluded that Biden offered benefits that the others could not match.

The name most often touted in the media as an alternative vice-presidential choice – that of Hillary Clinton – was never a serious possibility. Back in June, the Obama campaign had engaged in a deft, if hard-edged, piece of political manoeuvring that made this clear. David Axelrod had known Patti Solis Doyle, the woman who had been forced out as Clinton's presidential-campaign manager in February, for 20 years. (Both were based in Chicago.) The Obama campaign recruited Solis Doyle and announced that she would serve as chief of staff for the as-yet-unnamed vice president. In theory, Obama could have chosen Clinton and redeployed Solis Doyle, who was no longer on speaking terms with the former First Lady. In reality, the appointment of the erstwhile Hillary aide was a smoke signal to Clinton supporters: don't get your hopes up.

Biden made his first appearance with Obama at a rally in Springfield, Illinois, on 23 August. His address was typical of his usual, idiosyncratic style: sometimes he mangled his syntax, sometimes he seemed to reach for the right word and pluck out the wrong one, sometimes his jokes seemed a little peculiar. (He promised the crowd they would soon meet his wife, Jill, whom he said was 'drop-dead gorgeous', before adding: 'She also has her doctorate degree, which is a problem.')

That said, no real gaffes were committed, and Biden's warmth and respect for Obama seemed real and strong. 'Ladies and gentlemen, I know I'm told I talk too colloquially,' he said, 'but there's something about this guy. There's something about this guy. There's something about Barack Obama that allows him to bring people together like no one I have worked with and seen. There's something about Barack Obama that makes people understand [that] if they make compromises they can make things better.'

The launch of Biden as Obama's running mate had gone as smoothly as anyone could have expected. But there were two other major figures in the Democratic Party who would soon be on their way to Denver. And no one knew whether they would give the party nominee anything close to the effusive praise that Biden had lavished upon him.

*

As the Democratic convention opened, no subject was more feverishly discussed in the bars and restaurants of Denver than the role Bill and Hillary Clinton might play.

The former president, more so even than his wife, was believed to harbour bitterness about the manner of Hillary's defeat. He had been conspicuously tepid in his backing of Obama. When asked in an ABC News interview at the beginning of August whether he believed that Obama was ready to be president, he replied: 'You could argue that no one's ever ready to be president.' Pressed by the interviewer on whether Obama was at least qualified for the job, Clinton said: 'The Constitution sets qualifications for the president.' Clinton did eventually say that he thought Obama would win the presidential election and deserved to do so, but that did not erase the impression created by his earlier, more grudging responses.

Around the same time, his wife made the peculiar suggestion that the convention should be used as an occasion for 'catharsis' for her supporters. 'There's incredible pent-up desire and I think that people want to feel like, "OK, it's a catharsis, we're here, we did it", and then everybody get behind Senator Obama,' she told supporters in California.

Obama left it to the next week before responding, on board his campaign plane. 'I don't think we're looking for catharsis,' he said drily.

There was, fortuitously, one powerful factor that was pulling in the right direction for the Democrats. As a matter of self-interest if nothing else, the Clintons were more or less obliged to throw their lot in with Obama. The calculations were obvious. Obama might win in 2008 whatever they did. If he lost, it was imperative for Hillary's future ambitions that she should not be seen to have contributed to that defeat by letting her ego or hurt feelings take pre-eminence over party loyalty.

191

The convention ran from Monday to Thursday. Hillary's unifying speech, delivered on the Tuesday night, was one of its most dramatic moments – and for the right reasons. She set the tone from the opening line: 'I'm happy to be here tonight: a proud mother, a proud Democrat, a proud American and a proud supporter of Barack Obama.' And just as she had in Unity, New Hampshire, she beseeched her supporters to back the man who had vanquished her: 'You haven't worked so hard over the last 18 months, or endured the last eight years, to suffer through more failed leadership. No way, no how, no McCain,' she said to cheers. 'Barack Obama is my candidate and he must be our president.'

The genuineness of the endorsement was open to question. Plenty of people, including me, had their doubts. But it was clear that Clinton, in her words at least, had done as much as anyone could reasonably have expected to solidify support behind Obama.

This was not to say that all her supporters had been transformed into Obama enthusiasts. I found one such fan, Janet Keller of Laguna Beach, California, soaking up the atmosphere on the convention floor in the minutes after Clinton's speech had ended. She blamed the former First Lady's defeat on 'sexism in the media'.

Keller, a middle-aged businesswoman, went on: 'Every woman of my age remembers sitting at the boardroom table, and you are still asked to get the coffee. But young women today don't feel like that. I'm heartbroken. I will never see a woman president in my lifetime.'

She said that she would vote for Obama, if only to try to ensure the election of a Democratic president who would appoint pro-choice judges to the Supreme Court. 'But will I do for him what I would have done for Hillary?' she asked. 'No.'

The Obama-Clinton battle ended for good the next afternoon. The official nomination process involves a chairperson calling upon each state to announce how many of its delegates are supporting any candidates whose names remain in contention. In all but the rarest instances, this is only a matter of ceremony. By tradition, the state whose delegates would put the winning candidate over the finishing line cedes the floor to the candidate's home state, which then has the honour of delivering the decisive votes.

As the vote began, rumours swirled that Clinton would appear at the climax of proceedings to bestow the nomination upon Obama. Security guards cleared a space on the floor where her New York delegation was seated. Those seated nearby craned their necks for any sight of the senator. As Obama edged close to the magic number required, the spotlight fell, as expected, upon his native Illinois. The state's nominated speaker then threw proceedings over to New York.

Clinton walked onto the convention floor. With several large men forming a protective cordon around her and cameramen doing everything but fight each other to get closest to her, the scene called to mind a boxer's journey towards the ring. Once Clinton finally made it to her allotted spot, she had to suffer through a long introduction from Sheldon Silver, the speaker of the New York State Assembly, who seemed intent upon acknowledging every prominent Democrat in the Empire State by name. Eventually, Clinton stepped to the microphone:

'On behalf of the great state of New York . . . with eyes firmly fixed on the future; in the spirit of unity; with the goal of victory; with faith in our party and our country: let's declare together, in one voice, right here, right now, that Barack Obama is our candidate and he will be our president.'

Clinton then moved to suspend the roll-call vote and said: 'I move Senator Barack Obama of Illinois be selected by this convention, by acclamation, as the nominee of the Democratic Party for president of the United States.'

Within moments, House of Representatives Speaker Nancy Pelosi, who was chairing proceedings, moved the vote of acclamation on Obama's behalf. I was about 20 yards away from where Clinton was standing. Several people around me were crying. 'We did it,' one young woman said in celebration, her arm draped across the shoulder of a friend. 'I don't believe we did it.'

Bill Clinton's speech later that night was just as emphatic as his wife's had been. 'Last night, Hillary told us in no uncertain terms that she is going to do everything she can to elect Barack Obama,' he said. Then he paused. 'That makes two of us.'

As the convention closed on Thursday night, after Obama's big speech in the stadium, the thousands of people filing out of Invesco Field seemed seized by optimism. Surely, they thought, the combination of the historic address and the events of the previous days would be enough to catapult their candidate into the commanding lead they believed he deserved.

'The convention exceeded all our goals,' David Plouffe said happily. 'We are not just unified, our party is electrified.'

Within days, it wouldn't just be the Democrats who were electrified.

*

The shock came as the next day dawned.

I sat blearily in my hotel room on the outskirts of Denver watching CNN coverage of a McCain rally in Dayton, Ohio. To great excitement from the crowd – but consternation from media pundits and even some members of her own party – a 44-year-old woman took the microphone to introduce herself to the American people.

Sarah Palin had been announced that morning as McCain's vice-presidential nominee. Palin was the governor of Alaska. Prior to assuming that role in 2006, her major achievement in public life had been becoming mayor of Wasilla, a town of approximately 10,000 residents. McCain's decision was the most surprising choice of a running mate in the twenty years since George H. W. Bush had selected Indiana senator Dan Quayle.

Choosing the right running mate was always going to be a challenge for McCain. He was still distrusted by social conservatives among the party's base, and he needed to reassure them if he was to have any chance of reaching the White House. But even if he did get the party activists on board, the election would then be won, as usual, by whichever candidate could best attract the floating voters in the political centre-ground. Ideally, then, McCain needed to find a nominee who would appeal to both moderates and conservatives, while also buttressing his independent image.

Virtually no one had predicted Palin. The previous day's *New York*

Times had reported that 'the top contenders remained the same three men who have been the source of speculation for weeks'. The newspaper was referring to Mitt Romney, McCain's old foe from the primaries; Minnesota governor Tim Pawlenty; and Senator Joe Lieberman of Connecticut.

Each member of the trio had his downsides. For all the political advantages Romney supposedly offered, McCain just didn't like him. Pawlenty was competent but dull. McCain, by many accounts, was more enthused about Lieberman than any other option.

Lieberman was officially an independent despite having been a Democrat for many years. He had been Al Gore's running mate in 2000 but his relations with his own party had been soured by his robust and enduring support for the Iraq war.

Selecting a long-time member of the opposing party would certainly boost McCain's maverick credentials. But therein lay the danger as well as the opportunity. Lieberman, hawkish though he was on foreign policy, still supported a raft of Democratic domestic and social policies that were anathema to the Republican base, notably the protection of a woman's right to choose. According to an October 2008 report in the *New Yorker*, McCain's aides told him in no uncertain terms that selecting Lieberman could lead to a disastrous convention, with social and religious conservatives rising up against the vice-presidential nominee. Reluctantly, he came to accept the advice.

Palin was a huge gamble, but it was easy enough to see why she held appeal for McCain's team. She was staunchly conservative, especially on social issues like gay marriage, gun control and abortion. At the same time, her gender, her youth and her much-remarked-upon good looks – she had been runner-up in a Miss Alaska beauty pageant in 1984 – might give her greater appeal to centrists, or so the thinking went.

At the introductory rally in Dayton, McCain told the crowd: 'She's exactly who I need. She's exactly who this country needs to help me fight the same old Washington politics of "me first and country second".'

Palin delivered an unremarkable speech, its main noteworthy

feature being a blatant attempt to appeal to disgruntled Hillary Clinton supporters. Palin noted that the rally came just after the 88th anniversary of women being guaranteed the right to vote in America, and added: 'I can't begin this great effort without honouring the achievements of Geraldine Ferraro in 1984 and, of course, Senator Hillary Clinton, who showed such determination and grace in her presidential campaign.'

Ferraro, like Clinton, was a Democrat – she had been Walter Mondale's running mate – and both women were staunchly pro-choice. It seemed more than a little patronising for Republicans to believe that female supporters of either Democrat would switch their backing to Palin – who believed that abortion should be illegal even in the case of women who were victims of rape or incest – purely on the basis of her gender.

Palin's initial appearance in Dayton was trouble-free but uninspiring. A large swath of the world's media was headed to the so-called 'Twin Cities' of Minneapolis and St Paul for the Republican National Convention the following week. Palin was about to get her chance on a much bigger stage.

*

The two weeks that followed were Obama's worst of the general election campaign. Sarah Palin was at the heart of the problem. She became the star turn of the Republican convention, eclipsing even McCain. The fire of conservative excitement she ignited threatened to consume everything. Obama's team seemed dazed, unable to understand the Palin effect, much less find an antidote to it. I couldn't blame them: I didn't understand it myself.

I was on the floor of the Xcel Center in St Paul when Palin delivered her address on the convention's penultimate night. Her performance struck me in much the same way as her initial appearance in Dayton had done: it was professional – neither awful nor out of the ordinary. More than anything, the speech cast her in the classic vice-presidential role of 'attack dog', savaging the presidential nominee of the other party while allowing her running mate to remain above the fray.

Its most potent passage came when Palin sought to strike back against those who had questioned her inexperience. She did so by mocking Obama's roots and alluding to the comments that had caused him such a headache in the run-in to the Pennsylvania primary.

'I guess a small-town mayor is sort of like a community organiser, except that you have actual responsibilities,' she said to uproarious applause. 'I might add that, in small towns, we don't quite know what to make of a candidate who lavishes praise on working people when they're listening and then talks about how bitterly they cling to their religion and guns when those people aren't listening. No, we tend to prefer candidates who don't talk about us one way in Scranton and another way in San Francisco.'

Palin's speech – and her allure, as it would reveal itself in the days that followed – was not really about specific policies. Her charm, to many Americans, was both cultural and visceral. She appealed to people who were distrustful of anything that carried the scent of liberalism. In its place, she offered up a ferocious traditionalism. In the convention speech, she presented herself as 'just your average hockey mom', then added: 'You know, they say the difference between a hockey mom and a pit bull? Lipstick.'

I had watched the speech from close to where the Alaska delegation was seated. Its members were ecstatic at seeing their heroine propelled into the global spotlight. Mel Krogseng, a 67-year-old delegate, told me it had been a 'brilliant and bold' move of McCain to pick Palin.

McCain's speech the next night was low-wattage by comparison. It was a workmanlike rhetorical amble through his biography that also included pledges of loyalty to various standard Republican principles. It pleased the audience but did not thrill them. In its aftermath, 20-year-old Sophie Stevens, a delegate from South Dakota, praised McCain but was much more enthusiastic about Palin.

'At first I was surprised that she had been chosen,' Stevens told me, 'but the more I got to know about her, the more I fell in love with her. I am so glad she is against abortion; so many lives have been lost.'

'Palin fever' soon took hold further afield. Obama fell sharply in the polls. Of 12 major nationwide surveys conducted in the immediate aftermath of the convention, the Democrat held the lead in only two. His advantage in both polls was just 1 percent. McCain, by contrast, was in front in 7 of the 12, in one case by a startling 10 percent. The size of the crowds that turned up for joint McCain-Palin appearances was far in excess of the numbers McCain had been able to draw on his own. The change in the atmosphere of the race was, for the Obama camp, sudden and disorientating.

As Democrats outside the campaign began to panic, David Plouffe tried to calm nerves in an interview with the *New York Times*: 'We have a game plan and a strategy,' he said. 'We're familiar with this. And I'm sure between now and November 4, there will be another period of hand-wringing and bed-wetting. It comes with the territory.'

The strength of Plouffe's language belied the intended message of steadiness. The pressure was evident everywhere. I joined a conference call on 12 September, for which the Obama team had drafted in Senator Dick Durbin of Illinois and Congressman Rahm Emanuel. The latter was one of the party's most ruthless bare-knuckle political fighters.

'John McCain is offering George Bush's economic policies and Dick Cheney's foreign policy,' Emanuel said, striving to stay on-message. But he grew testy when asked about states like Florida, which Obama had once had high hopes of winning. Now McCain seemed to be enjoying a commanding lead there.

'I'm not ready to concede the notion of losing ground,' Emanuel said. 'You start with a whole field of races and you get focused [later] on where the game is really going to be played.'

The problem for Obama was that his path to victory seemed to be narrowing by the day. Aides were forced to confront more starkly than ever the idea that he could come up short on Election Day. Only two weeks after the euphoria of Denver, they could sense what defeat would taste like.

11

BREAKING THE DEADLOCK

On a Friday evening in mid-September, I stood outside the New York Stock Exchange, trying to get traders to speak to me on the record as they left for the day. I wasn't alone. Reporters from as far afield as France and Germany were also hovering by the exchange's exit. The traders mostly scuttled away with their heads down, keen to avoid any discussion of the dreadful preceding days.

Eventually, one man, Dan Ryan, did agree to speak. His verdict sounded apocalyptic: 'It's going to sell off again,' he told me, referring to the market. 'There's nothing good in the world.'

The election of 2008 had already taken strange twists. Now came a new one that served to remind those of us who had become immersed in the campaign that the daily, tactical moves in the political chess game could seem very trivial indeed compared to the bigger forces swirling in American society.

The US economy had been ailing for months. Then it entered a tailspin. The situation was so severe – with credit markets seizing up, blue-chip companies collapsing and the stock market crashing – that the country soon became embroiled in the biggest financial crisis since the Great Depression.

The problem had been building for a long time. At its core it dated back to the 1980s, when the American mortgage industry had been deregulated. Two key changes had taken place. First, people with opaque or mediocre credit histories were for the first time able to get mortgages, often with minimal preconditions. (These loans would become known as 'subprime mortgages'.) Second, rather than the old-style, straightforward arrangement under which a mortgage was essentially a contract between a customer and a bank, with little third-party involvement, the lending institutions were now rolling tens of thousands of mortgages together, repackaging them and selling on these 'debt products' to other companies. Those companies then repeated the process and passed the debt down the line in increasingly arcane garb.

The process hummed along smoothly while the American housing market was booming in the late 1990s and early 2000s. But when that market slowed in 2006, things came unstuck. A large number of sub-prime-mortgage holders began to default on their repayments. As a consequence, anxiety started to nag at the lending institutions. Mortgage debt had been repackaged so many times that it was almost impossible to work out the solidity or otherwise of any given institution's portfolio. In layman's terms, no one knew what cards they were holding. The result was fear – and a creeping freeze in the availability of credit.

The problem had been worsening throughout 2008. In July, Bush's treasury secretary, Henry Paulson, had put together a $25 billion plan to prop up Fannie Mae and Freddie Mac, the American mortgage behemoths that together backed about half of the nation's $5 trillion in home loans. It didn't work. In early September, more action was needed. Paulson placed the companies under the direct control of their federal regulator and announced that any profits they made in the future would accrue to the government. The administration gave the scheme a nice name – 'government conservatorship' – but, really, the firms had been nationalised.

The following weekend, chaos exploded. Merrill Lynch, a huge name in investment banking, saw its fiscal health decline so rapidly that it was left with no option but to sell itself to Bank of America. The deal was agreed on Sunday 14 September. The next morning, another big and well-respected company, Lehman Brothers, filed for bankruptcy. The two pieces of news combined to send the Dow Jones index into a mini-meltdown. The index lost 504 points, or 4.4 percent of its value, that day.

When another government bailout, this time of insurance giant AIG, was announced later that week, the feeling of panic became all-encompassing. 'I have never, ever seen it like this before,' Liz Claman, an experienced business journalist and an anchor on the Fox Business Network, told me. 'People are not having an intelligent discussion on the value of things. They are just in the middle of all this emotion.'

The political implications of the economic turmoil were indisputable. On the Monday of that week, the *Real Clear Politics* website, which publishes an authoritative moving average of major opinion polls, had McCain ahead of Obama nationwide, albeit by a small margin. By Wednesday – when the Dow took another massive tumble, this time of 449 points – the two were level. By Thursday, the Democrat was in the lead. Beyond that, the opinion poll graph came to resemble an open pair of scissors, Obama's ratings jagging up as McCain's shot downwards.

Even the most committed members of the Obama team would not have attributed their candidate's rise, at least in those initial few days, to any great moment of genius. His performance was steady rather than stellar. In a speech in Colorado on the first day of the crisis, he noted that the news from Wall Street was 'very serious and troubling', and added: 'I certainly don't fault Senator McCain for these problems. But I do fault the economic philosophy he subscribes to.'

Perhaps that was all he had to do. After all, the mere occurrence of the economic crisis was enough to hurt McCain badly. The Republican could assert his independence from Bush until he was blue in the face, but in the circumstances, any candidate of the incumbent party was doomed to suffer some damage.

McCain made matters infinitely worse for himself, however. As Obama showed that he could keep a steady hand on the wheel, his opponent careered all over the road. On 15 September, he made the kind of mistake that haunts candidates. Speaking at a rally in Jacksonville, Florida, he insisted to the crowd: 'The fundamentals of our economy are strong.' Either side of those fateful words, he mentioned 'tremendous turmoil' and 'very, very difficult times', but the soundbite was the problem. It fed directly into the message that the Obama campaign had been trying to push. McCain, they kept insisting, was out of touch with the general public. The Republican's comment was grist for their mill. 'This says in one sentence what we've been trying to say about McCain for months,' an unnamed Obama aide told the *Politico* website gleefully.

McCain exacerbated his initial error in the process of trying to erase it. Speaking later that day in Orlando, he admitted: 'The American economy is in a crisis.' The rapid switch from the reassuring words he had offered earlier in the day only buttressed yet another Obama argument: that McCain was rash and prone to erratic behaviour.

Presented with an opening, Obama struck hard. He picked up on McCain's 'fundamentals' comment on the day it was made, asking rhetorically: 'Senator – what economy are you talking about?'

By the next day, the Obama campaign had a new ad being broadcast across battleground states. It repeated the audio clip of McCain's remark three times, while on-screen text asked the question: 'How can John McCain fix our economy if he doesn't understand it's broken?'

The Republican would struggle with that question for the rest of the campaign.

*

McCain was soon to make another tactical blunder that would be seen as even more serious.

As the market gloom deepened, Paulson and the chairman of the Federal Reserve, Ben Bernanke, became convinced that drastic action was needed to prevent credit markets from drying up completely. Their initial plan was to ask Congress for $700 billion that would be used, in essence, to buy up potentially dodgy debt products that were crippling confidence in the nation's banks.

Winning the approval of the Senate and the House of Representatives for the proposal was always likely to be a challenge. After the idea was first announced, lawmakers reported receiving a flood of phone calls from angry constituents demanding that they vote against the package. Many taxpayers were furious that their money could be used to rescue institutions that, as they saw it, had caused the problems in the first place through greed and recklessness.

Around 8.30 AM on 24 September, with a televised address from the president planned for that evening, Obama called McCain to suggest that the two candidates put out a joint statement on the crisis. He did not get through to his opponent directly, but in the early afternoon McCain called back to say that he was prepared to sign on.

The statement was duly issued. It stated that the Paulson proposal was 'flawed' but emphasised that 'the effort to protect the American economy must not fail'.

Then came the bombshell. To the consternation of the Obama campaign, a statement was sent out from McCain's headquarters announcing that the Republican would suspend his campaign the following morning and return to Washington, purportedly to advance the tense negotiations about the Paulson bailout on Capitol Hill.

The statement strove for a statesmanlike tone. 'We must meet as Americans, not as Democrats or Republicans, and we must meet until this crisis is resolved,' it said. The statement also included a call for the first presidential debate, which was then just two days away, to be postponed.

There was some pressure on Obama, even from his own advisors, to make a similar move. They feared that, if he stayed on the campaign trail, he could be cast as prioritising the search for political advantage over the good of the nation. But Obama resisted such counsel.

'I didn't believe it,' he later told *Time*. 'I have to tell you, one of the benefits of running this 22-month gauntlet is that you have been through some ups and you have been through some downs. And you start realising that what seems important or clever or in need of some dramatic moment a lot of times just needs reflection and care.' It was one of his best decisions, protecting him from any sense that he had been obliged to follow a trail blazed by McCain.

The Republican's gamble did not pay off. Lawmakers on Capitol Hill had not called for either McCain or Obama to return to help them work on a deal, in part because they feared that the injection of presidential politics could stymie the negotiations. So it proved. A deal that had seemed to be in the works began to unravel as McCain and – at Bush's request – Obama arrived for a White House meeting.

Even McCain's ideological comrades seemed unimpressed by his tactics. Mike Huckabee told reporters that, as a candidate: 'You can't just say, "World, stop for a moment, I'm going to cancel everything."' The media took an even harsher view. A *Boston Globe* editorial referring to his campaign suspension as 'this impulsive new stunt' and a column from the *Washington Post*'s Harold Meyerson asserting that his 'ploy was transparent' were just two voices amid a chorus of criticism.

Things got even worse in the days that followed. In the early hours of Sunday 27 September, optimism briefly peeked through: congressional leaders came to a verbal agreement on a bailout deal. Normally, legislation is not brought to a vote on the floor of either the Senate or the House of Representatives unless the leaders of both parties are sure they can deliver its safe passage. The House vote was set for Monday. In a stunning outcome, it went down to defeat by 228 votes to 205. By the end of that day, 7 percent had been wiped off the value of the Dow Jones. Its 778-point decline was the largest one-day drop in history.

In the immediate aftermath, McCain's poll ratings continued to slide. Obama's lead across the nation now stood at an average of about 6 percent. Battleground states like Florida, which had seemed to be slipping away from him only two weeks before, were leaning towards him once again.

*

In the midst of the economic crisis, there was also the first debate to deal with. As it turned out, the most dramatic thing about it was McCain's threat not to participate. Presidential debates are often damp squibs, despite the hype that attends them, and this one, held at the University of Mississippi, was no different.

There were few genuinely memorable lines, and the candidates stuck fast to their established positions. The lines of attack were similarly predictable, with McCain accusing Obama of being ultra-liberal and Obama continuing his efforts to tether McCain as tightly as possible to Bush. McCain, in a move that was later seen as somewhat counter-productive, accused Obama on a number of occasions of failing to 'understand' or 'get' various points.

Obama perhaps had the night's most memorable soundbite when he attacked McCain for his erroneous predictions about the Iraq war: 'At the time when the war started, you said it was going to be quick and easy. You said we knew where the weapons of mass destruction were. You were wrong. You said that we were going to be greeted as liberators. You were wrong. You said that there was no history of violence between Shiite and Sunni. And you were wrong.'

In the so-called 'spin room' – the place where aides gather to try to persuade reporters to view things favourably for their candidate – Robert Gibbs said that Obama had reminded voters during the exchange on Iraq that he had shown 'the kind of judgement that is necessary to lead this country'. As for McCain, Gibbs opined that 'what he spent the last 90 minutes doing was advocating more of the same. . . . I think he looked erratic, I think he looked rattled, quite frankly he looked perturbed.'

'I think Senator McCain really gave Senator Obama a lesson on foreign policy,' countered Rudy Giuliani, who had been specially drafted in by the Republicans for the occasion. 'It seemed like, any number of times, Senator Obama didn't know any of these issues.'

I thought the debate was a draw. But a CBS News poll of previously uncommitted voters indicated that 39 percent of them thought Obama had won, while only 24 percent gave the nod to McCain. In a national poll of debate-watchers conducted by CNN, 51 percent thought Obama had done a better job in the encounter, as against 38 percent for McCain. Perhaps more importantly, both polls suggested that, by a margin of over 20 percent, more Americans believed that Obama would be better able to address the country's economic troubles.

It seemed like Obama was making rapid progress in putting voters' worries about his maturity to rest. If he could continue to reassure them, the dismal economy – and McCain's unsteady responses – looked ever more likely to deliver him victory.

*

The day after the debate, I travelled to Fredericksburg, Virginia, to see Obama and Biden address an evening rally in the open air at the University of Mary Washington. The attendance was huge. The official estimate of the crowd, supplied by the local authorities, was 26,000: 12,000 at the location itself and a further 14,000 who had to be turned away.

It was not just the numbers that mattered. The confidence of the candidate, his aides and his supporters seemed more palpable, more concrete, than it had been even at the Denver convention. Virginia had last voted for a Democrat for president in 1964, when Lyndon Johnson had won a national landslide in part because of lingering sympathy over John F. Kennedy's assassination the previous year. But Obama had made the battle for the state more than competitive. The last major poll conducted before the Fredericksburg event put him ahead by five points.

'I think we may just turn Virginia blue this time,' he told the crowd soon after taking the stage. They had waited for him through a torrential downpour; Obama evidently wanted to make clear that their dedication had been noted. 'I'd like to cover everybody's dry-cleaning bill tonight,' he told them, 'but I can't 'cos I gotta use it on the campaign. So consider it one more modest contribution to our efforts to change the country.'

The body of his stump speech held no surprises. Instead, he sought to make the weather a semi-serious metaphor for the race. 'This won't be easy,' he cautioned. 'The storm hasn't quite passed yet. Sometimes the skies look cloudy. You think the rains will never pass. But here's what I understand: that as long as all of us are together, as long as we are all committed, there is nothing we can't do. . . . These young people know that these clouds will pass and a brighter day will come.'

Afterwards, Linda Douglass, a veteran TV and print journalist who had joined the Obama campaign as a senior strategist and campaign spokesperson back in May, continued enthusing about Obama's performance at the debate the previous night. 'I think it is really beginning to sink in with those of you who write about the debate that he won last night,' she told me. 'I mean, clearly the voters concluded that he won last night in all the polling that was done. He made a very strong case for change that came through very clearly to voters.'

Douglass also struck back with force at McCain's oft-repeated insistence that Obama did not 'understand' various things. 'The answer to that is: John McCain – his problem is he doesn't get it,' Douglass said. 'He doesn't understand what people in this country are going through. . . . I mean, he's a guy who's demonstrated over and over again, when he says the fundamentals of the economy are strong, that he's out of touch. So he can use insulting phraseology if he wants to. It didn't go over very well with the voters, by the way. Voters did not like that kind of nasty rejoinder.' As if anyone was liable to forget, Douglass reiterated the point that 'the economy is the central issue'.

That same morning, David Plouffe had held a conference call to enthuse about the shift in the dynamics of the race. 'I do think that the two candidates' responses over the last couple of weeks may be seen as a turning point in the election,' he said. 'First of all, going back to the famous Monday where John McCain said the fundamentals of the economy are strong: that, we think, broke through. . . . People are paying attention out there, and when they see John McCain say the fundamentals of the economy are strong, I think it was really shocking to people.

'During these couple of weeks, Barack Obama has been very steady,' Plouffe continued. 'McCain has kind of been all over the lot, very erratic. There were days where it looked like he would oppose the bailout, then he was going to be for it, then he comes in again suggesting he's riding in on his white horse and kind of disrupts things. And I think people are looking for steady leadership and not someone who seems to be chasing news cycles.'

Plouffe was propagandising for his candidate, of course. But it was difficult to find obvious fault with his analysis. And Obama kept rising in the polls.

*

There was another factor driving Obama's surge – or, perhaps more accurately, hastening McCain's fall. The excitement about Sarah Palin had worn off rapidly, everywhere but among the most hardcore Republican supporters. In its place came serious worries about the Alaska governor's capabilities.

Her decline had begun on 11 September, when an interview she had conducted with Charles Gibson of ABC News aired. Palin made an unconvincing attempt to wriggle away from a quote Gibson had unearthed in which she described the American mission in Iraq as 'a task that is from God'. She seemed uncomprehending when he asked her a question about the Bush Doctrine. (In fairness, that doctrine had never been spelled out as clearly as her detractors suggested.) Most embarrassingly of all, when questioned about her lack of foreign policy experience, Palin suggested that she would have special insight into Russia because 'they're our next-door neighbours and you can actually see Russia from land here in Alaska'.

The remark instantly made her the butt of jokes on America's late-night TV talk shows. Even so, the missteps in the Gibson interview were not disastrous, and they might have faded from the public's memory had Palin regained her footing. Instead, she humiliated herself in some style. Another major TV interview, with Katie Couric of CBS News, was an unmitigated public relations catastrophe.

Couric had honed her skills as an anchor on the most popular of America's breakfast shows, NBC's *Today*. Her air of cheeriness – the adjective 'perky' seemed to appear in almost every profile of her – disguised a canny interviewing style that often lured people into unexpected confessions. The material she extracted from Palin was so powerful that it was stretched over several nights, producing an effect that more than one Republican compared to the agonising drip of Chinese water torture.

In the first instalment, aired on 24 September, Palin was asked to give some examples of McCain supporting regulation or oversight of the financial industry. The Alaska governor floundered, trying with ever-decreasing effectiveness to parry three successive questions on the issue. Eventually, in a move that must have horrified her handlers, Palin adopted a tone of forced jollity and told Couric: 'I'll try to find you some and I'll bring 'em to ya.'

The following night, viewers were treated to the spectacle of Palin again trying to defend her comments on how her home state's proximity to Russia gave her special expertise in foreign affairs. Her response this time was even worse than it had been during the Gibson interview – so bad, in fact, that even some conservative pundits began suggesting that she was suffering a crisis of confidence.

'It's very important when you consider even national security issues with Russia,' she began. 'As Putin rears his head and comes into the airspace of the United States of America, where do they go? It's Alaska. It's just right over the border. It is from Alaska that we send those out to make sure that an eye is being kept on this very powerful nation, Russia, because they are right there, they are right next to our state.' This was gobbledegook, and it fed the impression that Palin simply had no idea what she was talking about.

There was more to come from the Couric interview the following week. In one instance, the Alaska governor displayed an inexplicable unwillingness to say what newspapers or magazines she read. 'All of 'em, any of 'em . . . that have been in front of me all these years,' she said. A series of questions about the Supreme Court that most college students in America could have answered with ease bamboozled her to such an extent that the exchange was difficult to watch.

The footage sent tremors through conservative circles. The syndicated columnist Kathleen Parker, who confessed to having been 'delighted' by the initial selection of Palin, forsook the Alaska governor in savage style.

'It was fun while it lasted,' Parker wrote. 'I've been pulling for Palin, wishing her the best, hoping she will perform brilliantly. I've also noticed that I watch her interviews with the held breath of an anxious parent, my finger poised over the mute button in case it gets too painful. Unfortunately, it often does. My cringe reflex is exhausted.'

En route to suggesting Palin should find a palatable excuse to bow out of the race, Parker noted: 'If B.S. were currency, Palin could bail out Wall Street herself.'

The most devastating criticism of all came from a very different angle, however. Tina Fey, a comic actress and writer, had been one of the stars of the hugely popular *Saturday Night Live* television programme but had left the ensemble show to pursue various other projects. Fey's resemblance to Palin was striking and she was lured back to *SNL*, as it was commonly known, to impersonate the vice-presidential nominee as a new series began.

The sketches featuring Fey as Palin became a smash hit. One skit, incorporating almost word-for-word repetitions of the real Palin's answers during the Couric interview, was particularly memorable – testament, again, to the ruinous nature of that encounter. The overall effect was devastating.

The influence of popular culture on politics is often exaggerated – but not in this case. Fey's impersonation of Palin helped boost *Saturday Night Live*'s ratings by around 50 percent, to a total viewership of over 10 million. Those 10 million people were seeing the vice-presidential running mate of a 72-year-old cancer survivor portrayed as a dangerous idiot. There was bound to be some political effect.

A vice-presidential debate was held between Palin and Joe Biden on 2 October. Expectations by this point were so low for Palin that her avoidance of serious gaffes was hailed as a major achievement. Even after that, though, few voices were raised on the Republican side to praise McCain's choice of the Alaska governor as his running mate. Whereas once she had seemed like someone who could turn the election against Obama, now she looked like just another in a series of factors – along with the economic crisis and McCain's personal volatility – that had moved the race in the Democrat's direction, without him having to do very much at all.

*

McCain responded to this downturn in his fortunes with a campaign that became increasingly negative, aggressive and plain dirty. This was standard operating procedure for any candidate who found himself losing ground in the polls and running out of time. But it was disappointing coming from McCain, because he had for years present-ed himself as someone who disdained such tactics.

Back in March, his campaign manager, Rick Davis, had sent out a memo to the press highlighting McCain's intention to run 'a respectful campaign focused on the issues'. Davis added that, during the primary, his candidate had rejected 'the type of politics that degrade our civics, and this will not change as he prepares to run head-to-head against the Democratic nominee'.

The following month, the candidate himself had acknowledged that negative ads might help move the polls but had nonetheless come out against them, asking rhetorically: 'Do we have to go to the lowest common denominator?'

He failed to live up to his own standards. The danger signs had been seen relatively early, with the Paris Hilton and Britney Spears 'celeb' ad that had followed Obama's foreign trip. Although the com-mercial was relatively harmless, it hardly elevated the tone of the polit-ical debate.

A much more serious example came in early September, with an ad accusing Obama of having supported the teaching of 'comprehensive sex education to kindergarteners' during his time as an Illinois state senator. The spot was excoriated by various independent sources, who found that Obama had backed actual sex education only for much older children but had supported programmes to educate the very youngest about inappropriate touching and other issues that would alert them to the dangers of paedophilia. An Obama spokesperson, Bill Burton, described the McCain ad as 'shameful and downright per-verse'.

The first shot in the dirty war that would dominate the final weeks of the McCain campaign was fired by Palin. During a campaign stop in Colorado on 4 October, she said: 'Our opponent is someone who sees America, it seems, as being so imperfect that he's palling around with terrorists.'

The accusation would have been potent had it been true. It was not. Palin's remark was a reference to a former radical named Bill Ayers. Obama knew Ayers, but the suggestion that he was 'palling around' with him was absurd.

Ayers had been a member of the Weather Underground, a far-left group that was prominent in the late 1960s and early 1970s. The organisation had carried out some domestic bombings, including attacks on the US Capitol and the Pentagon. In an interview that – in a conspicuous piece of bad timing – appeared in the *New York Times* on 11 September 2001, Ayers said: 'I don't regret setting bombs. I feel we didn't do enough.' (Ayers later insisted that the newspaper had twisted his meaning, which he said was that the anti-war movement had self-evidently not done enough to end the Vietnam war sooner.)

In any case, Ayers had rehabilitated himself into mainstream society long before that. He became a professor of education at the University of Illinois. His overall outlook was sufficiently inoffensive for Chicago mayor Richard Daley – a Democrat but hardly a liberal – to become one of his strongest defenders.

Back in the mid-1990s, when Obama was readying himself to run for a state Senate seat – and when he was still on good terms with Alice Palmer, the woman he would replace in Springfield – there had been a party at the house shared by Ayers and his wife, another former Weather Underground member called Bernadine Dohrn. The meeting was not a fundraiser, as conservatives would later claim, nor was there anything particularly unusual about it. It seems to have been arranged largely to enable Palmer to introduce Obama to her liberal circle.

Obama and Ayers had also sat on two boards at the turn of the century. One was a school reform project, the Chicago Annenberg Challenge, and the other was a philanthropic organisation, the Woods Fund. The suggestion that either body was some kind of front for subversive activity was ludicrous. The Annenberg Challenge got its name from its patron, Walter Annenberg, a billionaire businessman who was a friend of Ronald Reagan and had served as an ambassador to the UK at Richard Nixon's behest. The Woods Fund was one of Chicago's most respected charities, having been set up in 1941 with the broad goal of helping the Windy City's less affluent citizens.

An exhaustive *New York Times* investigation into whatever connections existed between Obama and Ayers, published the day before Palin made her 'palling around' comment, noted that while Obama may at times have 'played down' his contacts with Ayers, 'the two men do not appear to have been close. Nor has Mr Obama ever expressed sympathy for the radical views and actions of Mr Ayers, whom he has called "somebody who engaged in detestable acts forty years ago, when I was eight".'

Ayers was clearly a weak hook on which to hang an attack on Obama. But by this point the McCain campaign had decided to start throwing anything that came to hand. Two days later, a Florida sheriff, in uniform, introduced Palin at a rally by urging the crowd: 'On November 4, let's leave Barack Hussein Obama wondering what happened.' The emphasis on Obama's middle name was clearly intended to suggest at best an exoticism that was not entirely American and, at worst, sympathy for Islamic extremism.

The barrage continued. On 6 October, the McCain campaign released a new TV ad, to be broadcast across the nation, with the title 'Dangerous'. The non-partisan website *Factcheck.org* found that the ad, which accused Obama of being 'dishonourable', 'recycles a misleading, 14-month-old charge that Senator Barack Obama disrespected US troops fighting in Afghanistan.'

Three days later came a Web-only ad that tied Obama closer than ever before to Ayers. It described Ayers as a 'domestic terrorist' and said of his relationship with Obama: 'They've worked together for years but Obama tries to hide it. Why?' It ended with the message that Obama was 'Too risky for America'.

As the campaign hardened its tone, outright threats against Obama began to be heard at Republican rallies. Cries of 'Terrorist' and 'Kill him!' rang out at McCain and Palin events. Spokespeople would later assert that the candidates had not heard the shouts.

Finally, on 10 October, McCain came face to face with the consequences of his actions. At an event in Lakeville, Minnesota, he opened the floor to questions. A man said he was 'scared' of an Obama presidency.

'First of all, I want to be president of the United States, and obviously I do not want Senator Obama to be. But I have to tell you, he is a decent person and a person that you do not have to be scared [of] as president of the United States,' McCain responded. He was booed and heckled for his trouble.

Around twenty minutes later, a woman rose to her feet. What followed was one of the most powerful moments of the campaign's closing stages. The woman stood only a few feet from McCain, who had given her his microphone.

'I gotta ask you a question,' she began. 'I can't trust Obama.'

McCain smiled approvingly and said: 'I got ya.'

Then the woman said: 'I have read about him and he's not, he's not . . . He's an Arab.'

McCain's jaw clenched. For about two seconds, it was not clear what he was going to do. Then he began shaking his head vigorously. 'No ma'am, no ma'am,' he said, taking the microphone back. 'He's a decent family man [and] citizen that I just happen to have disagreements with on fundamental issues.'

It was an increasingly rare glimpse of the honourable man he had once seemed to be.

*

The day after McCain's tactics had come back to embarrass him in Minnesota, I once again caught up with the Obama campaign, this time in Philadelphia, where he had scheduled four public events in one day.

The city was solidly Democratic, and Obama's candidacy was especially celebrated among its African-American community, who represented almost half the population. The contrast with McCain's increasingly sepulchral tone was stark. At both places where I saw Obama, in a rough-hewn area of north Philadelphia in the morning and at a sunlit street-corner meeting in the west of the city in the afternoon, his criticisms were certainly forceful. He spoke of corruption on Wall Street and the money that had been wasted in Iraq. But there was little personal animus towards McCain apparent in his message. Instead, he emphasised values like solidarity and community. This approach might have seemed almost quaint had it not proven so effective in his campaign to date. 'We're all in this together,' he exhorted the crowds.

That weekend, there was just over three weeks left before Election Day. The picture could hardly have looked better for Obama. The polls now had him almost 8 percent ahead of McCain on average. Early the next week, David Plouffe talked about the enthusiasm for Obama's candidacy and the awesome get-out-the-vote operation he believed had been built. 'It's a gathering storm out there and [the Republicans] are going to see it crashing on their beachhead on November 4,' he promised.

The final debate loomed the next night. (The second debate, held on 7 October in Nashville, had been a crushing bore, enlivened only by McCain's odd reference, accompanied by a dismissive hand gesture, to 'that one', meaning Obama. Novelty T-shirts carrying slogans like 'I'm voting for That One' appeared for sale shortly afterwards.)

In the final head-to-head match-up, McCain set a much more aggressive tone from the start, raising the Ayers issue and accusing Obama of planning to increase taxes. The Democrat remained calm, almost mild-mannered. Obama rolled up big margins of victory in the instant polls afterwards. Viewers polled by both CNN and CBS believed, by margins greater than 20 percent in each case, that he had done better than McCain.

Having thwarted McCain in what looked like the older man's last set-piece chance to alter the momentum of the race, Obama was in prime position. He had one thing to worry about: complacency. The day after the debate, he spoke in New Hampshire: 'We are nineteen days away from changing this country. Nineteen days!' he said. 'But for those who are getting a little cocky, I've got two words for you: New Hampshire. I learned right here that you can't let up or pay too much attention to the polls. We've got to keep making our case for change; we've got to keep fighting for every vote; we've got to keep running through that finish line.'

A man whose bid for the presidency had seemed so quixotic when it first began was now so far ahead that his main worry was his supporters taking his victory for granted.

It was a good complaint to have.

12

The Final Push

The currents of the campaign kept flowing in Obama's favour in the last days, shunting him towards the White House with ever-greater force.

Several Republican strongholds were in his sights by mid-October. According to the polls, he led in Indiana, which, like Virginia, had not backed a Democrat for president since 1964; he led in North Carolina, last won by a Democrat in 1976; and he led in Ohio, without which no Republican had ever won the presidency. In other states where recent Democratic presidential candidates had been unable even to put up a decent fight – places like Georgia, North Dakota and Arizona – he was breathing down McCain's neck.

'The Big Mo' was a phrase that had been coined almost 30 years before by George H. W. Bush to describe the kind of momentum Obama was enjoying. Bush had posited that, once the Big Mo was with you, it could pull every star into alignment. For Obama, as Election Day neared, it sometimes felt like that was exactly what was happening.

On 19 October, with just over two weeks to go, Colin Powell endorsed the Democrat. There was good reason to be sceptical about the power of endorsements, but Powell's was different. Its distinction lay in part in the retired general's unusual position in contemporary American life. Although he was a Republican, he had considerable cross-party appeal and his long military service made his patriotism unimpeachable.

Powell's intervention was also important because of the manner in which it was made. If the former secretary of state had merely issued a statement endorsing Obama in broad terms, that would have been one thing. Instead, he went on *Meet the Press* to give full vent to his feelings about the McCain campaign. Powell's delivery was polite; the content of his message was brutal. It amounted to a comprehensive dismantling of the case his Republican colleague was trying to make.

Powell scorned the attempts to damage Obama by connecting him to Bill Ayers: 'To suggest that because Mr Barack Obama had some contacts of a very casual nature – they sat on an educational board – over time, is somehow connected to his thinking or his actions, I think, is a terrible stretch,' he said. 'It's demagoguery.' He cited the ginned-up controversy as just one reason he had been 'disappointed, frankly, by some of the approaches that Senator McCain has taken recently'.

The retired general expanded on this point after the interview was over. Speaking to several reporters outside the TV studios, he made reference to a Republican congresswoman, Michele Bachmann, who had appeared on MSNBC's *Hardball* two days before. Bachmann had caused uproar by suggesting that Obama 'may have anti-American views'. She had called on the media to investigate other members of Congress for any anti-American sympathies they might harbour.

The congresswoman appeared to be advocating a return to the McCarthyite witch-hunts of the early 1950s. The usually diplomatic Powell left no doubt what he thought about that. 'We've got to stop this kind of nonsense and pull ourselves together,' he spat.

Bachmann was only half a step further to the right-wing extreme than her party's nominee for vice president. The day before Bachmann's toxic TV appearance, Sarah Palin had pepped up a crowd in North Carolina by referring to 'pro-America areas' of the country, terminology that seemed to imply that regions which leaned liberal had forfeited their right to be considered patriotic.

For his part, Powell delivered a clipped, crisp verdict on Palin: 'Now that we have had a chance to watch her for some seven weeks, I don't believe she's ready to be president of the United States, which is the job of the vice president.'

The Obama campaign was exultant about Powell's performance. On the morning it happened, I was in Fayetteville, North Carolina, at an Obama rally. David Axelrod was so delighted by Powell's intervention that he agreed to be interviewed while his candidate was addressing the crowd. Powell's words, he told me, had 'slammed the door' on attempts by Republicans to question Obama's love of his nation.

Axelrod asserted that Powell was 'seen as an American statesman, and people understand that. When he makes an endorsement, he makes it from the standpoint of the country.' He added that the retired general's comments would likely be 'a source of encouragement' to voters who had been reluctant to cast off doubts about Obama. 'For Republicans who are disaffected, I think he articulated their views very, very well,' he added.

The strategist also argued that the way the Republican campaign was being conducted was ultimately aiding Obama. 'There are a lot of voters who are disgusted with the tone of the Republican campaign, and part of that has been manifested in increased small donations to our campaign,' he said. 'I think Senator McCain and Governor Palin have helped us immeasurably. I don't necessarily think it's good for the country, but I think people are expressing themselves by volunteering, by showing up at rallies and by contributing to the campaign.'

About a hundred yards away, Obama was sounding similar points. Describing Powell as 'a great statesman', he tackled the rhetoric used by the likes of Palin and Bachmann head-on. 'We can have a tough contest . . . but we've got to have a line that we don't cross,' he said. 'There are no real or fake parts of this country. We are not separated by the pro-America and anti-America parts of this country – we all love this country, no matter where we live or where we come from.'

The lines got one of his biggest cheers of the day.

*

I had a good vantage point on the Obama team's reaction to the Powell endorsement, since I was travelling on the campaign jet at the time.

Access to *O Force One*, as the plane had become known, was limited to a relatively small number of reporters, in part because the cost of securing a seat was prohibitive for most news organisations. The media reimbursed the Obama campaign for the flights, as well as for food and accommodation, but the expense could never be calculated with confidence in advance: it was determined by the number of journeys the campaign might deem necessary in any given day, and the number of people on board.

The rule of thumb for flight costs was $1,000 per person for every hour in the air. Most of the flights were short but if, for instance, Obama had to return unexpectedly to Washington from a campaign stop in a western swing state like Nevada, any news organisation with a person on the plane would instantly be liable for about $5,000 more than it had expected. The likes of the *New York Times* and CNN did not blanch at that kind of expenditure, but many smaller outlets did.

Foreign media organisations that were willing to foot the bills customarily had their requests for access turned down anyway, for the simple reason that the people running the campaign viewed them as unimportant. An interview with the smallest swing-state newspaper or television station could shift more undecided voters in Obama's direction than a similar encounter with the biggest of the non-US outlets, and the priorities of the campaign reflected that reality. To the best of my knowledge, I was the only Irish journalist on the Obama campaign plane at any point – and I got access only because I was travelling under the auspices of the *New York Observer*.

The plane itself was separated into several compartments. At the front, in the equivalent of first-class on a commercial jet, were four individual chairs, and a dining table around which another four people could be seated. Obama's seat, which had a small table that resembled a lectern beside it, was embroidered with the campaign logo and the words 'Obama '08 President'. Aside from the candidate, this section was typically reserved for key supporters or Obama's closest aides. Obama made full use of the space in unexpected ways. Getting off the plane at one stop, I found myself a few feet from a grinning presidential candidate, who was amusing himself by throwing mock punches at the shoulders of the ever-lugubrious Axelrod.

The plane got less plush the farther back one went. Behind Obama's compartment was a roomy, but less luxurious, section that was home to the junior members of the travelling staff. Behind them sat about 20 secret service agents who accompanied Obama everywhere. Finally, in economy seats in the rear, sat the media.

Some of the journalists, especially the so-called 'embeds' affiliated with TV networks, and the photographers, had been with Obama almost every day since the primary campaign began – and it showed, in good ways and bad. Chronic fatigue had set in months before, and they were increasingly jaded by the demands of life on the trail. On the other hand, they had done their best to personalise the otherwise sterile environment. The luggage racks and walls of the press section were festooned with photos – sometimes of Obama or aides like Robert Gibbs, but more often of members of the media mugging for each other. A keen appetite for the oddest Obama memorabilia was much in evidence. The bathroom had a packet of 'Obama Condoms' (slogan: 'Use with Good Judgment') prominently taped up above the toilet. In the main cabin, a lemon yellow 'Obama Nation' T-shirt, replete with a comically bad caricature of the candidate, adorned the space above one row of seats.

The journalistic value of a seat on the plane lay in part in the access to inside information that came with it. The Obama campaign was – to the great frustration of the media – one of the most disciplined anyone could remember, and almost never leaked damaging internal stories. But aides at least offered up interesting titbits during the flights. On one of Axelrod's excursions to the press section, for instance, he insisted – with what at least seemed like candour – that the campaign had not known exactly what Colin Powell was going to say on *Meet the Press* until the programme was broadcast. Three different statements had been pre-prepared for release in the aftermath of the interview, including one to cover the possibility that the former general would 'say nice things about us', as Axelrod put it, yet stop short of a full endorsement.

These small details were consumed hungrily, in part because

opportunities to question Obama directly were almost non-existent. During my time on board, one reporter asked press aide Jen Psaki if she would bring the candidate to the back of the plane to conduct an informal news conference. She looked at him with wry amusement, as if he had taken leave of his senses, and let it be known that the campaign did not intend to organise any such encounters before Election Day. The reasoning was clear enough, even though Psaki did not spell it out: Obama would have nothing to gain from the exchange, and plenty to lose.

The renewed intensity of the campaign rallies offered some compensation for the lack of access to the candidate. On a Saturday afternoon, Obama and the trailing media pack arrived in the city of St Louis, in the crucial swing state of Missouri. As we all clambered up a grassy incline to the open-air event site, a crowd that was colossal even by Obama's standards hove into view. The local police department estimated attendance at 100,000. It was the largest domestic event of Obama's campaign to date, and second only to Berlin as the biggest audience he had ever addressed. That same evening, 75,000 people showed up to see him in Kansas City.

In both places, the candidate pounded away at the same themes: that McCain offered a continuation of Bush's policies, that the straitened state of the nation was proof that those policies did not work, and that it was therefore time to embrace change. The message worked better and better as the economic situation became worse and worse.

The expanding enthusiasm for Obama could be seen in other ways besides the size of the crowds. The campaign motorcade – it comprised a handful of sleek 4x4s carrying Obama and his retinue, some security vehicles and two press buses, all surrounded by a massive fleet of police outriders – would attract shouts and waves from the people arriving for rallies. This was perhaps only to be expected; more startling was that the same thing happened miles from Obama events. The police would block off subsidiary roads to allow the convoy through, and long lines of cars would build up. But many of the people whose journeys had been interrupted, and who might have been expected to sit in frustrated silence, instead got out of their vehicles to applaud and cheer the passing candidate. This happened everywhere. In Kansas City, I watched a woman driver, one foot still inside her vehicle, her upper body poking out the door, whirling a sweatshirt around and around above her head and roaring her approval.

The sights were extraordinary enough from the press bus; you had to wonder how they looked through the eyes of Obama, sitting a few vehicles in front.

*

Good news for the Democrat kept coming. As Axelrod was praising Powell's endorsement, David Plouffe was releasing a video message to supporters from the campaign's Chicago HQ.

Plouffe's message was one of gratitude: the campaign had raised $150 million in September alone. The figure was far above what any other candidate had ever raised in a single month. Fully 632,000 new donors had come on board, bringing the total number of contributors to around 3.1 million. The average contribution to Obama's war chest remained under $100 – including September's totals, according to Plouffe, it was $86.

That money was being used to support an organisational effort the like of which America had never seen. On a conference call the following week, Plouffe introduced the campaign's field director in the battleground states, Jen O'Malley. The numbers O'Malley had to report were eye-popping.

Obama now had 1.5 million active volunteers across the country, knocking on doors and making phone calls. This meant that roughly one out of every 200 people in the nation was volunteering for him. If any politician in the Republic of Ireland could replicate that level of involvement, he or she would have an army of 22,000 unpaid workers at their disposal.

The money that had poured in, even before September's bonanza, had allowed the campaign to open 770 offices across the US. According to O'Malley, volunteers were contacting around 400,000 people every day. They had reached 1.5 million voters in Ohio and 1.3 million in Florida in the previous seven weeks.

Among the people helping elsewhere in the country was Beverly Downes-Phillips, a medical physicist whom I had met at one of Obama's Philadelphia rallies. Downes-Phillips was a native of Jamaica, but she had immigrated to the US in 1968. She had met Obama shortly before he announced his candidacy for president, when he headlined a fundraiser for a local Pennsylvania politician held in a private home. (He had won over Downes-Phillips during the event when, to her embarrassment, her mobile phone had begun ringing during his speech and she had been unable to find it to turn it off. Rather than show displeasure, Obama had begun dancing to her 'When the Saints Go Marching In' ringtone.)

By the closing stages of the race, she told me, the office in downtown Philadelphia from where she made phone calls encouraging Obama supporters to get to the polls was 'mobbed, just wall-to-wall with people'.

Downes-Phillips said she was almost sure Obama was going to prevail. She had only two concerns: that chicanery would interfere with the integrity of the voting process, robbing him of victory; and that, win or lose, his safety might be in danger. 'Look at all the ones they shot,' she said quietly. 'Bobby Kennedy, John Kennedy, Martin Luther King. I just hope Barack doesn't get caught off-guard or get too exuberant someday.'

*

Things seemed to be going a little too perfectly – and reality bit back on the night of 20 October. In the early evening, I had watched Hillary Clinton join Obama at a rally that attracted 50,000 people in Orlando. But during the flight between Orlando and West Palm Beach, where the campaign would rest up for the night, Robert Gibbs appeared unexpectedly in the aisle of the plane's press section. For a while he did not say anything at all, which only heightened the sense of curiosity. Then he announced that some events scheduled for later in the week would not happen and that Obama would instead be going to Hawaii, of all places.

The spokesman then began to read a statement about 'the nature of the visit': 'Senator Obama's grandmother Madelyn Dunham has always been one of the most important people in his life. Along with his mother and his grandfather, she raised him in Hawaii from the time he was born until the moment he left for college. As he said at the Democratic convention, she poured everything she had into him. Recently, his grandmother has become ill, and in the last few weeks her health has deteriorated to the point where the situation is very serious. It is for that reason that Senator Obama has decided to change his schedule on Thursday and Friday so that he can see her and spend some time with her. He will be returning to the campaign trail on Saturday.'

Gibbs took only a few questions, explaining that Obama's grandmother was at home, having been released from hospital the previous week. He would say nothing about the nature of her illness 'for privacy reasons' but added: 'I think everyone understands that the decision Senator Obama is making to go to Hawaii underscores the seriousness of the situation.'

The news caused a flurry of activity among the media, yet the political ramifications of the announcement seemed to be slight. It was a mark of Obama's confidence that he could take time off from the campaign trail so close to the election. But the decision would have been reached in the knowledge that it would be hard for McCain to exploit his opponent's absence without appearing callous.

The story's power resided in its central, human element. Gibbs' words had left little doubt that Dunham's life was coming to a close. Obama – not yet 50 but with both his parents long gone – stood on the brink of the presidency. At that very moment, the woman who had played such a big part in raising him was dying. It was an ineffably sad turn.

*

While all this was going on inside the Obama campaign bubble, McCain continued on his unhappy course. The Republican was starting to get the worst of all worlds: his campaign's increasingly negative tone was besmirching his vaunted reputation for decency, but it was also flailing. He was making no headway in the polls.

On 17 October, the *Huffington Post* broke a story that perfectly encapsulated his fall from grace. The website noted that the McCain campaign appeared 'to have turned to the same political consulting firm that was responsible for spreading vicious smears about the senator during the 2000 South Carolina [Republican] primary'.

The 2008 McCain team had, it transpired, employed a company called FLS-Connect to conduct 'robocalls'. The term refers to phone calls made to voters in which either a pre-recorded message or a person reading from a script levels a series of negative, and often disingenuous, accusations against an opponent. In McCain's case, many of the calls were being used to push innuendoes about Bill Ayers' connection with Obama. A direct precursor of FLS-Connect (Feather, Hodges, Larson & Synhorst, or FHLS) had worked for Bush against McCain in South Carolina at the turn of the century. The company denied that its particular calls were the ones used to deliver the smears during that scorched-earth primary campaign, though the *Washington Post* suggested otherwise.

As the *Huffington Post* story noted, McCain had once referred to robocalls as 'hate calls'. Now, his unseemly embrace of such tactics hammered another nail into the coffin of his reputation as a maverick. By this point, even McCain's supposed comrades had begun to desert him – though whether this was out of genuine distaste for his strategy or because they did not want to be associated with a campaign that appeared certain to go down to defeat was open to debate.

On the same day as the *Huffington Post* story appeared, a spokesperson for Senator Susan Collins of Maine – a Republican, a close friend of McCain's, and his campaign's co-chair in her state – released a statement saying that Collins believed his robocalls should 'stop immediately'. Soon afterwards, three other Republican senators – Olympia Snowe, also of Maine, Norm Coleman of Minnesota and Gordon Smith of Oregon – suggested that the calls should be ended. Snowe termed them 'regrettable and inappropriate'. Chris Shays, a Republican member of Congress from Connecticut involved in a hard battle for re-election (which he eventually lost), gave an interview to the *Yale*

Daily News in which he asserted that his party's standard-bearer had 'lost his brand as a maverick' and 'did not live up to his pledge to fight a clean campaign'.

Alongside those who made specific criticisms of the robocalls, there was also a steady trickle of Republicans who had suddenly discovered an enthusiasm for Obama. Scott McClellan, President Bush's former press secretary, and William Weld, a Republican who had previously been governor of Massachusetts, both endorsed the Democrat. Charles Mathias, a former Republican senator from Maryland, wrote an opinion article in the *Washington Post* declaring his allegiance to Obama.

There was another factor compounding the McCain camp's gloom. Relations between the candidate's staff and Sarah Palin had turned glacial as Palin's approval ratings kept going south. (Two days before the election, a CNN/Opinion Research poll would find that 57 percent of American believed that Palin did not have the qualities required of a president. Forty-eight percent viewed her unfavourably – roughly twice as many as had done so after she was first selected by McCain.)

It was easy to understand why the McCain people were feeling the strain. In addition to her actual missteps, Palin had begun displaying an infuriating tendency to go intentionally off-message. Early in October, she had seemed to press the Republican campaign to attack Obama more harshly, telling William Kristol, a conservative columnist with the *New York Times*, that she could not understand why Jeremiah Wright had not been mentioned more on the trail. She added, somewhat forlornly: 'I guess that would be a John McCain call on whether he wants to bring that up.' (McCain had months earlier ruled out making Wright an issue, and, to his credit, he largely stuck to that pledge.) By 19 October, however, Palin seemed to be moving in the opposite direction, raising questions about the effectiveness of the infamous robocalls and deriding them as 'one of the old conventional ways of campaigning'.

Three days later came another embarrassment – though it seemed that the vice-presidential nominee herself was not solely to blame. A story posted on the *Politico* website on October 22 revealed that the

Republican National Committee (RNC) had spent $150,000 on clothes, make-up and accessories for Palin since she had first been unveiled as McCain's running mate. In one blow-out at the Neiman Marcus store in Minneapolis, $75,062.63 had been spent. The sums of money involved were discordant with the everywoman image Palin was trying so hard to project, and the story evidently rankled with her.

Four days after its publication, Palin told a rally in Tampa, Florida, that 'those clothes, they are not my property', adding: 'just like the lighting and the staging and everything else that the RNC purchased, I'm not taking them with me'.

Those comments in turn provoked some vicious in-fighting, which was laid bare in a story posted on the CNN website by Dana Bash, the network's de facto McCain correspondent. Bash reported that, after Palin had made her comments, a senior McCain adviser had told CNN that her words 'were not the remarks we sent to her plane'.

Bash went on to quote other unnamed members of the McCain team as saying that Palin had 'gone rogue'. In a particularly scathing move, one McCain aide said of the Alaska governor: 'She is a diva. She takes no advice from anyone. She does not have relationships of trust with any of us, her family, or anyone else. Also, she is playing for her own future, and sees herself as the next leader of the party. Remember: divas trust only unto themselves, as they see themselves as the beginning and end of all wisdom.' Yet another McCain team member described Palin's 'lack of fundamental understanding of some key issues' as 'dramatic'.

Palin loyalists fought back against this onslaught, asserting that the vice-presidential nominee had been poorly handled by McCain's people. They argued that the Alaska governor had, foolishly, been sequestered from the media in the days immediately after the convention, only to be thrown to the lions, in the shape of experienced, big-name broadcasters like Charles Gibson and Katie Couric, afterwards.

Obama's advisors stayed well out of the way. If their opponent's team wanted to form a circular firing squad, that was fine with them.

*

As the election entered its final week, I returned to Florida to see one final display of Democratic unity. Obama and Bill Clinton were due to address a late-night rally in Kissimmee, a suburb of Orlando.

The crowds for Obama were now customarily in the tens of thousands. This event was no different: 35,000 people showed up to see the last Democratic president and the man who looked like he would become the next one.

The two men walked to the stage in the cool night air shortly after 11 PM, Obama's hand occasionally draping itself supportively around Clinton's back. The former president was clear and powerful in his endorsement of Obama. It was 'not a close question [as to] who can best get us out of the ditch', he said.

'We can't fool with this,' Clinton added, in reference to the election. 'Our country is hanging in the balance. And we have so much promise and so much peril. This man should be our president. . . . And he's going to be our president, unless the American people forget what the election is about.'

Obama paid extravagant tribute to Clinton, referring to him as 'a great president, a great statesman, a great supporter in our campaign to change America'. He also said, of the former president and his wife: 'I am proud to call them my friends' – a sentiment that sounded good even if few people present entirely believed it.

Obama's oratory regained its lyricism in the very last days of the campaign. It was almost as if he had accomplished all that he could with the concrete, heavily specific stump speech that he had used so often in the previous weeks. Now, his job – just as it had been back in the days before Iowa, when the momentum had first shifted to him and animated his renegade candidacy – was to inspire.

'In six days, you can put an end to the politics that would divide this nation just to win an election,' he said. 'In six days, you can give this country the change we need. We began this journey in the depths of winter. . . . We didn't have much money. We didn't have many endorsements. We weren't given much of a chance by the polls or the pundits. We knew this would be a steep climb.

'But I also knew this: there are times in our history when the size of our challenges outgrows the smallness of our politics. And I was convinced that, when we come together, our voices are more powerful than the most entrenched lobbyists, or the most vicious political attacks, or the full force of the status quo in Washington that wants to just keep things the way they are.'

The crowd filed out, a mixture of anticipation and nervousness in the air.

Earlier that evening, Obama had sought to use his overwhelming financial muscle to copper-fasten his opinion poll lead. His campaign bought 30 minutes of airtime across seven TV networks at a cost of roughly $4 million. Those minutes were filled with a long-form, glossy political broadcast. Narrated by Obama and featuring several American families who were grappling with bread-and-butter problems, its message, fundamentally, was one of reassurance: it sought to connect Obama to the American mainstream and position him as someone in tune with the concerns of the general public.

The audience across all the networks amounted to over 30 million people. More people watched the broadcast on NBC and CBS than had watched the prime-time fare those channels had shown in the same time-slot the previous week.

After the rally with Clinton, I asked Jen Psaki about the thinking behind the huge airtime buy. 'It was an opportunity for people to see, unfiltered, what Senator Obama's priorities would be in the White House,' she said. 'It just served as an opportunity for people to learn more about what his priorities are.'

The McCain team had already fallen back on their standard response to such developments. They accused Obama of conceit and presumptuousness. Psaki would have none of that: 'We're not going to get into their silly game of distractions,' she said.

There was no point in having money in the bank after the election was over; instead, the Obama campaign would all but empty its coffers trying to swamp McCain.

The final days before the election threatened to become a blur. The candidates zipped across the country. They drafted in celebrities to appear alongside them: Bruce Springsteen for Obama, Arnold

Schwarzenegger for McCain. Schwarzenegger, the governor of California, came to McCain's aid for a rally in Columbus, Ohio, which drew around 10,000 people. Springsteen helped Obama bring 80,000 people out onto the streets of Cleveland.

*

There was one final, poignant turn of events. When Obama woke to begin his last day of campaigning at around 8 AM on Monday 3 November, he learned that his grandmother had died, at home in Hawaii, about three hours before. If she had survived just until the following night, she would have known the result of the election. She had cast a ballot for her grandson during Hawaii's early voting period; it would still count, despite her death.

Obama said nothing about his grandmother at his first engagement of the day. Later, in Charlotte, North Carolina, he called her 'one of those quiet heroes we have across America, who aren't famous . . . but each and every day they work hard. They look after their families. They look after their children and their grandchildren.'

Obama had prefaced his remarks about his grandmother by saying: 'I'm not going to talk about it long because it's hard to talk about.' His capacity to keep his emotions in check was becoming famous. But on this day, standing on the threshold of history but with personal loss bearing down upon him, he began to cry. Photos of him at the podium, a tear rolling down his cheek, flashed around the world.

His last pre-election gathering took place late that night in Manassas, Virginia. Almost 90,000 people came out. Obama reprised one of the oldest stories of his campaign. It revolved around an event very early on, when his candidacy was in its infancy and seemed to be going nowhere. He had shown up, in a bad mood, to a sparsely attended event in Greenwood, South Carolina. Trying to counter this depressed atmosphere, a small woman in late middle age had begun a chant. 'Fired up!' she said. 'Ready to go!'

Obama joked that he at first thought she was 'stealing his thunder'. After a few minutes, though, he had joined in with the shout. So had everyone else. And their gloominess had lifted. Since then, 'Fired Up!

Ready to Go!' had become the campaign's unofficial motto, chanted in unison at Obama's biggest rallies.

'Here's my point, Virginia: that's how this thing started,' he said. 'It showed you what one voice can do. One voice can change a room; and if a voice can change a room, it can change a city; and if it can change a city, it can change a state; and if it can change a state, it can change a nation; and if it can change a nation, it can change the world.'

After almost 21 dramatic and exhausting months, he was finished electioneering.

By that point, I was in Chicago. The evening was unseasonably warm and I walked through the city streets to Grant Park, which would host Obama's election night rally in 24 hours. Caterers were readying equipment inside marquees. Lights were already burning in the booths from which TV networks would broadcast. Technicians were at work on the podium where Obama would speak, adjusting the lectern and checking camera angles.

Obama was way up in the final polls. Still, doubt ate away at his supporters. One question above all plagued them: would America's voters, in the end, turn away from electing a black man as their president?

The answer would be revealed soon enough. As I stood there, looking at the lights of Chicago's skyscrapers, a cameraman and his colleague completed a final run-through and departed for the night. Workers pulled back the protective wrapping from the long blue carpet that had been laid out on the stage.

Everything was ready.

13

CHICAGO

He won, of course.

On election night in Grant Park, almost a quarter of a million people gathered. The result came just after 10 PM local time, when the polls on the West Coast closed. Suddenly, on the big screen that was broadcasting CNN, there was a picture of a smiling Obama and, in huge block letters, the words 'ELECTED PRESIDENT'.

The polls may have predicted it, the early results may have confirmed it was coming, but when it happened, the sheer enormity of the moment was extraordinary. I stood on the edge of the crowd. Strangers were embracing, thousands of voices yelling out.

Obama's old state Senate colleague, Terry Link, was standing in one of the backstage tents reserved for special guests. 'Tears were trickling down my face,' he told me a couple of days later. 'You remember all the time you've spent with this person – the times I had played cards with him or played golf with him kept running through my mind. It was extremely moving.'

Celebrations were bursting out all across the nation. They would last all night. Times Square in New York erupted into joyous mayhem. Car horns sounded up and down the gritty streets of south central Los Angeles. At Martin Luther King's old church in Atlanta, Ebenezer Baptist, veterans of the civil rights movement savoured an event that felt like the culmination of their struggle.

The man at the centre of it all had begun his day just after 7:30 AM, when he turned up with his family to vote at the local school that served as his polling station. He narrowly avoided what would have been a bizarre and awkward moment: Bill Ayers, who still lived in the neighbourhood, cast his ballot just minutes before Obama. The presidential candidate and his wife filled out their voting papers at adjacent booths. Michelle seemed to struggle with the complexities of the weirdly large ballot, which was about the size of a bathroom mirror. Later in the day, Obama would jokingly tell reporters that his wife took so long filling it out that he had to check who she was voting for.

He held fast to his Election Day tradition of taking to the basketball court. His motorcade pulled up at a gym on the west side of his adopted hometown in mid-afternoon. He brought a group of friends along with him for the game.

Later, he watched the results come in with his family, his running mate and his closest advisors at the Hyatt Regency Hotel. The only public record of the evening came in the form of pictures taken by the campaign's official photographer. The most noticeable thing about them is the lack of exuberance on display. In almost all the shots, Obama is either expressionless or smiling gently. In one image, striking because of the mood of relaxation it conveys, he sits alongside Michelle, his feet up on the table in front of him, gazing at the TV. In other photos, Michelle's mother and other members of her extended family mill around. If you didn't know who Obama was – and you could ignore the sight of aides like Axelrod and Plouffe hovering in the background, anxiously checking their Blackberrys – you could be forgiven for thinking the photos were of an upscale wedding reception or a family reunion.

When I spoke to Robert Gibbs later, he confirmed that the atmosphere in the hotel suite was far from out of control. 'I shook his hand, gave him a hug and said "Congratulations, Mr President-Elect," ' Gibbs recalled, as matter-of-factly as he could.

*

Despite all the fears and doubts about the reliability of the opinion polls in advance of the election, the actual results unfolded with smooth predictability. The only surprises for Obama supporters were pleasant ones. Victory came early in Pennsylvania, the only state of any significant size that the McCain camp truly believed they had a chance to grab from the Democrats. (It had voted for John Kerry, but by a very narrow margin, in 2004.) Thwarted there, the Republican candidate's path to victory almost vanished. Ohio, the state that had carried George W. Bush to victory in 2004, fell to Obama at 8.35 PM Chicago time, and the race was to all intents and purposes over.

In Grant Park, Linda Douglass acknowledged with a smile, and wry understatement, that the campaign was 'heartened' by the results up to that point. She was not prepared to tempt fate by declaring victory just yet. But she was willing to ponder certain aspects of the campaign. She still held that the pivotal phase was the economic crisis and the way the candidates had reacted to it. That period, she argued, had made voters see McCain as the riskier choice.

The negative attacks that had rained down upon Obama's head with increasing ferocity in the closing days of the campaign had not worked. Democrats in the past had been broken by that kind of assault, yet the Illinois senator had proven immune to them. Douglass offered one explanation for this: 'I think it just got harder and harder for them to make the case that Barack Obama was a scary guy who had terrorist friends and might be part of some radical Muslim sect. The ads were more and more ridiculous and shrill. You could see, through all the polling, that people became irritated that they were forced to wade through all these personal smears in order to find out: "Is anybody going to help me keep my job?" So, number one, the attacks weren't credible after a while, and number two, they weren't speaking to what was on voters' minds.'

There would be plenty of time for further analysis in the days ahead. For now, the big news was that McCain had called Obama at 10 PM to concede the election. According to Robert Gibbs, the new president-elect had thanked McCain for his graciousness and said he wanted to discuss how the two men could work together in the future.

The Republican soon emerged to give his concession speech. The contrast between Obama's huge rally and McCain's election night event, a sullen affair in a hotel in Phoenix, Arizona, told its own story. Still, McCain delivered a magnanimous address that reminded many independents and moderates why they had once held him in such high esteem.

'The American people have spoken, and they have spoken clearly,' he said. He highlighted the historic nature of Obama's win, saying of the election: 'I recognise the special significance it has for African-Americans and the special pride that must be theirs tonight.'

In defeat, the candidate sounded a note of true patriotism: 'Today, I was a candidate for the highest office in the country I love so much. And tonight, I remain her servant. . . . Tonight, more than any night, I hold in my heart nothing but love for this country and for all its citizens, whether they supported me or Senator Obama. I wish Godspeed to the man who was my former opponent and will be my president.'

McCain, for all his lapses into slimy tactics during the campaign, remained in ways a more generous person than some of his supporters. As he spoke, he repeatedly had to gesture at those present to stop booing every mention of Obama's name. At times, it looked like the famous McCain temper might break through. He held himself in check, just about.

Obama watched McCain's speech from his hotel room. Soon, it was time to leave. At 10:39 PM, his motorcade departed for the short journey to Grant Park. Canvas screens had been put up in the backstage area of the park to create a makeshift corridor towards the podium. Michelle and Malia led the way; Barack, holding Sasha's hand, followed close behind. They walked out onto the stage. The cheering went on for a long time.

*

Obama matched the biggest occasion of his life with one of the best speeches of his life. For so many people, his election said something profoundly optimistic about America, after a period when – for liberals and others to the left of the political centre, at least – a darkness had seemed to envelop the country.

His speech began with an affirmation of that optimism. 'If there

235

is anyone out there who still doubts that America is a place where all things are possible, who still wonders if the dream of our founders is alive in our time, who still questions the power of our democracy, tonight is your answer,' he declared. 'It's been a long time coming, but tonight, because of what we did, on this date, in this election, at this defining moment, change has come to America.'

Just as he had done all those months before, on the night he had won the Iowa caucuses, he paid tribute to the countless people who would never get, or expect, a name-check from the podium. 'I will never forget who this victory truly belongs to. It belongs to you,' he told the crowd. 'Our campaign was not hatched in the halls of Washington. It began in the backyards of Des Moines and the living rooms of Concord and the front porches of Charleston. It was built by working men and women who dug into what little savings they had to give $5 and $10 and $20 to the cause. It drew strength from . . . the millions of Americans who volunteered and organised and proved that . . . a government of the people, by the people, and for the people has not perished from the Earth. This is your victory.'

Obama and his speechwriters had faced one obvious difficulty. The occasion seemed to call for soaring rhetoric; on the other hand, the severity of the problems America was facing militated against words that could seem too self-congratulatory or bombastic. They resolved the conundrum by enumerating the problems, but then placing them within the context of a deeper faith in the nation's capacity to meet all challenges.

The president-elect spoke about the wars in which the US was enmeshed, and about his fellow citizens who were facing economic hardship. 'The road ahead will be long. Our climb will be steep,' he cautioned. 'We may not get there in one year or even in one term. But, America, I have never been more hopeful than I am tonight that we will get there. I promise you, we as a people will get there.'

(The final line struck me as the one discordant and odd part of the address. It echoed – intentionally, I assumed – a famous Martin Luther King speech. 'I just want to do God's will,' King had said on 3 April 1968 in Memphis, Tennessee. 'And he has allowed me to go up to the mountain. And I've looked over and I've seen the promised land. I may not get there with you, but I want you to know tonight that we, as a people, will get to the promised land.' The passage was well-known because it was disturbingly prophetic. King was shot dead the day after he delivered it. The podium from which Obama spoke in Chicago was positioned between two thick slabs of bulletproof glass. In that setting, invoking King's final speech brought forth unsettling thoughts.)

The speech concluded with another story built around the 'Yes We Can' motto that had become a rallying cry for Obama supporters. This time, the president-elect spoke of a 106-year-old woman, Ann Nixon Cooper. She had cast her ballot that day in Atlanta.

'Tonight, I think about all that she's seen throughout her century in America: the heartache and the hope; the struggle and the progress; the times we were told that we can't, and the people who pressed on with that American creed: Yes we can.

'This is our moment,' Obama continued. 'This is our time: to put our people back to work and open doors of opportunity for our kids; to restore prosperity and promote the cause of peace; to reclaim the American dream and reaffirm that fundamental truth, that, out of many, we are one; that while we breathe, we hope.'

The TV cameras picked up Jesse Jackson, weeping in the midst of the crowd just in front of the stage. Oprah Winfrey was crying too, on the shoulder of a man standing just in front of her. So too, beside me in the press area now, was Linda Douglass, the months of tension on the trail finally granted release.

A group of young Obama aides were taking photos of each other nearby. One of them, a young woman whom I knew, turned to me. She had a broad, dazed smile across her face.

'This can't be happening,' she said, not quite trusting the evidence of her own eyes. 'Stuff like this doesn't really happen, right?'

*

The celebrations spread across the world in the hours that followed. Obama's praises were sung from Kenya to Britain to Australia. People were cheering the US for the first time in a long time, enamoured not just by its new leader but by the populace that had elected him. The *Guardian*'s editorial the next day began: 'They did it. They really did it.'

For Obama supporters who had followed his progress from the start, the result was a sweet validation. Jennifer Tuttle, the volunteer who had toiled for him in Rochester, New Hampshire, was watching the election night events at a party in New York.

'I cried like a baby through his acceptance speech,' she said. She had left the party with her husband shortly afterwards. 'People were literally running through the streets screaming. It was unbelievable. It was like the war had ended and the soldiers were coming home.'

Almost 1,800 miles away, in San Marcos, Texas, Kaitlin Murphy, the student whom I had met in the crowd at an Obama rally in February, was also at an election-watch party. As various early results came in, she kept knocking on wood for good luck. Her knuckles were raw by the end of the night.

'It restored so much hope,' she said, of the result. 'Before, I had been thinking that people were always going to be resistant to change. What happened completely turned that around.'

There was one other person I knew I needed to speak to. I had stayed in touch with Brenda Williams, the doctor who had introduced Obama when he spoke in Sumter, South Carolina, just before the state's Democratic primary. I had grown to like her a lot. The 56-year-old was an extrovert who could talk all day. Prone to addressing people of either gender as 'Sugar-pugar', she laughed easily.

The good humour and flamboyance could sometimes obscure the fact that Williams was a bit of a rebel. Before Obama had come to the fore, she had often written in the name of a candidate of her choosing when she went to vote, so dissatisfied was she with the choices available. She had exposed a local church to the media after she found out about the dismal conditions it had let fester in a low-income housing project it owned. More generally, she burned hot about the indignities so often visited upon those who merely had the misfortune to 'come up on the rough side of the mountain', as she put it.

The voter registration efforts she had begun before the primary had continued afterwards. She had taken to visiting jails in her area: the inmates, so long as they had not been convicted of a serious crime, were eligible to get onto the electoral rolls. She had personally registered over 1,000 new voters since March.

On election night, she organised a party, with a live band, in a local hall. Admission was free – so long as the attendees could show evidence that they had voted earlier in the day. A widescreen TV had been set up for the occasion and Williams spent most of the time with one eye on the returns as she danced and talked with her husband.

'I don't drink but I was intoxicated with excitement, with energy,' she told me. The band, she remembered, were playing 'Ain't No Stopping Us Now' when the night's biggest news flashed up on the screen. 'When it was announced that Barack had won – my God, I just screamed,' she said. 'Everybody was just jumping up and down.'

Williams had been born and raised in Savannah, Georgia. As a young girl, she had to sit in the back of public buses, even if the vehicles were otherwise empty, because of the colour of her skin; she remembered walking through muck to her neighbourhood's neglected 'black' school, while white children nearby went to lessons in pristine buildings on carefully tended lawns; her father would take her to civil rights marches but would sometimes warn her in advance that the Ku Klux Klan had organised a counter-demonstration and that if things 'got rough', they would have to leave.

Her father, Frederick Chapman, had been a stalwart member of the NAACP. During her childhood, he had signed up as one of several plaintiffs in a civil rights case. Shortly after the case became public, a cinder block came crashing through the window of the bedroom he shared with his wife. It had a piece of paper wrapped around it, the Klan's symbol of a burning cross drawn on it. His wife and children slept in a back bedroom for the next few weeks, while he sat on the porch with a shotgun, waiting to see if the Klansmen would return. Chapman died in 2002. His daughter still carried his 1961 NAACP membership card in her purse, she told me.

Williams had gone with the youngest of her three daughters, Aisha, to a huge Obama rally in the nearby city of Columbia in December

2007. Looking around, she allowed herself to believe for the first time that America was changing.

'There were all these white people with Obama T-shirts on,' she said to me, laughing. 'I had to call my husband. I told him: "You have to see this. Look at all these white folks going around with a black man's face on their chest."' There was, she decided, 'something revolutionary going on in America'.

That revolution came to fruition on election night. 'I felt so much happiness. But there was sadness mixed in with it, too. I wished that my parents could have witnessed this, and my grandparents. I thought about all the struggles they had to endure. I thought about the Klan attack and I thought about my daddy's NAACP card.'

Her voice petered out and, down the phone line, I heard her begin to cry. It had been a long road from there to here.

*

A few days after the election, I went to see Jesse Jackson.

The headquarters of the organisation Jackson led, the Rainbow/PUSH Coalition, were a five-minute walk from the Obamas' home in the city's Hyde Park district. The taxi from the city centre to Jackson's building passed by police roadblocks that now cut off every street close to where the president-elect and his family lived. The driver, for whom English was not a first language, gestured vaguely and turned back to me with a grin. 'Obama!' he announced cheerfully.

I had met Jackson before, when Obama gave his convention speech in Denver, and he seemed less vigorous than he had then. He looked tired; someone he knew well had just died, and he was in a philosophical mood.

'I accept the time in which I have to live,' he mused, with a touch of melancholy. 'I watched our struggle evolve. I was arrested July 16, 1960, for trying to use a public library in Greenville, South Carolina. I was arrested in Greensboro, North Carolina, trying to use a cafeteria.'

The battles against segregation – and the memory of those who had given their lives for the cause – had come back to his mind as he stood in the Grant Park crowd. 'I looked at the results the other night, and I began to weep. In my heart there was joy over the achievement of the civil rights struggle, but pain over the martyrs and the price they had to pay to get us here. Schwerner, Goodman, Chaney – two Jews and a black – were killed; Medgar Evers killed; all these innocent people killed. But their sacrifices were redeemed the other night. America is being redeemed.'

(Michael Schwerner, Andrew Goodman and James Chaney were the three civil rights activists whose murders in 1964 at the hands of white racists became the basis for the film *Mississippi Burning*. Medgar Evers, an NAACP activist, had been shot dead by a Klansman the previous year at his home, also in Mississippi.)

I asked Jackson whether he had been surprised that the presidential election results showed no sign of the Bradley Effect. 'I was delighted, because more whites are maturing,' he replied. 'The fear of blacks was always unfounded. We always reached out to say "Let's just be human beings together", but that always met with cultural and legal and theological rejection. Much of that is changing.

'When there are walls,' Jackson continued, 'often there is fear of what is on the other side of the wall – and there is ignorance, fear, hatred and violence. The civil rights movement has torn down walls. We see each other more clearly and are now building bridges. So America is changing for the better.'

For all the evident emotion he felt about Obama's success, Jackson was not going to get carried away. When I asked him what effect the election of the first black president might have on the expectations that African-American children have for themselves, he pivoted towards more concrete concerns.

'The expectations are psychological. The needs are economic. There is a great sense of hope in the ghetto [because of Obama's election] but unemployment, structural inequality, second-class schools – that has not changed. While we feel better about each other, those structural inequalities have not been altered yet, and we hope that the Congress will honour President Obama's vision and make it happen.'

Jackson was warming to his subject now, shrugging off his weariness. 'Dr King would say that the freedom movement didn't cost a thing but for some emotional adjustments against barbarism. Sitting in the front of the bus? After all the drama, it cost white America nothing. The Voting Rights Act finally granted? It cost nothing. But to offset the devastation and neglect will require investment, and that is where the challenge comes in. Is America willing to invest in evening the playing field, willing to invest in addressing structural inequalities in health care and education?

'Black America is Number One in infant mortality; Number One in short life expectancy; Number One as victims of job discrimination. There are 2.4 million Americans in prison – a million are black, 500,000 are Latino. That's the objective facts. I mean, our spirits are soaring high, but we want to go from hope to fulfilment.'

Even if Obama did indeed decide to focus on the problems that Jackson mentioned, he would not articulate the issues in the same ethnically based way as the civil rights leader. That did not, obviously, render Jackson's points invalid. The questions he raised were important in other ways too, since they raised the question of what Obama was going to do with the power he had acquired only three days before.

*

Earlier, before I met Jackson, I had attended Obama's first press conference as president-elect, held in a Chicago hotel.

He was still getting used to the demands and customs of the office. When he walked in, the same members of the press who had been following him around for the past two years rose up from their seats respectfully, and he flinched in surprise. Later, he made an off-the-cuff joke about Nancy Reagan – he implied that the astrology-loving former First Lady had conducted seances in the White House – and ended up having to make an apologetic phone call to her as a result.

Sideshows apart, there was serious work to be done, and the economy loomed above all else. Standing in front of an array of economic experts who were advising him during the transition period, he stressed the importance of passing a fiscal stimulus plan. Such a package was needed, he said, to 'jump-start' economic growth. An extension of unemployment benefits was equally urgent.

As for the broader issues, he declared: 'We cannot afford to wait on moving forward on the key priorities that I identified during the campaign, including clean energy, health care, education and tax relief for middle-class families.'

This reflected a view among some of his advisors that it was best to try to make progress on as many fronts as possible while his mandate was fresh and his popularity ratings high. The reality, however, was that a failure to at least stabilise the nation's economy was almost certain to jeopardise his other plans. His assertive comments at the press conference seemed to sit uneasily with a candid warning he had given in a CNN interview just before the election. 'None of this can be accomplished if we continue to see a potential meltdown in the banking system or the financial system,' he said.

In the international arena, a winding down of the war in Iraq seemed certain to be the most dramatic consequence of Obama coming to power. He had always made clear that he would seek the counsel of commanders on the ground as to how best to accomplish a withdrawal of US troops; but he had been adamant that such a withdrawal was necessary. Many of the troops removed from Iraq would likely be used to beef up US efforts in Afghanistan, which Obama had long regarded as much more central to the so-called war on terror.

His arrival in the White House was also likely to bring a different tone to America's dealings with the rest of the world. That may be an abstract change but it would be an important one. The Bush White House, during its first term at least, seemed to take perverse delight in offending other nations. It was only later, when the adventure in Iraq ran aground, that it realised the value of maintaining stronger international alliances. Obama needed no tutoring on that score: during his victory speech in Chicago, he made a point of addressing 'all those watching tonight from beyond our shores' and assuring them that 'our stories are singular but our destiny is shared and a new dawn of American leadership is at hand'.

After that first post-election press conference, I asked Robert Gibbs whether there was a danger that expectations for Obama, at home and abroad, could rise too high.

'Absolutely,' Gibbs nodded. 'But I think that's why he said today, said in his speech on Tuesday night, and, I think, said every place he went on the trail, that none of this is going to be easy. We are going to have to make some extremely difficult choices. As he said, we are in a hole that it is going to take a lot to get out of. He is committed to pushing through the things he talked extensively about over the past two years, but he believes and he hopes people understand that it isn't going to happen overnight.'

One of the open secrets about the American presidency is that it is almost impossible to tell in advance who will be good at the job and who will be a dismal failure. No one, however accomplished, can honestly claim to be well-prepared to shoulder such colossal responsibilities. Obama has shown good political judgement throughout his career, has delivered calm, reasoned responses on issues ranging from the economic crisis to the Jeremiah Wright furore, and has run a presidential campaign of rare discipline and collegiality. It is entirely possible that he might lose all that in the White House. His natural cautiousness could harden into hesitancy and indecision. It is not yet known whether he will hold his nerve when faced with critical choices. And the array of problems the country now faces could be too much for any president to resolve.

On the other hand, Obama's intelligence, his curiosity and his equilibrium might serve his country very well. It is, at a minimum, unthinkable that he will replicate the rashness and dangerous certitude of the man who preceded him. He could turn out to be a disappointment as president; it is harder to imagine him being a disaster.

In any case, his 2008 presidential campaign has an enduring value all of its own. His quest, and its exhilarating conclusion, gave America back a sense of itself that had almost been lost. It reminded the rest of the world that the superpower had once been an object of affection, even yearning.

America had once seemed a place of generosity and openness, and those values endured whether its leaders were liberal or conservative. George W. Bush did great damage to that precious image. His America was a cold and dank place, of torture at Abu Ghraib, internment at

Guantánamo Bay, and intolerance and avarice all around.

On 4 November 2008, more than 65 million Americans rejected that vision of their nation. They watched the negative ads telling them that the Democratic Party's candidate for president was risky, dangerous and un-American, and they rejected those, too. They looked at Barack Hussein Obama, with his Kenyan father, his Indonesian childhood, his background devoid of wealth and influence, and they asked themselves whether he would be a good person to lead their country. Then they answered 'Yes', and voted for him.

It was a wondrous thing. Regardless of how well or otherwise Obama performs in office, the wonder of it will never quite be erased.

A friend of mine emailed me the day after the election. In New York, he wrote, the atmosphere was 'like a liberation. I can't describe it any other way.' The previous night, I felt the same sense of relief and release in Chicago. In the days that followed, I watched video footage of Americans, from the Atlantic to the Pacific, streaming out onto the streets on election night, waving their nation's flag and sometimes singing their national anthem with an ardour that I had never heard before. I think I understood what they were celebrating. They had got their country back.

I kept replaying in my mind the moment in Grant Park when a disembodied voice introduced the next First Family of the United States, and out into the bright lights strode Barack, Michelle, Malia and Sasha Obama.

They stood there, waving and smiling, and every person watching realised that it was a moment for the ages. At that instant, on that mild November night, those four people were emblems of a nation where it seemed, once again, that astounding things could happen.

It was a place full of promise, luminous with possibility.

ACKNOWLEDGEMENTS

My thanks are due to all those who helped bring this book from conception to completion. Deserving of particular praise are Seán O'Keeffe, Peter O'Connell, Orlaith Delaney and Daniel Bolger at Liberties Press, Bharat Ayyar of Yale College, and my agent, Jonathan Williams. Thanks also to Conor O'Clery, who provided the initial encouragement that set all else in motion.

At the *Sunday Business Post*, thanks are due to a multitude of staff members past and present. Notable among them are Cliff Taylor, Martha Kearns, Fiona Ness, Helen Boylan, Gavin Daly, Simon Carswell, Jennifer O'Connell, Ted Harding and Damien Kiberd.

At the *New York Observer*, Josh Benson and his predecessor, Terry Golway, proved themselves to be deft and thoughtful editors on more occasions than I can recall. I owe them a lot. Katharine Jose has many of the same attributes, and a greater zest for coining amusing nicknames. Thanks, K-Jo. Thanks also to editor-in-chief Peter Kaplan, and to all those writers with whom I have happily shared the *Observer*'s pages, especially Steve Kornacki and Jason Horowitz.

At the *Guardian*, a debt of gratitude is owed to Georgina Henry, Richard Adams and Seumas Milne.

Editing *Magill* was an immensely rewarding experience. Stephen Flanagan, Andrew Lynch and Paul O'Brien were among those who made it so.

I will always be grateful that I took my first real steps in journalism at *Hot Press*. Niall Stokes and Mairin Sheehy have piloted the ship for more than three decades now. My thanks to them. My days at *Hot Press* also gave me several of my closest friends. Thanks and love to Sharon Connelly, Liam Mackey, Simon Roche and Olaf Tyaransen.

Way back in Belfast, John McGurk encouraged me to prolong my efforts in journalism beyond a week of work experience at the *Irish News*. Thanks, John.

In relation to TV and radio work, thanks to Wendy Guarisco in Atlanta, Larry Conroy in New York, all at the BBC, especially *Good Morning Ulster*, and at RTÉ, especially *The Tubridy Show* and *The Late Debate*.

Writing this book was an intense experience. I was, and am, blessed to have the friendship of some amazing people who carried me through the troughs and made the sweet moments sweeter.

Two couples – Oistin Mac Bride and Fiona Shanley, and Mark and Cathy McElhinney – have been extraordinarily supportive for as long as I have known them. Thanks for so much.

I am envious of Emma Brockes's writing talent – so it's just as well she was such terrific company from the snows of Iowa to the sweltering heat of the New York summer. Ta, love!

Nadine O'Regan has my love and respect always.

Ben Harrison supplied encouragement and good humour throughout this project. He was also generous enough to read the manuscript as it was being written, his suggestions making the text much clearer and crisper than it would otherwise have been. Tip o' the hat to you, sir!

Sahar Habibi has helped me with research for close to three years now. She also did the bulk of the fact-checking for this book. Sahar is a brilliant assistant, and a friend with whom I have had a thousand laughs. The manuscript would not have been delivered on time without her efforts, and my life would be duller without her presence. Thank you.

One final thank-you: to Dr Brenda Williams of Sumter, South Carolina, quoted elsewhere in these pages. These days, I am honoured to call Dr Williams a friend. As we spoke and emailed in the months after our first meeting, her words were a constant reminder as to why the events described here mattered so much to so many people. To her, and to all the other interviewees who took time to speak with me, my deepest gratitude.

A Note on Sources

This book draws primarily on my own reporting and research. I have sought to make clear within the text itself where quotations that were not gleaned directly by me first appeared. On occasions when I have not done so, the quotation often comes from a press conference, a media conference call or a prepared statement.

If any quotation that should have been attributed has fallen through the gaps, or has been sourced imprecisely, my apologies. Anyone who spots such an omission or error should get in touch with the publishers, so that such lapses can be corrected in future editions.

In Chapter Two, the recollections of Barack Obama come from his books, *Dreams From My Father* and *The Audacity of Hope*, unless otherwise stated. Obama noted in the introduction to the first book that he had used some composite characters and that some events 'appear out of precise chronology'. Points of information from that memoir that are mentioned in these pages have either been independently verified or are undisputed.

In a broader, informational sense, I am indebted to the outstanding work of so many political reporters during this campaign. Especially indispensable were newspapers such as the *New York Times*, the *Washington Post*, the *Chicago Tribune*, the *Chicago Sun-Times*, the *Los Angeles Times* and the *Wall Street Journal*; magazines like the *New Yorker*, the *New Republic*, the *Atlantic* and *Vanity Fair*; and websites including *Politico*, *The Page*, *Slate* and *Salon*.

A special mention should also go to David Mendell, whose work both for the *Chicago Tribune* and in book form in *Obama: From Promise to Power* is essential reading for anyone seeking to understand the future president's early years in Chicago politics.

INDEX